KIERKEGAARD

KIERKEGAARD
A Life of Allegory

Naomi Lebowitz

Louisiana State University Press

Baton Rouge and London

Manufactured in the United States of America

Designer: Barbara Werden

Typeface: Linotron Garamond # 3

Typesetter: G & S Typesetters, Inc.

Printer and binder: Edwards Brothers, Inc.

LIBRARY OF CONGRESS CATALOGING IN PUBLICATION DATA

Lebowitz, Naomi.
  Kierkegaard, a life of allegory.

  Includes bibliographies and index.
    1. Kierkegaard, Søren, 1813–1855. I. Title.
B4377. L39 1985   198'.9   84-12618
ISBN 0-8071-1186-4

The author gratefully acknowledges permission to reprint from the following: *Christian Discourses*, trans. and ed. Walter Lowrie, by permission of Oxford University Press. The three-volume series *Edifying Discourses: A Selection*, trans. David F. Swenson and Lillian Marvin Swenson, ed. Paul Holmer, by permission of Augsburg Publishing House. *Søren Kierkegaard's Journals and Papers*, trans. and ed. Howard V. Hong and Edna H. Hong, with assistance of Gregor Malantschuk; *The Concept of Irony*, trans. and ed. Lee M. Capel; *"Armed Neutrality" and "An Open Letter,"* trans. and ed. Howard V. Hong and Edna H. Hong; *Kierkegaard's Attack Upon "Christendom," 1854–1855*, trans. Walter Lowrie. All reprinted by permission of Indiana University Press. *The Point of View for My Work as an Author: A Report to History*, trans. and ed. Walter Lowrie, copyright © 1962 by Harper and Row, Publishers, Inc.; *"The Present Age" and "Of the Difference Between a Genius and an Apostle,"* trans. Alexander Dru, copyright © 1962 by Alexander Dru; *Purity of Heart Is to Will One Thing*, trans. Douglas V. Steere, copyright 1938, 1948 by Harper & Row, Publishers, Inc.; *Works of Love: Some Christian Reflections in the Form of Discourses*, trans. Howard V. Hong and Edna H. Hong, copyright © 1962 by Howard V. Hong. All reprinted by permission of Harper & Row, Publishers, Inc. *The Concept of Dread*, trans. Walter Lowrie, copyright 1944, © 1972 by Princeton University Press; *Stages on Life's Way*, trans. Walter Lowrie, copyright 1940, © renewed 1968 by Howard Johnson, published by Princeton University Press; *Concluding Unscientific Postscript*, trans. David F. Swenson and Walter Lowrie, copyright 1941, © 1969 by Princeton University Press; *"Fear and Trembling" and "The Sickness Unto Death,"* trans. Walter Lowrie, copyright 1941, © 1969 by Princeton University Press; *Philosophical Fragments*, trans. David F. Swenson, copyright 1936, © 1962 by Princeton University Press; *Letters and Documents*, trans. Henrik Rosenmeier, copyright 1978 by Princeton University Press; *Repetition: An Essay in Experimental Psychology*, trans. Walter Lowrie, copyright 1941, © renewed 1969 by Princeton University Press; *Either/Or*, trans. David F. Swenson and Lillian Marvin Swenson, copyright 1944, © 1972 by Howard A. Johnson, published by Princeton University Press; *Training in Christianity*, trans. Walter Lowrie, published by Princeton University Press; *"For Self-Examination" and "Judge for Yourselves!"* trans. Walter Lowrie, published by Princeton University Press. All reprinted by permission of Princeton University Press.

For Al, Joel, Judith, and Sophie

A Man's life of any worth is a continual allegory—and very few eyes can see the Mystery of his life—a life like the scriptures, figurative—which such [shallow] people can no more make out than they can the Hebrew Bible. Lord Byron cuts a figure—but he is not figurative—Shakespeare led a life of Allegory; his works are the comments on it.

JOHN KEATS
The Selected Letters of John Keats

A philosopher who has traversed many kinds of health, and keeps traversing them, has passed through an equal number of philosophies; he simply *cannot* keep from transposing his states every time into the most spiritual form and distance: this art of transfiguration *is* philosophy. We philosophers are not free to divide body from soul as the people do; we are even less free to divide soul from spirit. We are not thinking frogs, nor objectifying and registering mechanisms with their innards removed: constantly, we have to give birth to our thoughts out of our pain and, like mothers, endow them with all we have of blood, heart, fire, pleasure, passion, agony, conscience, fate, and catastrophe. Life—that means for us constantly transforming all that we are into light and flame—also everything that wounds us; we simply can do no other. And as for sickness: are we not almost tempted to ask whether we could get along without it?

FRIEDRICH NIETZSCHE
The Gay Science

For the only pleasure the melancholic permits himself, and it is a powerful one, is allegory.

WALTER BENJAMIN
The Origin of German Trauerspiel

CONTENTS

ABBREVIATIONS

AN   *"Armed Neutrality" and "An Open Letter."* Translated and edited by Howard V. Hong and Edna H. Hong. Bloomington, Ind., 1968.

AC   *Kierkegaard's Attack Upon "Christendom," 1854–1855.* Translated by Walter Lowrie. Princeton, 1946.

BA   *On Authority and Revelation: The Book on Adler.* Translated and edited by Walter Lowrie. New York, 1966.

CA   *The Concept of Anxiety.* Translated and edited by Reidar Thomte with Albert B. Anderson. Princeton, 1980.

CD   *The Concept of Dread.* Translated and edited by Walter Lowrie. Princeton, 1973.
       [The two immediately preceding translations were used according to my preference.]

CI   *The Concept of Irony.* Translated and edited by Lee M. Capel. Bloomington, Ind., 1965.

CrA   *Crisis in the Life of an Actress.* Translated by Stephen Crites. London, 1967.

CrD   *Christian Discourses.* Translated and edited by Walter Lowrie. Princeton, 1974.

CUP   *Concluding Unscientific Postscript.* Translated by David F. Swenson and Walter Lowrie. Edited by Walter Lowrie. Princeton, 1968.

ED   *Edifying Discourses: A Selection.* Translated by David F. Swenson and Lillian Marvin Swenson. Edited by Paul L. Holmer. Minneapolis, 1943–46.

E/O   *Either/Or.* Volume I translated by David F. Swenson and Lillian Marvin Swenson with revisions by Howard A. Johnson; Volume II translated by Walter Lowrie with revisions by Howard A. Johnson. 2 vols. New York, 1959.

F/T *   *"Fear and Trembling" and "The Sickness Unto Death."* Translated and edited by Walter Lowrie. Princeton, 1974.

GS   *"The Gospel of Suffering" and "The Lilies of the Field."* Translated by David F. Swenson and Lillian Marvin Swenson. Minneapolis, 1948.

JC   *"Johannes Climacus or De Omnibus Dubitandum Est" and "A Sermon."* Translated by T. H. Croxall. Stanford, Calif., 1958.

J/P   *Søren Kierkegaard's Journals and Papers.* Translated and edited by Howard V. Hong and Edna H. Hong; assisted by Gregor Malantschuk. 7 vols. Bloomington, Ind., 1967–1978.

PA   *"The Present Age" and "Of the Difference Between a Genius and an Apostle."* Translated by Alexander Dru. New York, 1962.

PF   *Philosophical Fragments.* Translated by David Swenson; commentary by Niels Thulstrup; translation revised and commentary translated by Howard V. Hong. Princeton, 1974.

PH   *Purity of Heart Is to Will One Thing.* Translated by Douglas V. Steere. New York, 1956.

PVA   *The Point of View for My Work as an Author: A Report to History.* Translated and edited by Walter Lowrie. Newly edited by Benjamin Nelson. New York, 1962.

Rep *   *Repetition: An Essay in Experimental Psychology.* Translated and edited by Walter Lowrie. New York, 1964.

SD   *"The Sickness Unto Death," in "Fear and Trembling" and "The Sickness Unto Death."* Translated and edited by Walter Lowrie. Princeton, 1974.

SE/JY   *"For Self-Examination" and "Judge for Yourselves!"* Translated and edited by Walter Lowrie. Princeton, 1974.

SLW   *Stages on Life's Way.* Translated by Walter Lowrie. Princeton, 1945.

TC   *Training in Christianity.* Translated by Walter Lowrie. Princeton, 1972.

WL   *Works of Love.* Translated and edited by Howard V. Hong and Edna H. Hong. New York, 1964.

---

*Although I have cited the Lowrie translation in almost all the passages from *Fear and Trembling* and *Repetition*, I occasionally used the new translation by Howard V. Hong and Edna H. Hong (Princeton, 1983). I shall designate the latter edition herein as *Rep* [2].

PREFACE

When James Joyce has Stephen Daedalus show off his outrageous construction of Shakespeare's life from his works, to impress his literary elders in the library and to rescue his own identity through that of the bard, it is tempting to believe that Joyce is playing out Keats's claim that men as great as Shakespeare lead lives of "continual allegory," that their works "are the comments on it." More certainly Kierkegaard demonstrates this notion in the way in which he makes his works rescue a life that could not marry, could not hold a public post, could not trust friends, felt continually misunderstood. His body would not be wasted if he could use it in the service of faith, turn its frustration into fulfillment by renunciation itself.

The purpose of Kierkegaard's literature is to stimulate the reader to make his own movements of faith, and this purpose had to be so compelling that it could sustain the pressure of psychological justification that rendered it suspect. The way that Kierkegaard pictures himself obsessively in his writings—in the *Journals* as in the pseudonymous works—the way that he talks about himself and his act of being a religious writer, a dialectical poet, is the major subject of his literature (as its major object is faith). This is the process by which he simultaneously gains his ethical authenticity and frees the reader to his. As Kierkegaard tells his story again and again, directly and indirectly, through discourse and fable, notebook and fairy tale, he transforms his psychological problems into possibilities for faith. His anxiety, registered through the compulsive and crablike rhythms of his repetitions, is his bond with the reader. His sick body, struggling through pseudonyms and styles to get into the right position for faith, functions like a character in a novel to attract the reader, to interest him, to rivet him, in order finally to reject him and thereby direct him into his own ethical education. Literature pictures the ways in which meanings depend upon the positions and perspectives its characters assume. To feel Kierkegaard spiritually, it is necessary to experience him literarily. The structure of

Fear and Trembling starts literary waves of fairy tales, legends, scene, picture, poetry, crashing against philosophical problems, overcoming the contradiction philosophy abhors and literature accommodates. The poet and the hero in Kierkegaard himself, the one who watches and writes and the one who acts, sees his writing as act, are pictured as a pseudonym and Abraham, and the tension between these parts of Kierkegaard is what renders the book passionate. The pseudonym's struggles to get in the right position in relation to Abraham is the subject of *Fear and Trembling*. Kierkegaard's enemies, principally Hegel, complacently believe that they are already in the right position, and they are doomed to live in the medium of Kierkegaard's literature as fixed allegory, as System, and as Speculation. But those who make the movements of faith, no matter how fully—Lessing, Socrates—frolic in that literature's experimental fields.

The constant flurry of debate and drama around definitions forces them to whirl through fiction's possibilities, the fairy tale's absurd promises, the anecdote's humor. Philosophy might posit "Truth is inwardness," but when Kierkegaard's literature takes this in, it must be surrounded by the "supposes" of literary communication until it is forced to undergo several metamorphoses by the end of *Concluding Unscientific Postscript* (*CUP*, 71). The definition never stands still, for Kierkegaard is not justifying doctrine but seeking the right position in relation to it, and it is literature, not philosophy, that moves its persuasions forward by the positions of bodies.

The literary talent of Kierkegaard was a painful privilege for him—both a blessing and a curse. It was the only agent through which his body could express itself in all its anxiety and depression. But it could not fulfill the body's desires, for it was neither life nor spirit. Kierkegaard had to sabotage the customary resolutions and expectations of literature (as of his body), while exploiting its transactions, in order to push the reader beyond it to faith. His work yoked together the spirit and the word in an agonizing oxymoron; we must feel the suffering each gave to the other if we would feel the inspiration of the life and thought. I have tried to put the reader through the characteristic literary motions of all of Kierkegaard's works, the journals (which the formal works frequently raid) and discourses as well as the pseudonymous ones, for they all demonstrate the figurative translations of his body and draw us to his movement of faith. I have elected not to do a thorough, conventional literary analysis of any of his texts (even of those like *Stages on Life's Way*, which seem to demand it), for such attention, by emphasizing Kierkegaard's derivative situations, stock caricatures, artificial structures, and pacing, would not only be reductive but would do a serious disservice to Kierkegaard's literary power. But these devices, as literary versions of the body's movements between psychological justification and faith, as comments on the life's allegory, become charged and moving, and Kierkegaard becomes a figurative artist of the first rank. Instead of attempting firm definitions of categories (a task tried many times by others), which generally lead to impasse and contradiction Kierkegaard did not intend, to restrictions of resonance, I have attempted to imitate Kierkegaard's cumulative and recapitulated approach to his central concerns, his *literary* approach, in which every principle is qualified by person, position, and perspective.

In a passage in *Works of Love*, Kierkegaard asks us to imagine:

> a man (and you need not even imagine him as possessing that perfection which characterizes the magnificent one who, repudiated by men, becomes the glory of his generation), imagine a man who was or became or was and remained so unhappy that earthly advantages and the goods of this world had lost their allure to his eyes, so unhappy that, "weary of sighing" (Psalm 6:6), he became, as we read in Holy Scriptures of the unhappy Sara (Tobit 3:11), "so despondent that he wanted to hang himself." Imagine, then, that precisely in the darkest hour of his need it became absolutely clear to him that in spite of all his unhappiness, which essentially would not be relieved even if he won all the world's goods, since their possession, by inviting happy enjoyment, would only painfully remind him of his wretchedness, an unhappiness which would not essentially be increased by earthly adversity, which like the dark weather in relationship to melancholy would rather harmonize with his mood—imagine, then, that it became absolutely clear to him that there still remained for him the highest: to will to love men, to will to serve the good, to serve truth for truth's sake alone, the only thing which truly could enliven his troubled mind and give him the joy of life for eternity. Imagine such a person in the world and you will perceive that it will go hard with

him; he will not win the world's love, he will not be understood, he will not be loved by the world. (*WL*, 126–27)

I have tried to imagine such a person, tormented by the "highest" and unconsoled by earthly success. He is Kierkegaard. This book is about the ways in which he imagined and effected, through his literature, a passage from the psychological source of his art, his suffering in the world, to faith.

ACKNOWLEDGMENTS

I would like to express my gratitude to all my colleagues who have listened to my weekly bursts of Kierkegaardiana, but especially to those who taught me Hegel, Plato, and Danish: Albert William Levi, George M. Pepe, and George Dolis; to my colleagues Richard A. Watson, Marcus P. Bullock, Wayne D. Fields, David Hadas, Pamela White Hadas, and Stanley Goldstein, for stimulating conversations about Kierkegaard, Schlegel, and Schleiermacher; to Arlis Ehlen and Ruth Newton for their intelligent, patient, and sensitive reading and commentary; to James Olney, an ideal reader; to my best editors and scriveners: Al Lebowitz and Kaye Norton; to those who encouraged and supported me: Iris Murdoch, John O. Bayley, Howard Nemerov, and Steven N. Zwicker; to my students who have helped me to teach Kierkegaard, especially Diana Marré, Sue Aydelette, Francis Ingledew, Lisa Sarkis, and Lisa Horton; and to Celia Baldwin and Rikke Vognsen for helping me with Danish.

KIERKEGAARD

He must feel how misunderstanding tortures him,
just as the ascetic felt every instant the prick of the
penitential shirt he wore next to his skin—and in fact
he has clad himself in misunderstanding in which it is
terrible to be, like the apparel Hercules received from
Omphale, in which he was burned up.
Stages on Life's Way

Introduction

EFORE Søren Kierkegaard turned misunder-
standing into a major weapon against Chris-
tendom—his scornful name for contemporary
Christianity that understood too well the nature
of suffering and the divine Paradox—he felt it as
a tragic condition.[1] As early as 1834 he identified
strongly with the nobility of such a fate in Christ,
Job, and the tragic hero. "Doubtless the most sublime tragedy consists
in being *misunderstood*. For this reason the life of Christ is supreme
tragedy, misunderstood as he was by the people, the Pharisees, the
disciples, in short, by everybody, and this in spite of the most exalted
ideas which he wished to communicate. This is why Job's life is tragic;
surrounded by misunderstanding friends, by a ridiculing wife, he suffers. . . . This is why the scene in Goethe's *Egmont* [act V, scene 1] is so
genuinely tragic. Clara is wholly misunderstood by the citizens" (*J/P*, I,

1. All of Kierkegaard's key terms turn toward both a positive and negative pole.
Some critics of his work, like Martin Thust, "Die Innerlichkeit der Berufung," in
Kierkegaard: Der Dichter des Religiösen (Munich, 1931), favor the negative emphasis of
misunderstanding as a state endured by Kierkegaard, besetting the age and the re-
viewers, but I think it most important to emphasize the active transvaluation of the word
into a positive one, for this is one of Kierkegaard's most characteristic defenses.

I

51; n. 118 [1834]). Like Rousseau, Kierkegaard desired so passionately
to be perfectly understood, and nevertheless judged innocent, that when
he felt he could not realize this ideal (for as a child he saw the picture of
Christ spat upon, crucified), he turned himself from a resigned sufferer
into a knight of misunderstanding.[2] By assuming as style what he experienced as disappointment, he could simultaneously protect the idea of
innocence by choosing guilt and compelling the need for grace, and
disguise his own guilt while he worked it through his literature. A self-
conscious Don Quixote, he perpetrated difficulties everywhere. He became one who, unlike his great cultural antagonist Hegel, would not
allow the "cunning of reason," by exploiting the patterns of philosophy,
psychology, and history, to heal the lacerated dreams of perfect communion between the subjective and objective worlds, not even provisionally.[3] Where Hegel soothed the pathos, even the tragedy, of inadequate forms of communion with the promise of higher consciousness
within the world's time, Kierkegaard chose to taunt these fantastic
shapes, mocking his own descriptions, so that the heart, in its frustration, would be forced past the world's words to the perfect silence of
God. He preferred to think of himself, in relation to the Professor
Heibergs who wrote appreciative reviews as well as to those who attacked
him, as "one who writes in order to be misunderstood" (*CrD*, 17).[4]

Kierkegaard takes as his most cherished model Socrates, who hid his
beauty behind the Silenus skin of a "hectoring satyr" (*satyrou . . .
hybristou*). "He spends his whole life," says Alcibiades in the *Symposium*, a

2. See *J/P*, VI, 145; n. 6389 [1849], and *TC*, 174–77.
3. This is Hegel's celebrated term (*die List der Vernunft*) to describe *Geist's* economic
use of the passions of history for its dialectical purposes. See, for example, G. W. F.
Hegel, *Lectures on the Philosophy of World History: Introduction—Reason in History*, trans.
H. B. Nisbet (Cambridge, England, 1975), 89.
4. Johan Ludvig Heiberg was a Danish playwright, poet, Hegelian critic, and editor
of Copenhagen's most influential literary paper in Kierkegaard's day. The witty and
sophisticated Heiberg circle had received Kierkegaard, who later became irritated by a
superficial review of *Either / Or* in 1843 and turned on Heiberg with ironic and sarcastic
references. Heiberg himself, then, excluded Kierkegaard from his circle and kept him at
bay. In the first chapter of his book, *Kierkegaard: The Myths and Their Origins*, trans.
George C. Schoolfield (New Haven, 1980), Henning Fenger claims that this crucial
estrangement stimulated Kierkegaard's self-conscious determination to view this literature as entirely religious from the start. See Kierkegaard's footnote in *CD*, 17, in which
he sarcastically takes Heiberg to task for a misleading review of *Repetition*.

favorite dialogue of Kierkegaard, "pretending and playing with people, and I doubt whether anyone has ever seen the treasures which are revealed when he grows serious and exposes what he keeps inside."[5] And he would imitate Christ, in whom everything is revealed and everything hidden, so that his words are heard as offense and stumbling blocks.[6] The spirit, necessarily pressed through the body of this world, must always be misunderstood. Christ suffered this humiliation; Socrates reveled in this game.[7] And Kierkegaard does both. He shares the agony of the victims of Phalaris, boiled in a brazen bull, whose screams came through pipes as music.[8] And like Scheherazade,[9] he taunts death by telling stories and makes insomniacs out of his readers (for insomniacs have spirit),[10] lest they, like the watchers of Abraham and Christ, fall asleep to escape what is beyond understanding. In the skin of Quidam, he compares himself to one who is sick and needs to carry cathartic narration with him wherever he goes. "So, alas must I have with me everywhere a brief summary of my story of suffering, so that I may orient myself in the whole situation—orient myself in the matter I have thrashed out by myself, in a way quite different from that in which a pupil thrashes out his lesson with the teacher" (*SLW*, 289). The story of the suffering of misunderstanding is teased through pseudonyms, doctored fairy tales, patriarchal legends, and Greek myths. And it is compulsively told backwards to keep the true tale dialectically tensed against its disguise; the teller is denied the demonic absorption into illusion as well as the demonic justification of the guilt. The assumed spell is like that of the fairy tale: "We read in fairy tales about human beings whom mermaids and mermen enticed into their power by

5. Plato, *The Symposium*, trans. Walter Hamilton (Hamondsworth, England, 1951), 111, 103.

6. Interest in the parallels between Socrates and Christ was not unusual in Kierkegaard's time. Kierkegaard refers to F.'C. Baur's discussion and its relation to his own thesis (*J/P*, IV, 205; n. 4243 [1837]).

7. In a footnote in *CUP*, 83, Kierkegaard describes Socrates as acutely aware of the comic aspect of the view of his praying without words, and mocks his own "instruction" of Socrates in his thesis.

8. This is one of Kierkegaard's favorite references. The first reference to it, I believe, is in *E/O*, I, 19.

9. This is another of his favorites. See, for example, *J/P*, VI, 72; n. 6274 [1848].

10. *F/T*, 39.

means of demoniac music. In order to break the enchantment it was necessary in the fairy tale for the person who was under the spell to play the same piece of music backwards without making a single mistake . . . the errors one has taken into oneself one must eradicate in this way, and every time one makes a mistake one must begin all over" (*E/O*, II, 168–69).

Throughout his work, while Kierkegaard speaks obsessively of telling his story backwards, he actually rolls back version after version of himself, sometimes as the same character—Abraham or the merman, for example—while working out the spell of guilt and anxiety. Playing himself back from claim to motive means misunderstanding that is tragic but also comic, for it is both an imposed disguise and an assumed one. As Quidam remarks, the tragic is preserved under the cloak of the comic, and true seriousness, as Socrates knew so well, "itself invents the comic" (*SLW*, 335). The frustration of the longing of Alcibiades for the love of Socrates, described in the *Symposium* in both its comic and pathetic aspects, is a successful tactic in the serious game of misunderstanding. Socrates stimulates it to force upon his admirer a nobler vision, for the illusion of understanding denies to the learner both freedom and expansion. Kierkegaard imitates this action but, moving toward Christian faith, goes one step further and coerces his own longing to be both innocent and understood into a renunciation of worldly realization that could be transposed to a higher and positive pitch of fulfillment—the absolute and passionate misrelationship between men and God. Socrates kept this possibility open, for he stood as a "*judge* on the border between God and man, watching out to see that the deep gulf of qualitative distinction be firmly fixed between them" (*SD*, 230). This was both the cause and function of his ignorance. For these gadflies, the "art of *communication* at last becomes the art of *taking away*" (*CUP*, 245), since only ignorance can look upon the divine Paradox without despair. Most to be envied is the Socrates, then, who learned and taught the ignorance that alone of all conditions does full honor to the double tone of misunderstanding. Kierkegaard's view of himself as a pupil of Socrates is affirmed in the *Journals*. "Can there be the slightest doubt that what Christendom needs is another Socrates, who with the same dialectical, cunning simplicity is able to express ignorance or, as it may be stated in this case: I cannot understand anything at all about faith, but I do believe" (*J/P*, I, 153; n. 373 [1848]).

Like Socrates, Kierkegaard wants to be heard as one who takes away understanding from the lover of truth and premature absolution from the would-be believer. He discovers that both the pupil and the teacher have the same task, and he imagines this metamorphosis: "There was a young man as favorably endowed as an Alcibiades. He lost his way in the world. In his need he looked about for a Socrates but found none among his contemporaries. Then he requested the gods to change him into one. But now—he who had been so proud of being an Alcibiades was so humiliated and humbled by the gods' favor that, just when he received what he could be proud of, he felt inferior to all" (*J/P*, V, 217; n. 5613 [1843]). Only through the comic disguise of ignorance will he transmit the desperate, chosen passion and the necessary pathos of man's need for faith. Only by this tough dialectic of tone and form can misunderstanding be preserved. Its cross-grained roughness chafes poetry and keeps the real from solving itself through fantasy. One way to prevent the poeticizing of life, suggests Johannes Climacus, is "to create difficulties everywhere" (*CUP*, 166). In the process of earnest jest, he muses, "Since it will be impossible to make anything easier than it has become, you must, with the same humanitarian enthusiasm as the others, undertake to make something harder" (*CUP*, 165–66). The comedy of difficulties has to carry the poetry of the spirit's passion. Kierkegaard's loyal insomniacs can testify that the words of this badgering gadfly stir us, as Alcibiades says of those of Socrates, "to the depths and cast a spell over us." The lover insists: "Nothing of this kind ever used to happen to me when I listened to Pericles and other good speakers; I recognized that they spoke well, but my soul was not thrown into confusion and dismay by the thought that my life was no better than a slave's. That is the condition to which I have often been reduced by our modern Marsyas, with the result that it seems impossible to go on living in my present state." [11] But Kierkegaard, who like Socrates loves his listeners by spurning them as disciples, would be quick to remind us that Alcibiades' enthusiasm is a sign of his rhetorical, not ethical, vulnerability and that he who would hear Socrates

11. Plato, *Symposium*, 101.

correctly would hear him soberly (*J/P*, IV, 221; n. 4300 [1854]).
Christ's words, too, express his passion through ignorance, the ignorance of misunderstood simplicity, as he works for unknowing and undoing: "In thy nature and in mine and in that of every man there is
something He would do away with; with respect to all this He repels
men. Lowliness and humiliation are the stone of stumbling, the possibility of offense" (*TC*, 153).

The harassing, both perpetuated and endured, of Socrates, Christ,
and Kierkegaard as teachers of ignorance is marked not by the relief of
climax but by persistence. Socrates' prodding and Christ's suffering, in
Kierkegaard, are daily passions. The prison and the cross are, chrono-
logically, merely the last scenes. Kierkegaard's actual death on the
street seems incidental; he represents himself as one who "historically
died of a mortal disease, but poetically died of longing for eternity"
(*PVA*, 103). The compulsive recapitulation of Kierkegaard's drama of
misunderstanding keeps it in time. He is harsh on poetry and Hegel's
System because he assumes they foreshorten the pathos of daily misunderstanding by the form of tragedy or the determinism of world-
historical necessity. Far more agonizing for Christ than the climactic
crucifixion, he insists again and again, is the persistence, moment by
moment, of the life in misunderstanding. The longing that Socrates
sets up to block climaxes of fulfillment and understanding can be a
guarantor of this strenuous perseverance and consequently an agent of
the real.

> The ideal of a persistent striving is the only view of life that does not
> carry with it an inevitable disillusionment. Even if a man has attained
> to the highest, the repetition by which life receives content (if one is
> to escape retrogression or avoid becoming fantastic) will again consti-
> tute a persistent striving; because here again finality is moved further
> on, and postponed. It is with this view of life as it is with the Platonic
> interpretation of love as a want; and the principle that not only he is in
> want who desires something he does not have, but also he who desires
> the continued possession of what he has. In a speculative-fantastic
> sense we have a positive finality in the System, and in an aesthetic-
> fantastic sense we have one in the fifth act of the drama. But this sort
> of finality is valid only for fantastic beings. (*CUP*, 110)

Kierkegaard's art continually humiliates these reconciliations and, instead, fosters a dialectic of the incommensurability of form with concept, "the challenging opposition between the experiment and the content" (*CUP*, 245). It corrects, too, its author's reductive version of Hegel's mediation between the inner and the outer, the subjective and the objective. Like the sleeping Socrates, Kierkegaard's literature denies Alcibiades an aesthetic satisfaction, giving the content only of a "father or an elder brother" to the form of the lover's longing.[12] For one of the intentions of Kierkegaard's works is to lead us to give up art's powers of consolation. His art rejects the completion and full embodiment of literary form and exploits, by compensation, the literary process. When concepts are carried by moving figures and figures of speech, their placidity is disturbed and their categorical stability made vulnerable. In this way the literary process markedly resembles the movement of faith and provides the necessary phylogeny whose frustrations develop the spirit.[13] When the existing subject is set against the Absolute, the rich dialectic between the desires of the flesh and the spirit is fully exposed. While the literary genre might find the solution in death or marriage, the literary process refuses to ease the tension by turning its figures into Hegelian world-historical types, or worse, into omniscient philosophers of consciousness.[14] Kierkegaard's rejection of genre and System for the sake of experiment allows him to link those who, "with an infinite passionate interest in an eternal happiness base this their happiness upon their believing relationship to Christianity" to those who, "with an op-

12. *Ibid.*, 107.

13. See Walter J. Ong, "Wit and Mystery: A Revaluation," *Speculum*, XXII (1947), 337. Ong is speaking of the similarity between poetry and theology, both resisting abstract reason. "For both poetry and theology, metaphor is a last, and not quite satisfactory, resort." This subject is more fully discussed in Chapter III.

14. This is a phrase commonly used by Hegel (*die Welthistorischen Individuen*)—see, for example, *Lectures on the Philosophy of World History*, 83—and parodically mocked by Kierkegaard. Kierkegaard's critical use of literary process to shame philosophy's ontological and epistemological pretenses might be seen as a prefiguration of the deconstructive pattern from Nietzsche to contemporary critics, though, of course, that the process is an agent of faith quite changes its status as demystifier and makes it particularly vulnerable to habits of idealization that Kierkegaard is always eager to check. What is more telling is that the antihierarchical tendencies of deconstructive thought in its dealings with family, time, and text render its practitioners remarkably similar to Kierkegaard's aesthetic figures, stuck in their compelled games.

posite passion, but in passion, reject it" (*CUP*, 51). Johannes Climacus hyperbolically states his case in an oft-quoted distinction: "If one who lives in the midst of Christendom goes up to the house of God, the house of the true God, with the true conception of God in his knowledge, and prays, but prays in a false spirit; and one who lives in an idolatrous community prays with the entire passion of the infinite, although his eyes rest upon the image of an idol: where is there most truth? The one prays in truth to God though he worships an idol; the other prays falsely to the true God, and hence worships in fact an idol" (*CUP*, 179–80). [15]

Socrates, Christ, Abraham—all the pseudonyms, mythical figures, and heroes of modern thought in Kierkegaard's work—are subjected to the perils of constant movement, especially when they have standpoints like Socrates and standstills like the young man in *Repetition*. No character in the literature of Kierkegaard transcends the motion of his medium to be enshrined in history, not even the best knight of faith who is "able to fall down in such a way that the same second it looks as if [he] were standing and walking," not even one who can "transform the leap of life into a walk, absolutely to express the sublime in the pedestrian" (*F/T*, 52). And certainly not Hegel. As early as his thesis, *The Concept of Irony*, which he later looked upon as the book of a still somewhat "Hegelian fool" (*J/P*, IV, 214; n. 4281 [1850]), Kierkegaard considered the evanescent moment of personal and universal history, apparently more mobile than a constant standpoint, as a Hegelian stasis. "But one forgets that a standpoint is never so ideal in life as it is in the system. We forget that irony, like every other standpoint in life, also has its tribulations, conflicts, defeats, and triumphs." (*CI*, 192). And one should not forget that the persistent and moving maieutic standpoint of Socratic irony can be reflected by the literary process, but the System cannot reflect it at all. Positions and postures in Kierkegaard that are vulnerable to the movements of misunderstanding, ignorance, and faith are, unlike Hegel's,

15. The absolute, passionate, and hyperbolic nature of the emphasis of Kierkegaard transforms Hegel's "reasonable" assumption in his discussion of feeling and reason in religion in his Introduction to *Lectures on the Philosophy of World History*, 45. "If we see someone kneeling in prayer before an idol and the content of his prayer is contemptible in the eyes of reason, we can still respect the feelings which animate it and acknowledge that they are just as valuable as those of the Christian who worships truth in symbolic form, or of the philosopher who immerses himself in eternal truth through rational thought. Only the objects of such feelings are different."

not fantastic but are precisely the most able to represent the individual.
As long as "what is in itself true may in the mouth of such and such a
person become untrue" (*CUP*, 181), the moving figures and viewpoints
in Kierkegaard's texts prevent positive knowledge from dominating
their form of passion, of ignorance. "The Socratic ignorance, which
Socrates held fast with the entire passion of his inwardness, was thus an
expression for the principle that the eternal truth is related to an existing
individual, and that this truth must therefore be a paradox for him as
long as he exists; and yet it is possible that there was more truth in the
Socratic ignorance as it was in him, than in the entire objective truth of
the System, which flirts with what the times demand and accommodates
itself to *Privatdocents*" (*CUP*, 180–81). The corpus of Kierkegaard's
enemies, which we must feel as static (for it cannot ethically free the
reader, only imprison him), that of Hegel in particular, is forced to
undergo the literary movements of Kierkegaard's work as penance for the
"objective truth of the System."

For this reason it is necessary to feel Kierkegaard in a literary way,
where no thought lives free of the body of style and emotion, to feel him
in a religious way. The disturbers of theology like G. E. Lessing, David
Hume, and Ludwig Feuerbach are of more value to Kierkegaard's battle
for faith than orthodox thinkers, for they explode certainty. The figure of
Lessing in *Concluding Unscientific Postscript* is a triumphant literary per-
petrator of misunderstanding and a hero of form. He would seem to have
contributed much to Kierkegaard's philosophical content: he opposes
the simple and direct transition from the reliability of a historical account to an eternal decision (*CUP*, 88); he maintains that accidental
historical truths can never serve as proofs for eternal truths of reason.

> That the Christ, against whose resurrection I can raise no important
> historical objection, therefore declared himself to be the Son of God;
> that his disciples therefore believed him to be such; this I gladly
> believe from my heart. For these truths, as truths of one and the same
> class, follow quite naturally on one another.
>
> But to jump with that historical truth to a quite different class of
> truths, and to demand of me that I should form all my metaphysical
> and moral ideas accordingly; to expect me to alter all my fundamental
> ideas of the nature of the Godhead because I cannot set any credible

testimony against the resurrection of Christ: if that is not a
μετάβασις εἰς ἄλλο γένος,[16] then I do not know what Aristotle
meant by this phrase. . . . That, then, is the ugly, broad ditch which
I cannot get across, however often and however earnestly I have tried
to make the leap.[17]

But Kierkegaard was quite aware of the Enlightenment aspects of
Lessing's beliefs, against which he would continually protest in the
course of his work: his weakening of the historical entrance of the
Paradox, which helped to prepare the way for David Strauss; his concentration on the accessibility and immanence of Christ's ethics in our
history and nature; and his contention that revelation gives nothing to
the human race that human reason could not arrive at on its own.[18] In
Concluding Unscientific Postscript, he approves of this celebrated claim of
Lessing: "If God held all truth in his right hand and in his left the
everlasting striving after truth, so that I should always and everlastingly
be mistaken, and said to me, 'Choose,' with humility I would pick on
the left hand and say, 'Father, grant me that. Absolute truth is for Thee
alone.'"[19] But Kierkegaard, perhaps feeling this as his own tendency,
severely qualifies it. "He was wrong insofar as this . . . smacks a little
too much . . . of wanting to regard the price as being more valuable than
the truth. But this is really a kind of selfishness and can easily become a

16. This Aristotelian phrase is one of Kierkegaard's obsessively repeated formulas.
See Niels Thulstrup's commentary in *Philosophical Fragments*, 236, note to 90, 1. 21.

17. Gotthold Ephraim Lessing, "On the Proof of the Spirit and of Power," *Lessing's
Theological Writings*, trans. Henry Chadwick (Stanford, Calif., 1957), 53–55. Lessing
was a hero for many Romantics and for many reasons, but Friedrich Schlegel's assessment
in his essay, "Über Lessing," seems most interesting in relation to Kierkegaard's, for he
honored what he stood for more than what he wrote, his spirit more than his art. "Er
selbst war mehr werth, als alle seine Talente. In seiner Individualität lag seine Grosse"
Friedrich Schlegel, 1794–1802; Seine Prosaischen Jugendschriften, ed. J. Minor (2 vols.;
Vienna, 1882), II, 151.

18. It is interesting to compare Hegel's criticism of Lessing's "religion of pure
reason," which although opposed to the inferior positive religion, nevertheless, by
having a subjective sense of righteousness as its only content, fails, too, to bring about a
free and rich mediation between objective and subjective standards of judgment. See
"Positivity of the Christian Religion," *G. W. F. Hegel's Early Theological Writings*, ed. and
trans. T. M. Knox and Richard Kroner (Chicago, 1948), 150; and H. S. Harris, *Hegel's
Development: Toward the Sunlight, 1790–1801* (Oxford, England, 1972), 292–94.

19. Lessing, *Lessing's Theological Writings*, 42.

dangerous, yes, a presumptuous error" (*J/P*, IV, 266; n. 4375 [1849]). And in another entry he suggests that Lessing is one who gives "a deep bow and meaningless respect" to Christianity because he denies it Tertullian's truculent dignity of exclusivity and fanaticism (*J/P*, III, 30; n. 2379 [1854]).

All the more clearly, then, can we see how emphatically Kierkegaard valued positions that promote movement but block smug beliefs as a corrective to the Christendom of his age. Lessing's figure in *Concluding Unscientific Postscript* is never superior to its movement and is, therefore, respected like the passionate idol worshiper. What counts most is his choreography as a hero of the disguise of misunderstanding. He sets himself up against his enemies as a moving target. In a *Journal* entry related to this section in *Concluding Unscientific Postscript*, Kierkegaard notes, "Lessing, as a subjective thinker, is aware of the dialectic of communication" (*J/P*, III, 27; n. 2371 [1845]), and it is the *form* of his thought that allows Kierkegaard to use Lessing most effectively as a weapon against his great enemy Speculation. In a comic version of Johannes de Silentio's straining after the meaning of Abraham, Johannes Climacus bobs up again and again with his delighted qualification of the certainty of Lessing's meaning, which remains without result, "Ah, if only I could be sure" (*CUP*, 61). The refusal of a leap between the historical and eternal that does not go through the absurd, a refusal that humorously and passionately emphasizes the subjective and bodily resistance to change, is certainly superior to an optimistic fellowship of leap that promises salvation. Kierkegaard has Johannes Climacus recount an exchange between Lessing and the German philosopher F. H. Jacobi (who was certainly, with his greater influence, closer to Kierkegaard's spirit). The enthusiastic Jacobi urges, "There is nothing very complicated about it . . . you merely step out on the spring-board—and the leap comes automatically" (*CUP*, 94) But Lessing, realizing the full difficulty, absurdity, and isolation of such a choice, responds, ironically, with his body, not his mind, that "he cannot ask even a preliminary step from his old legs and heavy head." [20]

Lessing is fully literary here because he counters a concept with the body. His particularity is assured. Kierkegaard tenaciously calls his own

20. This is my translation from the German in *CUP*, 20. Compare *F/T*, 47.

form back to this dialectical Socratic humor that confounds understanding and disturbs the ease and consolation of fellowship, conventional wisdom, discipleship. Lessing is to be honored *because* "even if I strove with might and main to become Lessing's disciple, I could not, for Lessing has prevented it" (*CUP*, 67). And Lessing, like Socrates, dialectically binds the negative to the positive, the comic to pathos, the habit of those always in a state of becoming, of striving (*J/P*, V, 275; n. 5793 [1845]).

Readers of Kierkegaard become intellectually exasperated if they extrapolate concepts from the body of their medium, for they will encounter contradictions and inconsistencies.[21] But bodies do not contradict themselves, for they have always denied consistency and invited misunderstanding. Montaigne, rejecting the scholastic protection of books against the accidents and frustrations of the body, takes this in stride when he claims that he never contradicts the truth of this inconsistency. Although it would be difficult to imagine a temperament more unlike his than that of the French essayist, Kierkegaard greatly admired the way in which Montaigne's body assaulted human presumptions, especially those of Reason. And it might be particularly fruitful to imagine this alliance because we often forget to read Kierkegaard's books through his body.[22] With Montaigne, we never forget. Obviously, this is in part because Kierkegaard feels physically tenuous, while Montaigne is perpetually tasting himself. Often he laments, "Humanly speaking, my

21. A literary approach has this advantage, too, that major terms in Kierkegaard's vocabulary, like "suffering" and "passion," are not unnecessarily restricted just because Kierkegaard wants, here, to emphasize this aspect and, there, another. The terms keep their full resonance because they are never closed by conceptual definition. In his book, *Kierkegaard on Christ and Christian Coherence* (New York, 1968), Paul Sponheim makes a good attempt to ride Kierkegaard's thoughts on his rhythms, but the conceptual gradually lures him into polemics about inconsistencies.

22. See Jean-Paul Sartre, "L'Universel singulier," in *Kierkegaard vivant: Colloque organisé par l'Unesco, 1964* (Paris, 1966), 59–60. This article has been translated by Peter Goldberger as "The Singular Universal," in Josiah Thompson (ed.), *Kierkegaard* (New York, 1973). The following passage is on p. 262: "Reading Kierkegaard I climb back as far as myself; I want to catch hold of him, and it is myself I catch. This non-conceptual work is an invitation to understand myself as the source of all concepts." We can profitably place Kierkegaard with thinkers as diverse and apparently antipathetic to his direction as Feuerbach, Nietzsche, and William James—"literary" philosophers whose unsystematic styles and structures grow out of their consciousness of body and temperament.

misfortune is that I am not sufficiently corporeal" (*J/P*, VI, 14; n. 6170 [1848]). We have to ask, then, how it is that we feel Kierkegaard as a physical being? His renunciation of Regine, his celibacy, his solitude, the compulsive nature of his authorship, the intellectual and polemical overriding at times of his airy pseudonyms by a didactic voice, even his repulsion of the reader—all of these have led critics to assume a degree of abstraction in his work that betrays his insistence upon the subject as a central consciousness. This is especially ironic since he so often censured Hegel for abstracting the subject out of his history of thought. In contrasting Kierkegaard and Hegel, Käte Nadler maintains that the former's melancholy, his despair, are not religious categories in the Christian sense because they derive from a false intellectual idealism.[23] He has not, Nadler contends, overcome the world, but merely abstracted it. He is accused of having only the negative freedom of the Hegelian beautiful soul which, quarantined from the drama of dialectical development, holds itself aloft in empty isolation. Kierkegaard himself feeds Nadler's thesis with frequent suspicions about the protective function of his melancholy against involvement with the world. Even his God, maintains the critic, is the hollow abstraction of positive religion. In comparison to Kierkegaard's universe, concludes Nadler, Hegel's is decidedly concrete. Torsten Bohlin argues that, in contrast to Martin Luther's full-bodied faith (and what, we imagine, would not Kierkegaard have given for Luther's conscious acceptance of his body?), Kierkegaard's faith, shaping itself against the intellectualism of Hegel, is, in its turn, intellectual and willed.[24] The radical qualitative split between God and man leaves man bereft of the *feeling* of faith. Stripping Kierkegaard of the dialectical disguise that is the felt life of his literary body, Theodor Adorno insists that we take him literally as a philosopher.[25] By exposing his form as a vain envelope of an idealist content, Adorno implies that it covers up an objectless subjectivity, an abstract aloofness from a political and social world to which he would only pretend to be bound.

23. "Käte Nadler, "Hamann und Hegel: Zum Verhältnis von Dialektik und Existentialität," *Logos*, XX (1931), 259–85, especially 265.

24. Torsten Bohlin, *Kierkegaards dogmatische Anschauung*, trans. Ilse Meyer-Lune (Gütersloh, West Germany, 1927), 527–31.

25. Theodor W. Adorno, *Kierkegaard: Konstruktion des Aesthetischen* (Frankfurt, 1966). See especially Chapters I and II and 243.

In his qualification of Nadler's thesis, Jean Wahl suggests, but I
think with too little force, that Kierkegaard's meditations on anxiety,
sin, and faith lead an individual to such an extreme position that concrete passion springs forth.[26] In fact, Kierkegaard uses his art to exasper-
ate *himself* into concreteness. It is sometimes difficult to accept that the
rhythm of Kierkegaard's figures, the longing that their thin mouths
strain to express in the world and in the world's language as they move
toward the great and final misunderstanding and back into lower
forms—this rhythm, refused full and satisfying conceptual or metaphorical embodiment, is what is felt as the passion of Kierkegaard's
body. It is the rhythm of the depressive's longing for the "animal attribute" (*J/P*, VI, 320; n. 6626 [1850]), that he feels he lacks or distances, since his body is a place of sexual guilt.[27] The reader who flicks
away Kierkegaard's psychological and aesthetic disguises and experiments, irritating and offensive, and attempts to grab his religious
thought directly will inevitably feel the experience of the books as
abstract. The reader who sees these disguises as mere self-protection,
self-correction, compulsive rectification, will feel only half his power.
The full experience of this distant, passionate man comes to us through
the strain of embodiment denied for the sake of a higher realism. It
comes, too, through his anxiety that his art, breaking literature's habit
of gratification, might not, even checked, be sufficient ransom for its use
as a ferry to faith. Like that Danish indicative that stands in for the
present participle of thought and customarily attaches itself to a concrete
position, the "existential thinker must be pictured as essentially thinking, but so that in presenting his thought he sketches himself" (*CUP*,
319). He does not have the advantages of supporting "secondary personalities, a scenic environment and the like, all of which help to maintain
the self-sufficiency of the aesthetic production, constitute breadth"
(*CUP*, 319). Somehow he must express concreteness through the collisions between the thinker as he lives and the intellectual categories he
inherits. Because it refuses historical and philosophical fulfillments, the
position of dialectical strain, while it may be seen as self-negation in the
author's work, is felt as positive in its passionate withholding.

26. Jean Wahl, *Etudes kierkegaardiennes* (Paris, 1949), 158*n*.
27. The conceit of the "negative body" will be further developed and expanded.

This anxious self-negation, Kierkegaard's negative body, may be set against the negative capability that Keats uses as a measure of the great figurative artist. He is speaking of the capability in the artist of becoming transparent to his subject, of hiding in the voices of his characters so completely that there is no strain between them. Nothing could seem further from the texture of Kierkegaard's art. He also hides in the voices of others, but he self-consciously aborts and qualifies this absorption by diluting the bodies of his projected pseudonyms, hammering wedges between his poets and his heroes. Ironically, this refusal of full identification, played with as temptation, keeps Kierkegaard from merely cutting a figure. In a celebrated version of the negative capability, Keats makes this rich and evocative distinction: "A Man's life of any worth is a continual allegory—and very few eyes can see the Mystery of his life—a life like the scriptures, figurative—which such [shallow] people can no more make out than they can the Hebrew Bible. Lord Byron cuts a figure—but he is not figurative—Shakespeare led a life of Allegory: his works are the comments on it."[28] It is impossible to come to the end of the meaning of this comment, but some implications can be considered more likely than others, since Shakespeare is the model of negative capability. While the works fully translate the life, they also protect it from exposure and direct appropriation. While they are full of their author, enough to sap biographical curiosity, they are also free of him. The reference to Lord Byron would suggest, too, that a high degree of

28. John Keats, Letter to George and Georgiana, February 18, 1819, in Lionel Trilling (ed.), *The Selected Letters of John Keats* (New York, 1956), 229. It is interesting to compare this idea with the argument of Walter Benjamin, which revises the conventional relationship between Goethe's life and art, in his essay "Goethes Wahlverwandtschaften," in *Schriften*, ed. Theodor W. Adorno and Gretel Adorno (Frankfurt, 1955), I, esp. Part ii. That language, knowing itself *essentially* appearance, is the agent of the real (unvalidated by the life behind it) and is a perspective that binds Schlegel to the deconstructive critics. Kierkegaard's literature is more shamelessly linked to the life since its job is to torture it *because* of its allegorical secrets and *for* the sake of its allegorical transformation. Of related interest is Benjamin's essay "The Image of Proust," in *Illuminations*, trans. Harry Zohn, ed. Hannah Arendt (New York, 1969), 201–216.

See Paul De Man's allusions to Kierkegaard in his discussion of the cooperation of allegory and irony, both intimate with renunciation from the romantic age on. Both allegory and irony break up false unions of the self with ideal selves, with the world, and through literature, preserve and reflect our fall from distant origins. "The Rhetoric of Temporality," in Charles S. Singleton (ed.), *Interpretation: Theory and Practice* (Baltimore, 1969), 173–209.

unselfconsciousness seems to attend the translation, and it is this spontaneity that promotes its aesthetic autonomy. Those readers of Kierkegaard who would take his negative body as either self-protection or aesthetic failure, instead of as passionate longing, would not be willing to link him to Shakespeare. More likely he would seem the anti-Shakespeare Virginia Woolf had in mind in her recognition of the fullness of Shakespeare's disappearance into his works. "The reason perhaps why we know so little of Shakespeare . . . is that his grudges and spites and antipathies are hidden from us. We are not held up by some "revelation" which reminds us of the writer. All desire to protest, to preach, to proclaim an injury, to pay off a score, to make the world the witness of some hardship or grievance was fired out of him and consumed. Therefore, his poetry flows from him free and unimpeded." [29]

Certainly Kierkegaard's work is highly self-conscious, and certainly it fails to give to its figures aesthetic autonomy. This is because Kierkegaard refuses to possess them as beings (a dangerous delusion, in the view of a Kierkegaard jealous for ethical integrity), instead experimenting with them as positions. With this control it would seem that Kierkegaard, like the tragic hero, would compulsively edit a "pure and elegant edition of himself" (*F/T*, 72) in which all losses are made good and accidents turned into Providence. He knows he cannot match the Shakespeare he envies, who guiltlessly offers to the naked and suffering hero "the fig-leaf of the word," who is "able to *express* everything, absolutely everything, precisely as it is" (*F/T*, 72). Kierkegaard's talent, by contrast, his need, is to force everything and everyone to become what they already are. This is an aggressive act, for all its experimenting disguises, that carries with it a suspicion of the demonic motive, of a pride and self-protection never dreamed of in Shakespeare's philosophy. But the compulsive nature of authorship, its urgency, is, in a writer like Kierkegaard, spontaneity, for its dedication to the dialectic of misunderstanding is passionate and persistent.

I would contend that Kierkegaard's life *is* figurative. His works are comments on its allegory because he experiments himself into positions, both demonic and divine, from seduction and despair to resignation and faith. He then twines his body, sick with anxiety, wracked by the

29. Virginia Woolf, *A Room of One's Own* (New York, 1929), 99.

dialectic of psychological and spiritual realism, around these possibilities, so that their lack of fullness expresses the pathos and pitch of continual longing and misunderstanding.[30] As an act reminding us that life is antagonistic to its expression in words, his renunciation is of a different sort from that of Shakespeare. But when he appears to be cutting a figure he is truly most figurative, for he *illustrates* misunderstanding. In his long discussion of pathos toward the end of *Concluding Unscientific Postscript*, Johannes Climacus, while speaking of existence as a "continual meanwhile" (*CUP*, 469), imagines one about to undergo the task of living in continual striving. At the moment he is ready "to cut at once a fine figure (*at slaae stort paa*) (which only can be done *in abstracto* and on paper, because the loose trousers of the abstractor are very different from the strait-jacket of the exister)," he discovers he must begin again upon "the immense detour of dying from immediacy," and then again, in guilt, which puts him into "thorough distress" in the "medium of existence." This backward movement of beginnings is also one that goes forward. Shuffling his pseudonym in this fashion, Kierkegaard transfigures himself into his medium and thereby avoids "cutting a figure." He is persistently in a dialectical motion in and with his art, and by this means he becomes, ironically, figurative.

Like Hegel, Kierkegaard saw Shakespeare as one who had, in a great romantic version of classicism, mastered irony. Here is an early judgment of Goethe that describes this process, a judgment soon to be completely reversed: "If this is the case, the particular poetic production will not have a mere external relation to the poet, but he will see in the particular poem a moment in his own development. It was in this respect that Goethe's existence as a poet [*Digter-Existens*] was so great: he succeeded in making his existence as a poet [*Digter-Tilvaerelse*] congrue with his actuality" (*CI*, 337). Kierkegaard's form of "congruence" exploits, romantically, a misunderstanding between the poet and his work. His irony struts as if it had mastered its author, and forces form to thwart its

---

30. This gives us a psychological truth that is far deeper and more significant than the literal truth of his "social" personality, by which a disguised fundamentalist like Henning Fenger, who claims to accept the right to life as literature but secretly resents it as a psychological cheat, qualifies Kierkegaard's religious choice (in *Kierkegaard: Myths and Origins*). What matters to one who has felt the authenticity of the struggle of Kierkegaard with faith in every one of his pages is that he makes his life *take* that direction.

content. Devoted to the dialectical relationship between misunderstanding and the truth, Kierkegaard's form, its disturbance of classical congruence, becomes, in fact, an agent of the real and of his own reality. It is evident that Kierkegaard, like Hegel's Hamlet,[31] does not have an accidental relationship to his content, but must, to guarantee that he does not, pretend that he does. The peril and possibility of the word's idealization of life must always be exposed by the anxiety they engender. His insistence upon the denial of a poetic mediation between the body and the Ideal accounts for Kierkegaard's disappointment in the ending of *Don Quixote*. The hero is a model for the real only as long as the two torture each other. "Don Quixote should not come to an end; he ought to be presented as going full speed, so that he opens vistas upon an infinite series of new fixed ideas" (*J/P*, I, 357; n. 771 [1847]). Cervantes sold out the dialectical fullness of his vision to a deathbed conversion. The fact that the don's imagination stays in the world, has permanently changed it, does not satisfy Kierkegaard, because the body that had struggled with it has died. So, too, the dialectic between one's fact and fiction must be supported. Not for Kierkegaard is Rousseau's persistent hope, in *The Confessions*, to be what he appeared.[32] The negative body incorporated in his authorship depends on the resistance between these two terms.

It is through this form that Kierkegaard is able to make new professions of faith that are both historical and current, orthodox and unorthodox (even his dogmatics depend upon the relation between categories, not the categories themselves). The literary process, in all its suppleness, works for the continual Christian transvaluation: "An existing individual is constantly in process of becoming; the actual existing subjective thinker constantly reproduces the existential situation in his thoughts, and translates all his thinking into terms of process. It is with the subjective thinker as it is with a writer and his style; for he only has a

---

31. G. W. F. Hegel, *Hegel's Aesthetics*, trans. T. M. Knox (Oxford, England, 1975), I, 243ff. For evidence of Kierkegaard's interest in Hegel's views on classical form, see the aesthete's discussion in *E/O*, I, 49–54.

32. See Jean-Jacques Rousseau, *The Confessions*, trans. J. M. Cohen (Baltimore, 1954), 88. Rousseau is here at the penultimate, still negative, stage before the fulfillment of his desire.

style who never has anything finished, but 'moves the waters of the language' every time he begins, so that the most common expression comes into being for him with the freshness of a new birth" (*CUP*, 79). Lessing could work for literature because his style never finishes his thought and for faith because, in this way, his ignorance prepares us for it. "*How* it is said—this is what is new. Understood in this way, it is true that everything is new. It is still new—even when someone out of prudence joins the chorus, even when a mimic repeats one or another old proverb with utmost carelessness. The new thing is that the old has become nonsense, a triviality" (*J/P*, I, 317; n. 678 [1850]).

In this important entry Kierkegaard, like a novelist, distinguishes the content of I Corinthians 2 : 2: "I know nothing except Christ and him crucified," in the mouth of the apostle, a witness of the truth, a poet, a pastor, in descending order of authority and value. The words bring forth, according to the speaker, death, persecution, suffering, good fortune, and a reputation for personal saintliness. The content comes into meaning only when it comes into relationship with a life, and between each life there is an "infinite distinction." The authenticity of the redoubling of life and style that we feel in Kierkegaard derives in part from the play of the world of spirit through these alternating perspectives. His rhythms continually mock the public, universal possibilities of appropriated Christian truths. They bristle with varieties of misunderstanding to free the reader to his own single and difficult journey. The "relief of speech" (*F/T*, 122) allows universal wisdom to be intelligible in direct communication. Since all words are mediation, it is Kierkegaard's task to use them to indicate the ideal quality of silence. Art can give relief neither to Kierkegaard nor to his reader.[33] For this reason, it is an all-important medium for the dialectic of misunderstanding. The tragic hero, "translated into the universal, does at last get to the end of

---

33. This is quite a different withholding from those of Gustave Flaubert and Kafka, who must use art itself for a place of salvation. Kafka writes: "In me, by myself, without human relationship, there are no visible lies. The limited circle is pure" [Max Brod (ed.), *The Diaries of Franz Kafka, 1910–1913*, trans. Joseph Kresh (2 vols.; New York, 1968), I, 300]. He suggests to us that, since there is no marriage for him beyond the celibacy of art, the only way it can remain bearably innocent is to restrict severely the expansion of style, character, even length—potentially guilty explosions of rebellion against the father and family.

his story" (*F/T*, 122). But Kierkegaard cannot come to the end. He, at least the physical part of him, must stay in "dread, distress, paradox" (*CUP*, 549) while he plies the "ambiguous art of thinking about existence and existing."

I am only a poet who loves what wounds.
Journals and Papers

To be made well with the aid of Christianity is not the
difficulty; the difficulty is in becoming sick to some
purpose.
Journals and Papers

A poet's life begins in conflict with the whole of
existence. The gist of it is to find an appeasement or a
justification; for in the first conflict he must always be
defeated, and if he is bent upon triumphing at once, he
is an unjustified exception.
Repetition

1 · *The Wound of Misunderstanding: The Condition*

 HE famous thorn in the flesh, to which Kierke-
gaard so often refers, shows up most powerfully
in his work as a secret and sinful sexual identification with the father, as the inheritance of that
father's melancholy and premonition of family
doom and of his youthful curse against God on
the heath. It shows up also as the despairing
inability to share this legacy with father or fiancée; in the works of his
commentators, the sexual guilt might derive from a brothel escapade
and an oedipal antagonism to the father.[1] But in the largest and most
important sense, the wound of Kierkegaard is the wound of misunderstanding, or the fear of being understood as guilty. The psychological

---

1. See Walter Lowrie, *Kierkegaard* (New York, 1962), I, 130ff. and 70ff., for a
discussion of the section in *SLW* called "Solomon's Dream" and its relation to Kierkegaard's secret sense of sin. Cf. the entry of 1843, in *J/P*, V, 236; n. 5669. That
Kierkegaard's father had sexual relations with the servant that became his wife *before* the
year of mourning for his first wife was up doubtless fed the legacy of sexual sin.

longing for pure motive is to be spiritually raised to the purity to will one thing, but the public passage always reflects the ambivalence of the private condition. While envying Shakespeare's ability to express everything without the sense that his words cover up sexual guilt, Kierkegaard muses himself into a relationship, wondering if perhaps the playwright did not reserve for himself a pang (the dread suspension of the tragic consolation) he spared his characters, a demonic secret "like the loved one whose name one cannot endure that the world should mention? For the poet purchases the power of words, the power of uttering all the dread secrets of others, at the price of a little secret he is unable to utter . . . and a poet is not an apostle, he casts out devils only by the power of the devil" (F/T, 72). Even when he appears most confident, Kierkegaard always anxiously walks the line between the use of misunderstanding for public revelation and for private protection.

That is why it was so important for him to establish misunderstanding, the pathetic version of his own actively guilty ambivalence toward the father, as the necessary base for all spirituality. William James notes the close relationship between sickness, spiritual passion, and the tendency to moral emphasis, and surely Kierkegaard was a genius of emphasis.[2] The wound, the most corporeal of his attributes, dialectically incites the spiritual as it binds him to the humiliations of Christ and Paul.[3] "In the New Testament, Christianity is the deepest wound that can be dealt to a man" (J/P, VI, 500; n. 6860 [1854]). He continually reminds us that the least of Christ's suffering was the cross. "No day passed, not an hour of any day, but that misunderstanding, as well as it can (and perhaps with greater tortures than bodily suffering) crucified Him" (TC, 170). Powerful self-idealization is often the sign of great capacity for spirit, but so strong is the identification that he must remind himself to

2. William James, *The Varieties of Religious Experience* (London, 1961), 38.
3. See Rachel Bespaloff, "En marge de 'Crainte et Tremblement' de Kierkegaard," *Revue philosophique de la France et de l'Étranger*, CXIX (1935), 47–48: "Il manquait à Kierkegaard pour accéder au réel, la pesanteur qui équilibre l'homme à son univers, l' 'inépuisible animalité'. Cet acrobate de l'infini perd pied dès qu'il touche au sol. Ce qui l'y rattache, c'est précisément l'épine qui lui rend la marche si pénible et le vol si aisé." ("For adjusting to the real, Kierkegaard lacked the weight that balances man with his universe, an inexhaustible animality. This acrobat of the infinite loses his footing as soon as he touches ground. What fastens him to it is precisely the thorn that makes his gait painful and his flight so easy" [author's translation].)

stave off the demonic pride and solace implicit in that comparison.[4] "Oh, let us never take the name of sacred things in vain. And yet how often have we not been accustomed to comfort earthly sorrows by using the thorn in the flesh as the highest and strongest consolation, without being willing to understand that before the wounds of comfort can bring healing, they must wound still deeper!" (*ED*, IV, 53). If he were as pure as his Abraham, his God-relationship would be compatible with a pedestrian gait; but Kierkegaard's often hysterical devices to disguise his suffering testify to a concern that he was too willing a Philoctetus, cherishing his wound as a sign of God's love. Perhaps he too much envied Job, for through the young man in *Repetition*, Kierkegaard reminds Constantine Constantius, his creator, "What is Philoctetus with his complaints, which constantly remain on earth and do not terrify the gods!" (*Rep*, 110). If he is, like Jacob, "instantaneously recognizable by his limp" as one "who in truth has become involved with God" (*J/P*, II, 123; n. 1405 [1850]), he must suffer continual possibilities of ambivalent motives and not allow his wound to close, for it is the impetus to dialectical extension. "But there is a kind of pietism, a tragic spiritual asceticism, which believes that the thorn in the flesh is given to a man merely so that he may sit and whimper and look at the thorn instead of using the thorn to rise higher; for that is how it is, however odd it is in a certain sense: with the help of the thorn in my foot I leap higher than anyone with feet in the best condition" (*J/P*, V, 3856; n. 6011 [1847]). Without social possibilities, Kierkegaard masters reality by means of the open wound.[5] It allows Father Taciturnus to imagine that diseased body as unable to "be humbled by any reality," but the Pyrrhic price is the consciousness of annihilation "as other men are not sensible of it" (*SLW*, 407). The wound is Kierkegaard's history: "absolute isolation is in this case identical with the profoundest continuity" (*E/O*, II, 221).

In an important *Journal* entry, Kierkegaard observes that the spiritual yearning for healing is brought on by a graduated series of misrela-

---

4. Cf. Ludwig Feuerbach's linking of the capacity for spiritual projection with the capacity for self-knowledge (as well as delusion) throughout *The Essence of Christianity*, trans. George Eliot (New York, 1957).

5. See *CUP*, 78: "He is conscious of the negativity of the infinite in existence, and he constantly keeps the wound of the negative open, which in the bodily realm is sometimes the condition for a cure."

tionships, beginning with the one between the mind and the body and advancing, in his case acutely, to that between father and son. Kierkegaard obsessively fingers this filial misunderstanding and feels it as the psychological basis for his spiritual impulsion. At first there is a strong bond of inherited suffering between the two. "An old man who himself was extremely melancholy . . . gets a son in his old age who inherits all this melancholy" (*J/P*, V, 334; n. 5913 [1846]). But the bond is one of despair, itself the symptom of a misrelationship between the eternal and the temporal in man (*J/P*, I, 25; n. 68 [1848] and *SD*, 145—50). This primary misrelationship leads to misunderstanding, since the father cannot question the son about his melancholy for fear of finding himself the source. "Who knows if after all I have not had an injurious influence upon him?" (*E/O*, II, 221).[6] The fear is mutual and leads to the fateful secret: "And the father believed that he was responsible for his son's melancholy, and the son believed that he was responsible for his father's melancholy; therefore, they never raised the subject" (*J/P*, I, 346; n. 745 [1844]). But the injury has already been inflicted, and secrecy does not heal it. "'Misguidance' about the nature of sin is often found, and the source may very well be someone with the best intentions. For example, a man who has been very debauched and, wanting to deter his son from the same, interpreted the sexual drive as sin—and forgot that there was a difference between himself and the child—that the child was innocent and therefore must necessarily misunderstand. Unfortunate one, who in this way would be hitched, even as a child, to pulling and hauling through life" (*J/P*, IV, 107; n. 4009 [1845]).

How terrible Kierkegaard had always felt this consciousness of sin to be, isolated from the solacing qualification of racial predisposition, is evident in an early *Journal* entry in which he blasts the smugness of bourgeois notions of Christendom and gives this Romantic rendition of its true nature: "They have never caught a glimpse of the idea which lies underneath when we are pushed through the hidden, mysterious door, open in all its terror only to presentiment, into this dark realm of sighs—when we see the crushed sacrifices of seduction and deception and the coldness of the tempter" (*J/P*, I, 89—90; n. 219 [1837]). No

---

6. We hardly need the *Journal* entries to confirm the biographical recapitulations in the texts, thinly disguised as generalizations, so full are these of private pathos.

ethical protection could ever shield Kierkegaard from the shudder of this homelessness; later, it willfully hovers, by compensation, as the "teleological suspension of the ethical" in *Fear and Trembling*. In a diatribe against the paternal influence, Kierkegaard apostrophizes: "O, wretched satire upon the human race, that providence has so richly equipped almost every child, because it knew in advance what it means to have to be brought up by 'parents,' i.e., to be messed up as much as it is humanly possible to be" (*J/P*, II, 31; n. 1171 [1849]). The father aborts the son's first immediacy (*PVA*, 80) and "slays his childhood and youth" (*J/P*, II, 49; n. 1215 [1848]). After the *Corsair* polemic, Kierkegaard notes from time to time the mocking of the citizens, especially of his uneven trouser legs, and here again he poignantly emphasizes the misrelationship between the child and the old man through the identification of their bodies.[7] "The fundamental misfortune of my whole life is that I was confused with being an old man, and this appeared also in my clothes" (*J/P*, VI, 136; n. 6379 [1849]). This confusion is possible because Kierkegaard has ever been but one age. "As a man I am personally a poor unhappy child whom a despondent old man in his love made as unhappy as possible" (*J/P*, VI, 36; n. 6220 [1849]).

But Kierkegaard sees the contagion from the other side as well, from that of the prodigal son who infects the father with grief. In a comparison of the misrelationships between father and son, between son and the present age, Kierkegaard comments: "Alas, it goes with me and so it will go with me and my age as it did with my father. I gave him much grief— then he died, and I inherited him" (*J/P*, VI, 36; n. 6222 [1848]). The compulsive parasitism is strong enough to be deserved. And here is a prayer from 1838, after Kierkegaard's youthful period of estrangement: "How I thank you, Father in heaven, for having kept an earthly father present for a time here on earth, where I so greatly need him; with your help I hope that he will have a greater joy in being my father the second time than he had the first time" (*J/P*, V, 120; n. 5328). His twinship with the prodigal son (a common Romantic representative of man's alienation from the divine) is patent in an entry of a decade later in which

7. The lampooning of Kierkegaard by the *Corsair*, a comic paper of Copenhagen, in the years 1845–46, a response to Kierkegaard's own provocation as he railed against his praise in its pages, is well documented. See, for example, Lowrie's chapter in *Kierkegaard*, II, 347–63.

Kierkegaard compares his brother with the upright son, calling himself
the prodigal brother (J/P, VI, 16; n. 6176).

However fateful the misunderstanding, the power of the relationship
is such that it can only be contrasted to the common, indifferent misunderstanding of a staid, bourgeois Christendom in which a whole age has
become a committee. "A father no longer curses his son in anger, using
all his parental authority, nor does a son defy his father, a conflict which
might end in the inwardness of forgiveness; on the contrary, their relationship is irreproachable, for it is really in process of ceasing to exist,
since they are no longer related to one another within the relationship"
(PA, 44–45). No, this is a dialectical misunderstanding that is, as
Father Taciturnus defines it, "a heterogeneity such as does not exclude a
relationship" (SLW, 378). It is rich, deep, agonizing, and permanent. It
must be loved so that, at last, the "inwardness of forgiveness" can make
"the child's obedience and the father's authority joyful" (PA, 45). Is it
any wonder that Kierkegaard was so continually moved by the picture of
Abraham receiving Isaac back with a joy that knew no resentment? This
is not just meant to be the dream of Regine's forgiveness. Kierkegaard
can never, not even at the end, have the immediacy of Abraham, strong
enough to overcome secrets. But he can project a severely economical
transfiguration by having the dialectical relationship prefigure that between human and divine, though there the misunderstanding is all on
the side of the petitioner.

> The point precisely is that he made me unhappy—but out of love.
> His error did not consist in lack of love, but in mistaking a child for
> an old man. To love him who makes one happy is to a reflective mind
> an inadequate definition of what love is; to love him who made one
> unhappy out of malice, is virtue; but to love him who out of love,
> though by a misunderstanding, yet out of love, made one unhappy—
> that is the formula never yet enunciated, so far as I know, but
> nevertheless the normal formula in reflection for what it is to love.
> (PVA, 77)[8]

While this formula leads the man to an acceptance of the unhappiness
that accompanies God's love, it leads the author to a rich misrelationship

8. Sponheim, *Kierkegaard on Christ*, 143, calls this process "a sado-masochistic
grammar."

with his work. In their love for one another, the author and his work make each other unhappy. His work has obvious relationships to Rousseau's *Confessions*, a book that greatly interested Kierkegaard and that turns private pain to public purposes. But Rousseau's words can be forged into guiltless weapons, since they are "compelled" by a persecuting society; they can describe for him, a passive pawn, the deep innocence of his flaws. However, Kierkegaard had to create difficulties and take responsibility for them, prodding his own wound, for the sin was felt to be deeply within him, not without.

In a passage in *The Concept of Anxiety* dealing with our relationship to Adam, Kierkegaard distinguishes our tired assumption of sin as fate from the spontaneous appropriation of the child who "wishes to be guilty along with the father" out of "sympathy and the persuasion of piety" (*CA*, 29). Like Aeneas, Kierkegaard would choose to bear his father on his shoulders from simple motives of piety, continuity, and recovery. But he cannot altogether be that child, nor can he be glad Abraham. Instead, he projects himself into his literature as a modern Antigone, a figure who bears secrecy and anxiety without support or sanction of history and myth.[9] She goes, in her ethical isolation, beyond the desired Hegelian reconciliation with her fate.

> She loves her father with all her soul, and this love transports her out of herself and into her father's guilt; as the fruit of such a love, she feels herself alienated from mankind; she feels her own guilt the more she loves her father; only with him could she find rest, as equally guilty they would sorrow together. But while her father lived she had not been able to confide her sorrow to him, for she did not know whether he knew about it, and consequently there was a possibility of plunging him into a similar pain. (*E/O*, I, 159)

The public exposure of the long shadow of tragedy that the father casts upon his child in the classical Antigone assures the heroine of the universal compensation and consolation of chorus and legend. Hegel's discussion of tragedy is closely bound to his praise of the ancient Antigone precisely for its agonizing but comprehensible mediation of a terrible collision of traditional values. Justice can be "grasped by thought" and

9. *J/P*, V, 236; n. 5669 [1843]).

the tragic form. It is true that Hegel considers that there is a higher "form of reconciliation" than that, involving an interiorization of fate. "The attitude of one-sidedness should be done away with in *the Subject* . . . the subject should have the consciousness of his wrong-doing, and . . . he should in his own heart put away his wrong-doing."[10] Kierkegaard's Antigone might represent this higher form of reconciliation, her Christian guilt making death "superfluous," but instead she is not available to the compensation of justice grasped by thought. She remains a one-sided Subject from a Hegelian point of view. He will not even give his stranded heroine the peace of death. And, like Kierkegaard himself, Antigone will have to deal endlessly with the collision between the paternal secret and marriage.

The only form of recovery, an ambiguous one indeed, is that of a renunciation of the possibility of sharing the secret, the son's sacrifice in his struggle for salvation "for his father's sake" (*CUP*, 522).[11] He cannot let the father go, no matter how cruel the love, any more than he can give up the Christianity that gives him so much pain. The identity with the father does not lead to a Hegelian mediation of private and public, particular and universal, subjective and objective. No, it is a base for a higher misrelationship. In this life, the collision is perpetually preserved in the heart of misunderstanding's transvaluation, just as cruelty is constantly a quality of God's love manifested in this world. When Judge William looks upon his son and worries about injuring him, he consoles himself with the thought that in choosing himself, the son "will repent my guilt that rests on him." And he continues, "It is a beautiful thing for a son to repent his father's fault" (*E/O*, II, 221). Kierkegaard qualifies this smug consolation by claiming elsewhere, in a harder voice, that such an equilibrium is no more possible than straightening out the absurdity of the Christian Paradox by straightening out its consequences. That would be "about as reasonable as to suppose that a son had retroactive

10. See G. W. F. Hegel, *Lectures on the Philosophy of Religion*, trans. E. B. Speirs and J. B. Sanderson (2 vols., London, 1895), II, 263–66, esp. 264, where the phrase "justice is grasped by thought" appears.

11. In *Søren Kierkegaard*, trans. T. H. Croxall (New York, 1978), 39, Johannes Hohlenberg notes: "It is as if each of them found and recognized himself in the other. It is as if each of them, without in any sense telling each other outright, was quite clear that a secret contract had been concluded between them, by which the son's life should be a sacrifice for the father's sin."

power to transform his own father" (*PF*, 119). And this is why Kierkegaard is so fierce in his objection to the mediation of infant baptism,
because "it is also a part of the earnestness of Christianity that it forces
itself disruptively, with the decisiveness of eternity, between parents and
child" (*J/P*, IV, 246; n. 4344 [1852]). This division is to assure the
freedom of the act of choosing the self in faith, which carries with it the
consciousness of guilt and sin. Yet, for Kierkegaard, does not Christianity keep apart only what, in fact, has already been tragically sun-
dered, and thereby sanction as holy the misrelationship between fathers
and sons?

The unhappy childhood of misunderstanding is gradually the very
means by which Kierkegaard is "transfigured into spirit" (*J/P*, II, 12;
n. 1123 [1848]), and the transfiguration, through an ascending, qualitative transposition of the same experience, repeatedly brings a second
and true childhood, not in spite of, but because of misunderstanding.
"But on not rare occasions it seems as if my childhood had come back
again, for unhappy as my father made me, it seems as if I now experience
being a child in my relationship to God, as if all my early life was
misspent so dreadfully in order that I should experience it more truly the
second time in my relationship to God" (*J/P*, VI, 84; n. 6298 [1849]).
In an interesting *Journal* note, Kierkegaard spots the humor, which
always precedes full spiritual transformation, "in a person who unhappily has been cheated of his childhood and then later becomes spirit and
simultaneously aware of childhood" (*J/P*, II, 11; n. 1123 [1848]). And,
indeed, the view of childhood as unconscious of guilt from the Christian
perspective regularly accompanies Kierkegaard's discussions of the relation of humor to the spirit; for humor shows us that real gain might come
from loss, dialectically tensed as it is between these two terms. It helps
us to reverse our ages, our metaphors. Baptism might come at maturity,
childhood might come at the end, and our first father might actually be a
poor image of our eternal one. By this reversed perspective, analogy is
kept in its humble place of mere reflection, so that art does not do the
work of the spirit, nor recollection that of repentance. The heavenly
Father lends his name to the earthly one.

If . . . you felt a certain sadness about taking the best there is on earth
to express the divine and it still did not reach up to heaven but along

the way dissolved and disappeared before your eyes, this is now not
the case, for now you have perceived that God is not called father
according to the earthly designation, but that it is the other way
around . . . so that even if you had the best father there could be on
earth, he is still only your step-father, only a reflection of the father-
love after which he is named, only a shadow, a reflection, a picture, a
metaphor, a dim expression of the fatherliness from which all fatherhood has its name in heaven and on earth. (*J/P*, V, 166; n. 5488
[1840–41], and see *ED*, I, 116–119)

The first child cannot have this vision, a reversal of Feuerbach's assumption of man's self-projection into God. He is often tortured by the doubt
that the unrest in the father's piety, the injuries caused by the best
intention, reflect weaknesses in God himself and even the possibility
that there may be no infinite love (*J/P*, II, 32; n. 1173 [1850]). He
might project from his earthly father, a bad-gift giver, onto the Heavenly One, taking the figurative for the real. But psychological projection
is as deceitful as art's poor spiritual analogies.

An expansion of vision might bring with it an apparent regression of
attitude to that of the child who unconsciously takes upon himself the
guilt for disorder to spare the parents, to keep them agents of the world's
order. But as a religious poet, Kierkegaard goes beyond this pathetic
assumption to the conscious transvaluation of regression into growth,
obedience (which, like renunciation, allows the will to protect against
exclusions, from the primal one to that of other marriages) into realism.
It is not surprising that the reluctance of a guilty son to go past the father
should flower into Kierkegaard's obsessive warning to the age not to go
further than faith. The child who takes on guilt is at least in the right
position, if not in the right mind, because (Luther is right) in front of
God we are always in the wrong. It must be understood backwards, too,
that in relation to the earthly father, the son is always in the wrong. This
is a deliberately difficult regression, and it is simply another way of
indicating that the correct position in this world (where intention has no
guarantee of effect), in relation to the absolute, must be measured by the
movement of misunderstanding and incommensurability. Again, working the metaphor down from the top, the notion of suffering innocently
before God must be reserved for Christ, for this assumption, humanly,

would press for a justification of God. This is precisely what Kant demands for Abraham who, when he hears God's voice demanding the sacrifice of Isaac, a command wholly incommensurable with the categorical imperative, should have protested: "That I ought not to kill my good son is quite certain. But that you, this apparition, are God—of that I am not certain." [12] The self may use art to ask for justification, but to use it for the justification rather than the demonstration of God would be to assume that God is not love. Because God is the father of lights "with whom is no variableness, neither shadow of turning," we are forever dialectical with his truth. [13] But our guilt assures us of God's love, for where there is need, there is forgiveness, though to believe that, especially for Kierkegaard, is the hardest of all acts of faith. That is why we so often feel the intimate relation in Kierkegaard between the compulsion to self-justification and the difficulty of accepting justification by Grace. No world could be more terrifying and impossible in Kierkegaard's eyes than one that continually sought and demanded justice and retribution for the kind of misunderstanding that exists between the finite and infinite in us, no life more impossible than one of constant litigation between fathers and sons. Although regularly refusing to imagine the autonomy, and hence reality, of God's love, Kierkegaard's admirer and parodist, Franz Kafka, describes best this "trial of guilt" in his characteristic blend of pathos and humor that readily distinguishes false guilt from existential guilt. "That one should consider it possible to argue about it as about any ordinary arithmetical problem which is so clear that it produces results for daily conduct, this I don't understand at all. Of course you are to blame, but then your husband is also to blame and then you again and then he again, since it cannot be otherwise in the living together of human beings and the blame piles up in endless succession until it reaches the grey Original Sin." [14] In *Works of Love*,

---

12. Immanuel Kant, *The Conflict of the Faculties / Der Streit der Fakultäten*, trans. Mary J. Gregor (New York, 1979), 115n. And see Geoffrey Clive, "The Teleological Suspension of the Ethical in Nineteenth-Century Literature," *Journal of Religion*, XXXIV (1954), 76, and Robert L. Perkins, "For Sanity's Sake: Kant, Kierkegaard, and Father Abraham," in Robert L. Perkins (ed.), *Kierkegaard's "Fear and Trembling": Critical Appraisals* (University, Ala., 1981), 43–61.

13. James 1 : 17.

14. Franz Kafka, *Letters to Milena*, ed. Willi Haas, trans. Tania Stern and James Stern (New York, 1953), 193.

Kierkegaard corrects the childish understanding that one could deceive those parents who, superior in wisdom and insight, have "also such superiority in true love for the child." He then asks, "Would it not be miserable and disgusting to see a father or mother who could therefore sink into unseemly wrangling with the child, become irritated and embittered over their own mistakes, because the father and mother childishly had the foolish opinion that it was the child who deceived them!" (*WL*, 222).

The most touching passages in relation to this imperative of order deal with the task of being always in the right as a father, for "to have someone around toward whom one is constantly in the right—this is a dangerous business" (*J/P*, II, 28; n. 1161 [1845]) and one that we know Kierkegaard would not willingly have assumed. It helps to account, perhaps, for the self-irony of his authorship. The young man in *Stages on Life's Way* pictures fatherhood as a most dreadful state. "There is no comparison between putting a human being to death and giving life to a human being; the first merely decides his fate in time; the other in eternity" (*SLW*, 58). The anguish of the father who sees his image in the son's eyes as incommensurable with his own feelings about himself leads both to the need for a higher father. Most moving is the long passage in the discourse, "The Joy in the Thought in Relation to God a Man Always Suffers as Being Guilty" (*GS*, 65–96). It is a great relief to one in such guilt as Kierkegaard to believe that innocence is not possible in any relation to the eternal, so that the greatest love between man and man may even hold to the desire "to be in the wrong, aye, to be the one guilty" (*GS*, 86). It is most terrible for a son to be in the right against his father, but if he is always in the wrong, then God is love (*GS*, 78). For, as long as man suffers as guilty, there is always task enough, always need, always hope. "If therefore a sufferer could be in the right as over against God, if it were possible that the fault could lie in God, aye, then would there be hopelessness and the horror of hopelessness, then would there be no task" (*GS*, 81–82).

It is easy to see, now, why Job is such a hero of suffering for Kierkegaard. For he suffers innocently from a human point of view, and, therefore, makes the notion of guilt before God as difficult as possible. "Nevertheless, Job was constantly in the wrong as toward God" (*GS*, 91). Only with this unconditional recognition do we rise above the child's interpretation of punishment, above the realm of fortune and misfortune. In the latter realm, one is guilty about this or that, but in the eternal perspective, man is *essentially* a sinner. Therefore, he is always guilty. By raising the guilt in the relation with the father and the fiancée to the position "before God," Kierkegaard justifies it. From the discourse in the "Ultimatum" of *Either/Or*, we know how much of himself he put into this reflection:

> You loved a person, you wished that with respect to him you might always be in the wrong; but, alas, he was unfaithful to you, and however reluctantly you admitted it, however much it pained you, you nevertheless would have to recognize that you were in the right in your behavior towards him, and in the wrong for loving him so dearly. And yet your soul insisted upon loving him thus, only in this could you find peace and rest and happiness. Then your soul turned away from the finite to the infinite; there it found its object, there your love became a happy love. God I will love, you said; He bestows upon the lover all things, He fulfills my dearest, my only wish, that against Him I must be always in the wrong. (*E/O*, II, 352)

In this relationship, the anxiety inherent in the passion for innocence is soothed. To hold God to account for the suffering from individual sins is to "subsume God under ethical categories" (*Rep.* 112). The secret wound is felt as essential sin, beyond psychological and ethical control. Around the edges of this release from exceptional misunderstanding prowls the suspicion of personal apology, but the beast is kept at bay by the relentless spin of transfiguration.

The second stage in the sanctification of misrelationship is the renunciation of marriage, a universal mediation. The fatal secret, the "dowry of pain" (*E/O*, I, 160) and of melancholy that the modern Antigone carries with her, assures a breach with the beloved. "To marry means making the relation to the ideal so difficult for oneself that ordinarily it is synonymous with giving up the ideal" (*J/P*, II, 306; n. 1824 {1854(?)}). The justification in this late entry is surer than in the early, all possibilities even of reconciliation having run out, but essentially the pattern does not change. To make Christianity more difficult takes one kind of courage, but to endure a life of marital misunderstandings when one needs "something majestic to love" (*J/P*, III, 144; n. 2624 {1854})

takes a faith strong enough to share the secret. It is no wonder that
Johannes de Silentio wants to draw so near to the humble Sarah of the
Book of Tobit, who had the faith to marry in the face of a curse of death, a
dowry of pain. "For what love to God it requires to be willing to let
oneself be healed when from the beginning one has been bungled without one's fault, from the beginning has been an abortive specimen of
humanity" (F/T, 113). Socrates set up marriage as a useful dialectical
hindrance to the spiritual (J/P, II, 306; n. 1824 [1854(?)]), but Kierkegaard did not have the boldness for this kind of comedy.[15] Like the young
man in Repetition, he could not trim himself into commensurability (Rep,
120). Only in a tragic sense is God "Regine's successful rival."[16] If
Socrates could say that he had learned from the words of a woman,
Kierkegaard could say, "I owe my best to a girl" (J/P, VI, 4; n. 6144
[1848]), for his best is renunciation. The idealizing religious action of
renunciation, too, can work with but a single love. Only when psychological complex cannot be or does not want to be fully transformed into
spiritual purpose, as in Kafka, will the lover renounce several times.
Regine could have been a Socrates to his Alcibiades had she been able to
endure the dialectical agony that would enable her to take unhappiness
for happiness (J/P, IV, 583; n. 5007 [1854]). But Kierkegaard has to
do the work of frustration. While the pretense of deceit on the part of the
lover is to free the beloved (Regine and the reader) who has not a great
enough God-relationship to understand direct renunciation, it ironically
reveals that the "seducer" has not faith enough, "faith that for God all
things are possible" (J/P, V, 176; n. 177 [1841]), faith enough to
endure dialectically the relationship between earthly marriage and the
Paradox. The greatest of all threats to the willed construction of Kierkegaard's life would be the possibility, the secret shared, of being understood only too well, that is, as guilty. Engagement is menacingly called

15. Cf. the claim of Nietzsche in The Birth of Tragedy and the Genealogy of Morals,
trans. Francis Golffing (Garden City, N.Y., 1956), 242: "Thus the philosopher abhors
marriage and all that would persuade him to marriage, for he sees the married state as an
obstacle to fulfillment. What great philosopher has ever been married? . . . I maintain
that a married philosopher belongs in comedy, and as for that great exception, Socrates,
it would almost seem that the malicious Socrates got married in a spirit of irony, precisely
in order to prove that contention."

16. This is the phrase of Martin Buber in his criticism of Kierkegaard, in Between
Man and Man, trans. Ronald Gregor Smith (Boston, 1955), 57.

"revelation" in "Diary of the Seducer" (E/O, I, 382). Marriage with
Regine, the reader, cannot be allowed, for the "comfort of temporal
existence is a precarious affair. It lets the wound grow together, although
it is not yet healed." It must be kept open "in order that the Eternal may
heal it" (PH, 149). But the references to the courage of Sarah, who could
marry with the knowledge that the wound would wound, and to that of
figures who might allow themselves to be saved by love are obsessive.
They reflect the difficulty Kierkegaard felt in accepting Regine's forgiveness, self-forgiveness, and the forgiveness of Grace, all of which
demand surrender of the will's control.[17]

In one of his many versions of the fairy tale of the king and the humble
maiden, Johannes Climacus seems to suggest, by the careful and passionate quality of his analogy betwen earthly and divine love, that his
author himself assumes, provisionally, the costume of the king. In the
world of fortune and misfortune favored by fairy tales, it is common for
the union of lovers to be frustrated. But in the world of spirit, which
providentially rises above fortune, the misunderstanding is necessary.
"The unhappiness of this love does not come from the inability of the
lovers to realize their union, but from their inability to understand one
another. This grief is infinitely more profound than that of which men
commonly speak, since it strikes at the very heart of love, and wounds for
an eternity; not like that other misfortune which touches only the temporal and the external, and which for the magnanimous is as a sort of jest
over the inability of the lovers to realize their union here in time" (PF,
31). This deeper grief is perpetrated by "the superior," by the king, since
"only he likewise understands the misunderstanding; in reality it belongs to the God alone, and no human relationship can afford a valid
analogy" (PF, 32). While the God can elevate through the Incarnation
and the "crucifixion of the understanding" (CUP, 531), what can a poor
king do? It is better to stay heterogeneous with the world, finally, to
choose the "single state instead of weddings and birthdays" (J/P, III,
145; n. 2626 [1854]), unless one is Abraham and can receive without
remorse, without guilt, and with a clear, undeviating faith in the hierar-

17. In her interesting book, Aparté: conceptions et morts de Søren Kierkegaard (Paris,
1977), Sylviane Agacinski illuminates the tension in Kierkegaard between imitation of
Christ and the acceptance of Christ as savior, and between the disguise of seduction of the
writer and fiancé and the passion of the Christian.

chy of misunderstandings. Kierkegaard's works are strewn with lyrical dreams of reconciliation between lovers, but they are crossed by the impossibility of relating "oneself with *eternal* faithfulness to that which in itself is *not* the eternal" (*WL*, 290). This misrelationship is a weak analogy to that between the understanding and the Christian Paradox, but its perpetuation is a preparation for the ultimate giving back of the self to God. Perhaps, fantasizes Kierkegaard, living out of wedlock like Hamann, the wife a concubine, perhaps that would keep the wound open and satisfy erotic longing (*J/P*, II, 204; n. 1558 [1847]). Without the sanction of the world, one could still remain heterogeneous with it.

He allows William to go past himself in *Stages on Life's Way* and to relate vividly the agony of the renunciation of erotic fulfillment within society's sanction. "He must so comprehend the breach as to understand that he who had found security in life . . . is now cast out into new perils and the most awful of mortal dangers" (*SLW*, 174). There is no consolation:

> Even if it is established that he could do no otherwise, yet by this step he has ventured out upon the trackless vast of infinite space, where the sword of Damocles hangs above his head if he looks towards heaven, where the traps of temptation try to catch his feet if he looks towards earth, where no human help is offered. . . . He is a rebel against the earthly; and the physical which when it is on good terms with the spiritual is a staff of support, as time is also, has become an enemy; for the physical has become a serpent to him and time has become the instant of the bad conscience. He supposes that it is so easy to triumph over the physical; yes, that is so when one does not incite it by wanting to destroy it. (*SLW*, 174)

Kierkegaard can, through the mouth of William, describe the marriage "on good terms with the spiritual" just because *he* has "a fervor such as a married man hardly has"; for "the torment of responsibility for the breach must keep his soul alert and vigilant in the contemplation of what he destroyed and the new responsibility requires him first of all to know what he did" (*SLW*, 173).

How to prevent the universal understanding and sanction from killing the God-relationship and still keep the human relationship, between father and son, between lovers, a conductor of a higher sort of incommensurability—this is a terrible dilemma, as is that of keeping art a conductor of the spirit when it falls so short of it. To keep the relationship in mind means to remember always the priority of misunderstanding. The father and the fiancée, who have made him as unhappy as possible (and whom he has made unhappy), were affectionate enough to make the son's longing sincere, his remembrance full and constant (*J/P*, VI, 13; n. 6167 [1848]). Abraham comes to his aid, the Abraham who might have told his son that he was a monster, a murderer, thus seconding a common opinion and, at the same time, strengthening the bond between the boy and God. In such a way, the father's oppressive, secret sense of sin drives Kierkegaard to a second father, and his own "murder" of Regine might release both to God (*FT*, 27ff and *J/P*, V, 224–25; n. 5640 [1843]). Rising above the universal, Abraham must deal with a collision that goes beyond that of Hegelian tragedy—a collision between the same God's contradictory command and promise (*J/P*, I, 404; n. 908 [1843]). Ultimately, Abraham's belief shames that of Kierkegaard, who presses after him like Johannes de Silentio. It is not for Abraham to sue for love from one whom he makes unhappy, a desire that Kierkegaard himself recognizes as one that "no man had the right to demand" (*J/P*, VI, 313; n. 6615 [1850]). The poet of the ideal despairs over "the pain he must bring upon men when the ideal is to be brought into actuality" and lived (*J/P*, VI, 324; n. 6632 [1850]), for he knows this pain intimately. To the degree that he cannot live the ideal, as a poet, his whole life is "an unhappy love affair" with it; needless to say, as he succeeds, he renounces his art.

If the religious poet cannot unhitch himself from the Platonic horses straining in opposite directions, he can and must see in the lower world the pattern of the higher, where the dialectic persists but sanctifies unhappiness and renunciation. "Unhappy love is the highest form of erotic love. The lover still says: I would ten times rather be unhappy with him and ten times as unhappy again than to be happy with someone else. So also with the religious person. It just has to be that one becomes unhappy, humanly speaking—it lies in the misrelationship between God and man; but still, still—what blessedness!" (*J/P*, III, 42; n. 2418 [1848]). The highest form of erotic love is out of the reach of Kierkegaard and Regine. But the love he has refused to Regine makes him a vessel of God's love, a love given with the understanding that he who carries it will "become an unhappy, piteous, wretched man, a byword among men, hated, exiled, persecuted by men, and finally deceived" by God (*J/P*, III, 54; n. 2447 [1854]). The Christian victim is also the pattern. The misrelationship testifies, too, to one term that never changes. "No, that God is love means, of course, that he will do everything to help you to love him, that is, to be transformed into likeness to him. As I have frequently said, he knows very well how infinitely agonizing this transformation is for a human being; he is willing to suffer with you—yes, out of love he suffers more than you, suffers all the deep sorrow of misunderstanding—but he is not changed" (*J/P*, III, 57; n. 2450 [1854]). Not by nature, but by dialectically assumed obedience can the other term imitate the pattern. "A faithful son loves unchangeably," but "in his heart he may . . . cherish a wish like that of the inhabitants who besought Christ to depart from their region, because He made them afraid" (*CUP*, 522).

The punishment does not change, but the conception of it can (*J/P*, II, 51; n. 1222 [1850]), and through this act suffering can be seen as the sign of God's love. The suffering of misunderstanding in love attests to the reality of that love (*SD*, 262). It is childish to see love and cruelty as Manichean antagonists. The child who receives punishment from the parent perceives "a cleft in the father's nature," for he "imagines that the father is the loving one, that punishment . . . is something a bad man has invented" (*PH*, 87). That punishment and love are dialectically wishboned is beyond his imagination. (Kierkegaard often takes Luther to task for splitting the devil's temptations from God's trials.) Here, then, is the "strenuousness" of the idea that "not only is the suffering to be endured but that it is a good, a gift from a God of love. Think of it! When a person inflicts suffering upon another man and then himself wants to be the cruel one who says: This is cruel—there is relief in this. But if the person who inflicts the suffering says: This is a benefit—that, humanly speaking is enough to drive one out of his mind" (*J/P*, IV, 266; n. 4375 [1849]). And yet, is it not the despair of Kierkegaard that he himself has to play this role with another, as it is played with him? What a monster! Could he compare his offense to that of Christ? Again, he must travesty imitation with the analogy of human love.

Let a lover say to his beloved, "My dear girl, I give thee thy freedom, we must part; to belong to me would signify (as I can tell thee with certainty beforehand) that thou, humanly speaking, wouldst become unhappy as possible! Let us suppose that she replied, "I will endure everything, for only then am I unhappy when I am parted from thee." Let us go farther, let us suppose that he replied, "Very well, but I must require one thing more if thou art to remain with me, that thou must maintain that to be thus unhappy with me is nevertheless the highest happiness." What then? Would not the girl be fully justified in saying, "This is madness." (*SE/JY*, 212)

The king obsessively returns to justify the transformation of common weakness into the pathos of superiority.[18] "Suppose a girl is loved by a man who is decidedly superior to her; the more sincerely he loves her, the unhappier he will make her—and out of love. He applies his standard; he cannot do otherwise; he loves her sincerely; and what happens—the very thing which he regards as the strongest expression for his love, precisely this will be too high for her and will disturb her" (*J/P*, I, 207; n. 514 [1850]). He cannot do otherwise, says Kierkegaard in this draft of himself, and the inevitability binds his standard to that of a disturbing God. Unlike Christ, he cannot make love equal. "It is the omnipotence of the love which is so resolved that it is able to accomplish its purpose, which neither Socrates nor the king could do, whence their assumed figures constituted after all a kind of deceit" (*PF*, 39).

The most extensive working out of the misrelationships between the Christian and worldly notions of love occurs in *Works of Love*. In a lyrical passage, Kierkegaard speaks of the suffering that derives from the love which stirs hate in the beloved "because there is the infinite difference of Christian truth between what the one person and the other understands by love" (*WL*, 115). Whatever the collisions of misfortune that love has suffered in the history of literature and life, nothing can compare to the absolute, qualitative misunderstanding between divine and human love

18. In *Kierkegaard's Psychology*, trans. Bruce H. Kirmmse (Pittsburgh, 1972), 298ff., Kresten Nordentoft alludes to Kierkegaard's terror of pity that would put him in an inferior position, suggesting that the entire authorship might be, in part, a revenge against the superiority of Regine. And see *F/T*, 113–14: "The proud and noble nature can endure everything, but one thing it cannot endure, it cannot endure pity."

"separated by a world of difference." In such a collision, "then, divinely understood, love means precisely to hold fast to the true, eternal conception, although the one or ones who are loved, if they have a merely human concept, may regard it as hate" (*WL*, 115). The identification of the misunderstanding of Kierkegaard with that of Christ comes fully into bloom as the passage swells, revealing his envy of the coupling of misunderstanding and innocence.

> We often complain about misunderstanding, especially when it is most bitterly blended with love, when we recognize in its every utterance that love is unhappily present, that we are really loved but are not understood, that everything is made so bitter because it is done out of love but through a misunderstanding: but to become misunderstood in such a way as no human being has ever, ever been misunderstood by another human being, to become misunderstood as Christ was misunderstood—and then to be love as Christ was love! One assumes that it was only ungodliness which had to collide with Christ. What a misunderstanding! No, humanly speaking, the best and most affectionate man who has lived had to collide with him, had to misunderstand him. . . . He made himself and his own as unhappy, humanly speaking, as possible. . . . No, it was—humanly speaking—madness: he sacrificed himself—in order to make the beloved as unhappy as himself. (*WL*, 115–16)

As the child must change his notion of punishment as time goes by, so too must those change who are serious about the God-relationship. They must come to know that "truly to love another person is with every sacrifice (even to become hated) to help the other person love God or in loving God" (*WL*, 119). Kierkegaard cannot marry. In fact, says Quidam, "I cannot go to any man, for I am a prisoner, and misunderstanding, and misunderstanding, and misunderstanding again, are the iron bars before my window" (*SLW*, 323). The pattern of the broken engagement is sanctioned as an imitation of Christ, but it remains bound to the neurotic rhythm of guilt, anxiety, obsessive recapitulation in the art. The misunderstanding of father, lover, is continually worked up to the divine offense, but can never of its own efforts get past it. Like the self going toward the God, it must "repeatedly arrive" (*CUP*, 75) and be described through mere analogy. The literature, oedipally bound to repetition, propitiation, and renunciation, never lets go of the father and the fiancée, and as Kierkegaard's surrogate body, it must foster misunderstanding in the reader it loves and break its engagement with him in the name of faith.

The offense of the Christian dialectic assumes the singularity of a man, conscious of living before God, with no sanction of shared secret. Like God's love, the sense of sin merely tempts us with the possibility of a common legacy before it brutally splits us off from such a consolation. "Sin, common though it is to all, does not gather men together in a common concept, into a society or a partnership . . . but it splits men into individuals and holds every individual fast as a sinner—a splitting which in another sense is both in correspondence with and teleologically in the direction of the pefection of existence" (*SD*, 251*n*). The sins of the father may, for the classical Antigone, carry with tragically determined doom the relief of legend, but for the modern Antigone, the secrecy secures "the possibility of offense" in the relationship with God, the climactic and isolated collision of the will with the Paradox. It is the common fate of any character of spirit to be vulnerable to offense, unavailable to parental or erotic reconciliations. Even Abraham's deepest life is hidden from Sarah, and Xantippe farcically pushes Socrates to his teaching. This life reminds the individual that he is separated from God, ethically and aesthetically, by a "yawning qualitative abyss" (*SD*, 253). However much apologists direct Kierkegaard's assurances of atonement to an ultimate overcoming of this split, there is no way we can question that the finest and most persuasive passion he sends us is through his body in its literary medium as it struggles with offense. Overwhelmed by the distance between God and man, between the emperor and the laborer, he asks to have enough faith to be the son-in-law, the individual who may register an offense that is an aesthetically tainted variation of unhappy love, "unhappy admiration" (*SD*, 216). It is the envy of the poet leaning into the life of Abraham, the poet who is a genius of possibilities but is troubled by the faith beyond him that alone can turn them into actualities. As a poet of Christianity, Kierkegaard cannot marry; he cannot receive Isaac back. He has not enough faith for that. But he can translate to us the positions of his body, pulled between the poem and its hero, posturing forth an imagination and a passion that can project us past offense, even while mired in it (*SD*, 215–16).

Putting aside for a moment the grace that makes the requirement unconditional, the individual might be tempted to haggle with God, who might even seem "in the face of the law and requirement" to "condescend to haggle with you . . . as if you still might be able to fulfill the law" (*J/P*, II, 354; n. 1910 [1852]). But through grace the individual and God are set at "an infinite distance once and for all." Job has a firmer faith than Kierkegaard, and he has justification; but even his complaint can only incite qualitative demonstrations of power and majesty. For love insists upon such misunderstanding that Kant's protests in Abraham's behalf and talmudic settlements can only fatten us up for the collision between the understanding and the cross. If God in Christ made love an agent of equality beyond all fairy-tale divisions of kings and maidens, he also "made sure of an infinitely higher majestic expression of distance: 'grace'" (*J/P*, II, 354; n. 1910 [1852]). Kierkegaard contrasts the relationship between human beings, who "the more they get to know each other, the more intimate they become," with the relationship between man and God: "The longer one lives with him the more infinite he becomes" (*J/P*, II, 118; n. 1393 [1849]). As a child, a youth, one dreamed of achieving this intimacy. But God's upbringing teaches about the distance of misrelationship; it is like a Socratic education in ignorance, "with which the beginning was not made but the ending—it ended with ignorance!" (*J/P*, II, 118; n. 1393 [1849]). Intimacy changes to ignorance in the relation to the divine, but is it really any different for Kierkegaard on the human level? And if what is necessary for God is evil in man, that "he transforms himself into the incomprehensible, and precisely by this repulsion he torments the adoration of devotion from the other" (*J/P*, I, 30; n. 77 [1850]), can we not see how close to the demonic is the breach with Regine, with his reader? The relentless storytelling is a symptom, before it is an educative force, of the anxiety that spots the intimacy between the desire to dominate, perhaps out of the terror of pity, and the desire to free. To have one's life "in what he cannot understand" (*J/P*, I, 30; n. 77 [1850]) is to be given as faith as well as gained. Is not the structure of marriage perilously close to the cozy compromise by which man converts the crucifixion to comprehension? (*J/P*, I, 30; n. 77 [1850]).

The perpetuation of the unhappy love of the child and the lover through story after story seems a desperate measure, a defense against exposure and the volatilization of that self developed *against* absorption into a communal life. With this in mind, it is instructive to contrast Kierkegaard's vision of the structure of love with that of Hegel as it is set forth in an early theological fragment at the turn of the century.[19] At this stage Hegel is already intent upon distinguishing his ethics from those of Kant, as he was to do more fully in the *Phenomenology*; and religious Love is playing John the Baptist to Philosophy's coming as the great god of dialectical harmony. In "The Spirit of Christianity and Its Fate," Hegel takes Kant's moral imperative to task by deeming it an inadequate form for service to life, to reality, akin to what he calls positive religion—that religion of the Jews, for example, which fed upon exclusion, external and authoritarian notions of leaders, Gods, and laws, served in slavery and obeyed without joy, pleasure, or love. The natural ethics of Jesus, which simply "are," are set against the "duty" of command, which assumes a breach between reason and inclination and is conceptually couched in a *thou shalt*. That Jesus' ethics are commands is merely a symptom of the alien quality of life to thought, expressed through the stiffness of diction. By contrast, Kant's commands are concepts inevitably colliding with life. "And it is on this confusion of the utterly accidental kind of phraseology expressive of life with the moral imperative (which depends on the opposition between concept and reality) that there rests Kant's profound reduction of what he calls a 'command' (love God first of all and thy neighbor as thyself) to his moral imperative."[20]

Kant's corrective diminution of love to "liking" in the performance of duties, which he claims cannot be commanded, only "falls to the ground," as Hegel sees it, "by its own weight, because in love all thought of duties vanishes." Furthermore, the tenuous respect he does pay to the ethics of Christ, that they are "an ideal of holiness unattainable by any creature," gathers no qualitative credit. "For such an 'ideal,' in which duties are represented as willingly done, is self-contradictory, since duties require an opposition, and an action that we like to do requires none. And he can suffer this unresolved contradiction in his ideal because he declares that rational creatures (a remarkable juxtaposi-

19. Hegel, "The Spirit of Christianity and Its Fate," *Early Theological Writings*, 182–301. Kierkegaard could not have known these fragments, which were not published in the nineteenth century, except as they were developed in Hegel's larger works.
20. *Ibid.*, 212–13.

tion of words) can fall but cannot attain that ideal." The universal masters the particular instead of lifting it. Love overcomes this opposition by a feeling of harmony in which "there is no universality," only because "in a harmony the particular is not in discord but in concord, or otherwise there would be no harmony." Hegel pays honor to Christ's ethics with the qualifying reminder that they failed in history. The community could not break out of its own positivity, its worship of a dead god, to the life-giving relationship such as that between the Greek citizen and state, so the fate was like "the nemesis raging against a too beautiful endeavor. . . . This restriction of love to itself, its flight from all determinate modes of living even if its spirit breathed in them, or even if they sprang from its spirit, this removal of itself from all fate, is just its greatest fate; and here is the point where Jesus is linked with fate, linked indeed in the most sublime way, but where he suffers under it." [21] If, later, Christianity was to be a vessel of subjectivity that could nourish modern man, it had to yield its place to Philosophy so that Jesus could come back into this world and the Incarnation remain immanent for the sake of man and his community. The Christian *thou shalt* brings Hegel's subject back into the world. It leads Kierkegaard's beyond, for his ethics are always on the point of being exploded by the requirement of the eternal.

While Hegel chastises the positive law that splits inclination from reason, love rendering it superfluous, Kierkegaard, who has so often been accused of clinging to the Law as a reaction against the too easy acceptance of grace in his age, characteristically sharpens what Hegel saw as the Kantian tension and contradiction, to the point even of the positive extreme: "Thou shalt *believe*! that is what was said in the old days, as soberly as possible and in so many words—" (*SD*, 246).[22] It is the poet, says Kierkegaard, who "idolises the inclinations and is therefore quite right—since he always has only erotic love in mind—in saying that to command love is the greatest foolishness and the most preposterous kind of talk." But so is Christianity right when "it de-

---

21. *Ibid.*, 212–13, 247, 278, 281.
22. In *Kierkegaards dogmatische Anschauung*, 25, Bohlin contends that Kierkegaard pits the *thou shalt* of offensive Christianity against orthodoxy's belief in natural man's reason, a protest against orthodoxy's concentration on historical detail at the expense of the absolute Paradox.

thrones inclination and sets the *shall* in its place," for it is thinking of Christian love (*WL*, 63). It is self-renunciation's love which loves one's neighbor, "whom one *shall* love" (*WL*, 66). Never would it enter his mind that in history Christ and Christianity could be anything but heterogeneous with the world, for never would he sanction the immanence of Hegel's Incarnation. Stephen Crites has suggested a telling contrast between Hegel's domesticity and Kierkegaard's celibacy ("Christianity . . . has thrust down erotic love and friendship" [*WL*, 59]) as a basis for their antagonistic visions.[23] And it is certainly true that the agony of being "unequal" in love, that of the king, and of Kierkegaard himself, is everywhere reflected in the *thou shalts* of *Works of Love*. The love "which has undergone the transformation of the eternal by becoming duty has won continuity" (*WL*, 47), and it protects from the despair attendant upon spontaneous and accidental love. It peoples the earth with neighbors. This is one of the most formidable of the offenses that continues to "guard the approach to Christianity" (*WL*, 71). It suggests a control of the arbitrary individual not by the state, the universal set against him, but by his position "before God." And this is an offense that not only exposes the lack of transcendental courage in Kant's Abraham, but refuses as well Hegel's claim for Abraham that he was so intent upon rejecting the communal powers of love that he wanted to destroy his love for Isaac, which gave him so much anxiety. "His heart was quieted only through the certainty of the feeling that his love was not so strong as to render him unable to slay his beloved son with his own hand."[24]

It is the collision of earthly and divine notions of love that Kierkegaard will not mediate, for where, in all his literature, do we find two who are equal in love through their mutual primacy of faith in God? Through Quidam, Kierkegaard reasons this way about the broken engagement: "What for me is the nerve of my spiritual existence, namely, equality in human relationships, she does away with. She cares nothing for this infinite passion for freedom." (*SLW*, 291). We can no more imagine two knights of faith helping each other (*F/T*, 82) than we can

---

23. Stephen Crites, *In the Twilight of Christendom: Hegel vs. Kierkegaard on Faith and History* (Chambersburg, Pa., 1972). For a discussion of the ethics of *WL*, see John W. Elrod, *Kierkegaard and Christendom* (Princeton, 1981).

24. Hegel, "The Spirit of Christianity," *Early Theological Writings*, 187.

imagine two beings engaged in freedom of spirit and passion for eternity
and to each other. "From the first time I saw her and while she was my
object in the form of hope I could imagine her dead without losing my
composure. I should have felt pain, perhaps all my life long, but eternity
would promptly have been at hand, and for me eternity is the highest.
Only thus can I understand that people love one another. In the consciousness of eternity, in the infinite, each of the partners is free, and this
freedom they both possess while they love one another. This higher
existence does not concern her at all" (*SLW*, 295–96). Where Hegel sees
the form of Christ's command as "accidental phraseology" attendant
upon the entrance of reflection into life, and sees it with equanimity,
Kierkegaard tortures himself over misunderstanding between two
worlds that can have love only as law. "Even though the law is abolished,
it stands here, still with power, and fixes an eternal yawning abyss
between the God-man and every other human being, who cannot even
comprehend but can only believe what the divine law must concede—
that he was the fulfilling of the law" (*WL*, 108). This is not the son of
God that Hegel wants. The rift between "explaining and being" (*WL*,
108) is a yawning abyss, Lessing's ditch, which Hegel leaps in one
paragraph. The "obligation to love," for Kierkegaard, "is an alteration
by the eternal," and does not "rise up in any human heart" (*WL*, 41).
And, of course, the breach with Regine is ever present.

> Worldly wisdom has a long list of various expressions for affection and
> devotion. I wonder if among them there are also found: out of love to
> hate the beloved, out of love to hate the beloved and thereby oneself,
> out of love to hate one's contemporaries and thereby his own life.
> Worldly wisdom knows a great many and a great variety of cases of
> unhappy love. I wonder if among these you find the suffering which
> has to appear to hate the beloved, which has to use hate as the last and
> only expression for its love, or the suffering which in reward for its
> love has to be hated by the beloved because there is the infinite
> difference of Christian truth between what the one person and the
> other understands by love? (*WL*, 114–15)

Perhaps there is not another passage in Kierkegaard's works that would
so tempt the reader to assume his use of Christianity for psychological
justification, yet it is precisely the greatness of Kierkegaard that he does

not allow us to separate the Christian from the case. That is why the recommendations in *Works of Love* may seem tortured from a psychological point of view, though they bloom into a moving and authentic spiritual transvaluation that seems realistic because it takes, by its dependence on the case history, full account of the tragedy of every life that loves.

So Christ is the Pattern of heterogeneity that rests upon an unchanging relationship between the divine and human worlds. And this heterogeneity, its reality, is reflected in the infinite difference in Christian truth between what two different people understand by love. Only when love is misunderstanding is it truly love, whatever Kierkegaard may say about the love between neighbors. The latter tortures itself into reality, but it does not torture itself with this disappointment. The former is the deepest love Kierkegaard would feel, for it compels man to need God. God, however, cannot rule over an ethically loveless world. The love that makes equals, the love of neighbor, is the love that enables Kierkegaard to keep the God-relationship in a world of universal measures. The two loves are themselves in a misrelationship, as they are not in Hegel. They cannot marry. They affirm the double perspective of dialectical reality. That is why Kiekegaard is so hard on fairy-tale misfortunes of thwarted lovers, because they deny the providence of this divorce. Since everything in Hegel's dialectic moves toward balance and reconciliation between subjective and communal love, the love between men, between equals when it is healthy, wards off the dreaded master-slave equation and marries the human and divine. This might explain why Hegel is drawn to the Greek representation of gods as human beings, since even the cleft between the majesty of godship and the abasement of man is narrowed.[25] In Kierkegaard, Christian love, far from bringing duty and inclination, spirit and flesh together, makes man doubly unhappy and the neighbor anything but a tamed sublimation. For the world ridicules what it deems difficult by calling it unnatural (*WL*, 196). The love between neighbors must be relentlessly described in all its difficulty, so that it cannot be a way out of misunderstanding. The text persecutes the term *neighbor* (as it persecutes the reader) into an ethical strenuousness that makes God in the world essentially agonizing.

25. Hegel, "Love," *Early Theological Writings*, 304.

Kierkegaard would bind us in love only by the presence of the third (the eternal, the spirit), but the isolation of each man's God-relationship is a block to intimacy. "Marriage is not really love and . . . therefore it is said that the two become *one flesh*—but not one spirit, since two spirits cannot possibly become one spirit" (*J/P*, III, 127; n. 2598 [1847]). This should be used to qualify the comfort of Judge William's notion of the *thou shalt* as leading marriage to the eternal (*E/O*, II, 152). For Hegel, Kierkegaard's equation would belong to that positive faith that "puts a mystery in the place of genuine experience of the divine life which we enjoy in love."[26] The Paradox, after all, stands between lovers in the community, putting the price high for freedom from possessive forms of "egotistic" binding. "Erotic love and marriage are really only a deeper confirmation of self-love by becoming two in self-loving. For this very reason married people become so satisfied, so vegetatively prosperous—because true love does not fit into earthly existence [*Tilvaer*] the way self-love does" (*J/P*, III, 127; n. 2596 [1847]). This is, finally, Kierkegaard's major emphasis:

> Within the race every individual is essentially different or unique. This superiority is the really human superiority. . . . Yes, if it were not so, that the single human being, honourable, upright, respectable, God-fearing, can under the same circumstances do the opposite to what another person does, one who is also honourable, upright, respectable, God-fearing—then the God-relationship would not essentially exist, not in its deepest sense. If one could with unqualified truthfulness judge every human being according to an established universal criterion, the God-relationship would essentially be done away with; then everything would turn outward, fulfilling itself paganly in political or social life; then to live would become much too easy, but also exceedingly empty; then exertion or the deepening of the self would be neither possible nor required, and yet precisely in the most difficult collision of infinite misunderstanding the God-relationship in a man develops. (*WL*, 217)

And it is that relationship which has priority and transcendence. The intimate relationship, that with Regine, is again worked through to this

26. Harris, *Hegel's Development*, 316.

pattern: "When a relationship is only between two, one always has the upper hand in the relationship by being able to break it, for as soon as one has broken, *the relationship* is broken. But when there are three, one person cannot do this. The third . . . is love itself, which the innocent sufferer can hold to in the break, and then the break has no power over him" (*WL*, 283). By this process of idealization, the "past has no power at all" over one bound by the eternal; then behold, "there is no break." The lover who "abides on the path with the one who hates him" does not really break the relationship (*WL*, 286).

If despair and anxiety are routed by the true love of neighbor, we know that Kierkegaard could rarely find peace in this transformation, even if he ardently believed in its form. Symptomatic of this conflict is the constant marveling at the power of Christ to endure misunderstanding even though he *was* Christian love. The fullness of Kierkegaard's passion always emerges from the struggle between the anxious process of transvaluation and the peace of the vision on the other side. That he never allowed the first to be mechanically suppressed is his heroism. It is that realism, that trenchant, tenacious realism, that would push him willingly toward doubters undeluded by a mythical, bourgeois Christianity, allies like Hume and Feuerbach; he even foreshadows the Freud who exposes, in *Civilization and Its Discontents*, in quite a different spirit from that of Kierkegaard, the unpsychological proceedings of the cultural superego that commands: "Love thy neighbor."[27] It is precisely the difficulty of this command that reveals the hidden reality of the imperative ("the suffering of unhappy love attests the reality of love" [*SD*, 262]), for Kierkegaard would deem any psychological development abortive and fantastic without the trial of the spiritual. The alterations of the eternal can never appear easy in this world, though they emanate from simplicity itself. Kierkegaard's fiercest impatience is reserved for those who would cheat reality of its full terror. Inclination and duty, being and thought, may be mediated in another world, but not in this.

27. Sigmund Freud, *Civilization and Its Discontents*, trans. James Strachey (New York, 1961), 90: "The commandment 'Love thy neighbor as thyself', is the strongest defence against human aggressiveness and an excellent example of the unpsychological proceedings of the cultural super-ego. The commandment is impossible to fulfill; such an enormous inflation of love can only lower its values, not get rid of the difficulty. Civilization pays no attention to all this; it merely admonishes us that the harder it is to obey the precept the more meritorious it is to do so."

Love cannot remove the offense from the world; it *is* offense. And to those who try to evade the full requirement, who dare not judge the Christian experience, to those he says: You are people who have "clean forgotten the Christian 'thou shalt'" (*SD*, 260). And so his very life, which yearns for intimacy and cannot achieve it, compensates for the impossibility, for guilt and envy, by shifting the standard of reality from spontaneity to a command, and by doing so with passion, establishes it.

Kierkegaard's own tragic sense of the misunderstanding between the finite and infinite in us, between erotic and Christian love, between fathers, sons, and lovers, is a human reflection (like the sense of the king whose standards are too high) of the sorrow God feels about the inevitability of misrelationship as a common base for the real and spiritual, a base that proves their identity. Kierkegaard speaks of the pathos of God's position that cannot change to accommodate the lover, a theme we have heard before.

> When Christ cried out, "My God, my God, why have you forsaken me," it was terrible for Christ, and this is the way it is usually presented. But it seems to me it would have been still more terrible for God to hear it . . . to be unchangeable this way and still to be love—what infinitely deep inscrutable grief!
>
> Alas, what I, a wretched human being, have experienced in this respect, this contradiction of not being able to change and yet to love—alas, what I have experienced helps me in a very remote way to get a faint notion of this suffering of divine love. (*J/P*, IV, 434; n. 4715 [1854])

To the Apostle, the unchangeableness of God is entirely comforting and consoling, "one of pure unmixed comfort, peace, joy, happiness. And this is indeed eternally true. But let us not forget that the Apostle's joy has its explanation in the fact that the Apostle is the Apostle, that he already long since wholly yielded himself in unconditional obedience to God's unchangeableness" (*ED*, 255). Kierkegaard continually denies himself apostolic privileges as he falls away from this comfort into circles of anxiety and despair. But it is an important part of our experience of the pathos of Kierkegaard's authorship that we hear him, as he is falling away, repeatedly comfort as if he were the apostle in his costume of edifying discourser. The falling is registered in the intensity with which the terms of transvaluation are pushed forward almost beyond patience, in a version of Johannes de Silentio straining after Abraham to render his difficulty. Kierkegaard's favorite text from James, "Every good and every perfect gift is from above and cometh down from the Father of lights, with whom is no variableness nor shadow of turning" (*ED*, 49), presents a becalmed version of the structure of recapitulation which knows that the apostolic word remains obscure. We do not hold onto it by understanding, however, and this what saves us. We hold onto it from need. How else could one grasp that the greatest love must make us unhappy?[28]

28. See Denis de Rougemont's comments on Kierkegaard in *Love in the Western World* (Garden City, N.Y., 1957), 337: "We need not seek anywhere but in his unquestionably unique vocation for being a solitary the explanation of his failure as a man. Others are endowed with some other vocation; they marry Regine, and passion lives again in their marriage, but then 'by virtue of the absurd'. And they are day by day astounded to find that they are happy. Such things are too elementary and too complete for words to interpose their dilatoriness between the question which they raise and the answer returned in our living experience."

> Disguise is my life, my element; to suffer, to make
> sacrifices . . . that I am willing enough to do, but
> disguise is a passion with me.
> *Journals and Papers*

2 · A Negative Body in a Negative Age: The Weapon

A NEGATIVE BODY

N part, Kierkegaard hung on to the *thou shalt* of the Old Testament as positive command because he was haunted by the demonic danger of being "self-important over against God" and men. "As in political life one becomes important by belonging to the Opposition, and in the last resort may well wish that there should be a government so that one might at least have something to oppose; so in the last resort one does not wish to abolish God—if merely with a view to becoming still more self-important by being the Opposition" (*SD*, 246). The reader suspects that Kierkegaard is warning himself against the forms of self-idealization that cover anger, hate, envy, guilt, and disappointment and are inherent in every public transformation of private pain. Walter Lowrie's feeling that Kierkegaard identified his despair with that demonic kind described in *Sickness Unto Death* certainly seems persuasive.[1] "Revolting against the whole of existence, it thinks it has hold of a proof against it, against its goodness. This proof the despairer thinks he himself is, and that is what he wills to be, therefore he wills to be himself, himself with his torment, in order with this torment to protest against the whole of existence" (*SD*, 207). The pride that uses

---

1. Lowrie, *Kierkegaard*, I, 126ff.

misunderstanding to protect self-importance, the silence of the God-relationship as a justification of silence toward others, the secret sense of secluded superiority to hide the fear of pity, of "being loved and having his weakness publicly recognized" (*ED*, IV, 108), are sketched as a form of self-love in the edifying discourse "Against Cowardice." Even in the last years, even when the decision had been made for direct communication, apology is fed by the desperate need to justify a whole life because the possibilities for development in the world had been so definitively curtailed.

> If I consider my own personal life, am I then a Christian or is my personal life purely a poet-existence, even with an addition of something demonic. In that case the idea would be to take such an enormous risk that I thereby make myself so unhappy that I would get into the situation for really becoming a Christian. But does this give me that right to do it dramatically so that the Christendom of a whole country gets involved? Is there not something desperate in the whole thing, something like the treachery of starting a fire in order to throw oneself into the arms of God—perhaps, for perhaps it would nevertheless turn out that I would not become a Christian. (*J/P*, VI, 172–73; n. 6431 [1849])

Turning misunderstanding from a condition to a weapon was fraught with expressive anxiety. Psychologically, Kierkegaard acutely worried about bad faith (Was his personal fate the public's fault?) and going beyond the father; spiritually, he worried that Christian action, in its purest example, was mute and passive suffering; politically, he worried that his literature might be a satanic temptation to turn his lack of fulfillment in the world to power over it. Was his dialectics, like that of the Socrates of Nietzsche, "only a form of revenge against his opponents?" [2] Was he countering the world's exclusion of him, and that of the parental bond, by his own act of exclusion, exposing the motive of vengeance before it became renunciation? No richer place of passion and torment, no more thrilling struggle, can be found in Kierkegaard than

---

2. Friedrich Nietzsche, *Twilight of the Idols and the Anti-Christ*, trans. and ed. R. J. Hollingdale (Baltimore, 1968), 32.

on that border between his sickness as fate and as polemic. Here he projects and enacts the offense and appeal of his diseased physiognomy. Could private sickness be transformed into public protest, suffering into polemic, psychological retreat into spiritual aggression, the negative body into positive spirit, without suspicion in a mind as acute and honest as Kierkegaard's? And could Kierkegaard imitate Rousseau's rite of passage, neutralize his private negation by making negative the age, so that he could feel his disguise of irony as "concealed enthusiasm"? (PA, 47). Most agonizing of all was the question of secrecy as a private defense or heroic necessity. That no absolute and final justification, similar to Rousseau's, could ever attend this process of transformation is the very sign of Kierkegaard's character; the relentless anxiety, almost strangling his literature, is the sign of his integrity.

As many commentators have observed, the presence of the fall in Adam never really convincingly works as an antidote to the stress on the qualitative isolation of the individual's confrontation with the consciousness of sin. The first man does not offer his fig leaf to the naked individual, perpetually estranged in Kierkegaard's literary structure and texture from history, community, and tradition. While Adam and each subsequent man share the pain of the qualitative leap into sin, Kierkegaard grants that for modern man "the future is reflected more than for Adam" (CA, 91) and that "psychologically speaking, this more may signify what is appalling" (CA, 91). What is interesting about this reminder is that Kierkegaard habitually demotes the quantitative measure in consciousness in relation to the qualitative, but the private sense of the extraordinary degree of his suffering led him to smuggle in the *more* of dread, like that of passion, oftener than we might suspect. If it is his necessary fate to have a spiritual "genius for reflection" (PVA, 73) in an age of philistine reflection, it is also a curse that such reflection intensifies the suffering. For Kierkegaard was one who desired more than others to have an innocent, healthy, silent body, to attain the faith that is immediacy *after* reflection.

Consequently, he had to spell out his guilt daily to sanction his sickness. Even Christ, he considers in a moment of despondency, might have missed one kind of intense suffering endured by his modern patient; for

Christ was not tested and tried in the suffering of illness, least of all in the most tormenting ones of all, where the psychic and the somatic dialectically touch each other—consequently it seems as if the prototype's life were easier in this respect. But then I say to myself: Do you believe, then, that if you were thoroughly healthy you would easily or more easily achieve perfection? Just the opposite: then you would yield easily to your passions, to pride if not to others, to an intensified self-esteem and the like. In that way sufferings, even though a burden, are a beneficial burden, like the braces used in the orthopedic institute.

To be thoroughly healthy physically and mentally and then to lead a truly spiritual life—that no man can do. This sense of spontaneous well-being immediately runs away with him. In one sense the life of the spirit is the death of immediacy. This is why sufferings are a help. (*J/P*, IV, 387–88; n. 4637 [1849])

The only health available is that which is "required in order to become aware and to know and acknowledge that one is sick" (*J/P*, IV, 239; n. 4329; [1849]). The man who is extraordinarily vulnerable to the world of spirit, who so closely binds body to belief, can he use his extraordinary suffering as a norm? Can he translate into a positive genre a life "like a satire on what it is to be a man"? (*J/P*, VI, 214–216; n. 6484 [1849]). Erik Erikson's words on Luther seem apt for Kierkegaard, too. "But the greatest advances in human consciousness are made by people who demand too much, and thus invite a situation in which their overstrained followers inevitably end up either compromisers or dogmatists."[3]

This was a possibility of which Kierkegaard, like his contemporary critics, was aware.

The reason I have always spoken of myself as being without authority is that I personally have felt that there was too much of the poetic in me, furthermore that I feel aided by something higher, and also that I am put together backwards, but then, too, because I perceive that the profound suffering of my life and also my guilt make me need an

3. Erik Erikson, *Young Man Luther* (New York, 1962), 143.

enormous measure of Christianity, while at the same time I am fearful
of making it too heavy for someone who may not need so great a
measure. Of course, neither the God-man nor an apostle can have
such a concern—but then I am just a poor human being. (*J/P*, VI,
289; n. 6587 [1850])

But more painful to him, I believe, was the problem of secret pride, of
self-indulgent relief in raising "his individual patienthood to the level of
a universal one and to try to solve for all what he could not solve for
himself alone."[4] In *The Book on Adler*, Kierkegaard establishes the familiar qualitative difference between the patient who jumps out of bed as an
author and indulges in colorful descriptions of his symptoms and the
sober physician who is interested in translating the sickness into health
(*BA*, 11). Luther, strangely, joins Adler as one who fails in the full
transformation.

> But the tragedy about Luther is that a condition in Christendom at
> a particular time and place is transformed into the normative. Luther
> suffered exceedingly from an anguished conscience and needed a cure.
> Well and good, but must Christianity therefore be converted *in toto* to
> this, to soothing and reassuring anguished consciences.
> The more I see of Luther the more clear it is to me that he also is a
> part of this confusion of mistaking the patient for the physician. He is
> an exceedingly important patient for Christendom, but he is not the
> physician; he has the patient's passion for expressing and describing
> his suffering and what he feels he needs to relieve it, but he does not
> have the physician's comprehensive view. And to reform Christianity
> requires first and foremost a comprehensive view of the whole of
> Christianity. (*J/P*, III, 101; n. 2550 [1854])

Who could help feeling that Kierkegaard was talking of himself when he
noted Luther's "passion for expressing and describing his suffering and
what he feels he needs to relieve it," but we also feel the active concern
about the exploitation of such passion. That is why it is crucial, for
Kierkegaard, to make Christianity more difficult, to imitate the model
of misunderstanding in those patient-physicians Socrates and Christ.
The consolation is to "wonder if it did not go with Socrates in his age as

4. *Ibid.*, 67.

with me. He came to be regarded as representing evil—and yet Socrates was in truth the physician" (*J/P*, IV, 355; n. 4555 [1850]). It is the dialectical strain of this double role—"my genius has really been my suffering" (*J/P*, VI, 214; n. 6484 [1849])—that gives "credence to what [he] writes." The suffering is cherished as that which gives the life its public standard: "The significance of my life corresponds directly to my suffering" (*J/P*, VI, 233; n. 6507 [1849]). Not as pure as the dialectic of Christ who came on earth precisely in order to suffer, Kierkegaard's role must be assumed after it is reflectively brought into consciousness. The physician and the patient are held together in dialectical difficulty. So Kierkegaard muses about *Sickness Unto Death*, "Perhaps there ought to have been, as first intended, a little postscript by the editor, for example: The Editor's Postscript. This book seems to be written by a physician; I, the editor, am not the physician, I am one of those sick" (*J/P*, VI, 252; n. 6535 [1849]). Is this not identical to that neo-Socratic claim, made so often by Kierkegaard in and out of pseudonyms that he can diagnose Christendom's disease because he knows he has the sickness of not being a Christian?

Because, then, he cannot be a Christ, he must will suffering into faith, though he would like to suffer innocently. Perhaps this is, after all, health, to know that one cannot suffer innocently, that one must attain a rebirth after reflection, guilt, sin-consciousness. Monastic asceticism is a false break, a break out of, not into, the suffering of existence, a way of easing guilt. In a fine distinction between irony and humor (*CUP*, 490), Johannes Climacus imagines a woman patting a child's head and envying the situation of his innocence. "Yes," says a humorist, this is to be envied, "and above all the happiness of childhood in getting a licking." The rejoinder is taken by the superficial as ironic, but as humor it holds together pain and sympathy by its consciousness of the eternal guilt of man, who has lost his innocence from the beginning. Monasticism is like the spanking, a "life-view something like that of a child, who suffers its punishment on a particular day and then forgetting it all becomes a good child again" (*J/P*, I, 66; n. 172 [1845]). The break with the world distracts from the task of the greater break into sin-consciousness. One can will to attain immediacy after reflection only by refusing the innocence of suffering, as Socrates attained ignorance *after* knowledge because "in radical ethicality he took his task to be that of preserving

himself in ignorance" (*J/P*, I, 424; n. 972 [1849]). This second innocence, or rebirth, comes precisely out of conscious acceptance of guilt
and sin and is continually renewed. It is to be severely contrasted with
the sentimental version of innocence represented by the child whose
immediacy is as pre-Christian as its misunderstandings: "They bring the
innocent child to God or Christ. Is this Christianity, the point of which
precisely it is that it is a sinner who has recourse to the paradox? It is
pretty and touching and becoming that an older person at the sight of a
child feels his guilt and sadly conceives of the child's innocence; but this
mood is not decisively Christian. For the sentimental conception of the
child's innocence forgets that Christianity recognizes no such thing in
the fallen race, and that the qualitative dialectic defines sin-
consciousness as an advance upon innocence" (*CUP*, 524). The child,
whom we envy, is merely "a sinner without sin-consciousness." Kierkegaard appreciates Schopenhauer's rage against the sentimentality of optimistic Christianity. But he makes a most important qualification when
he takes Schopenhauer to task for his contention that to exist is to suffer.
"Christianity proclaims itself to be suffering, to be a Christian is to
suffer, but now if to exist at all, to be a human being, is to suffer, then
Christianity is robbed of its dialectic" (*J/P*, IV, 31; n. 3881 [1854]).
Kierkegaard is, then, as intent upon choosing his suffering as on choosing despair, so that the sickness can be turned into a weapon in the battle
for Christianity as reality.

A touchy aspect of the expression of this transference is the dialectical
relationship between defense and offense. He has the example of the
Christian cause itself, whose apparent passivity is active and needs iron-
ists, not defense attorneys. "The Christian cause . . . is aggressive; to
defend it is of all misrepresentations the most inexcusable—it is *unconscious crafty treachery*. Christianity is aggressive; in Christendom, as a
matter of course, it attacks from behind" (Epigraph to *CrD*, 168). So
Kierkegaard can send forth thoughts that "wound from behind"[5] in
imitation, not defense, of Christianity. But what about the recognition
that the "defense and attack are within a single hair of being one" (*J/P*,
VI, 245; n. 6523 [1849]), when personal psychology, the need for
justification, is dialectically related to imitation? Then we have the

---

5. This is the title of a section of edifying addresses in *Christian Discourses*.

complication of anxiety that habitually hangs between both positions
without allowing a decision. As Kierkegaard wounds Regine, he feels it
necessary to make it appear that Regine has wounded him, so that there
is specifically and reflectively established a perspective in which defense
and attack are almost one. Here is the accounting:

> Just as that general who personally gave the order when he was to
> be shot, so I personally have always given the order when I was to
> be wounded. But the skirmish itself, which she had to wage, was in
> the grand style and admirable. In a way I put the bow in her hand, set
> the arrow, showed her how to aim—my idea was—and it was love
> —either I become yours or you will be allowed to wound me so
> deeply, wound me in my melancholy and in my God-relationship so
> deeply that I, although parted from you, yet remain yours. (*J/P*, VI,
> 201–202; n. 6473 [1849])

The attack ("accentuating her"), that frees the disciple both displaces
Kierkegaard's sexual aggression and disguises the subsequently guilty
need to suffer and renounce, and that is why Kierkegaard calls this
dialectic a "religious collision" (*J/P*, VI, 202; n. 6473 [1849]). The
equation is, from the earliest time, this: "To conquer means to conquer
in an infinite sense, which in a finite sense means to suffer" (*PVA*, 78).
Still this identifies him as the one who loves, for Christ, who was
sacrificed, was the loving one (*TC*, 195). With the primacy of the
presence of the infinite, the chorus of legend, the common support of the
tragic hero, falls away; "for to make sacrifices, or to be sacrificed (which
may in fact be the consequence of declining to entertain the thought
of becoming a power of a material sort), does not interest the world"
(*PVA*, 132).

These are the problems of expression when one is sick to some purpose. He must find a way to interest this modern world, rejected as a
chorus, in the sacrificial act, though sacrifice is not universally sanctioned. Wasn't Christ's offense the boundary of his healing, of his love?
Could version after version of Kierkegaard's own chosen tactic, the
perpetuation of the misunderstanding between offense and defense, seduction and liberation, raise his patienthood to a common need for faith?
If misunderstanding is the protective, pathetic version of an active,
guilty, psychological ambivalence toward those he loves, could it lead

the religious poet to its sanction for all by Paradox? To effect this passage, Kierkegaard characteristically takes all the parts in his dramas, both offensive and defensive, as we do in dreams. He is not only the seducer but Cordelia as well, just as Christ, who deceives, is also deceived (Cordelia and Christ share at two spheres' remove the cry: "Why has thou forsaken me?"); he is not only Abraham but Isaac, too (who is not just Regine); he is not merely warring against his age but sacrificing himself to it. He makes his body realize its immediacy only as metaphor descended from the divine prototype. Its action of suffering is a paltry imitation of that miracle on the cross. "He did the miracle of love, that without *doing* anything but by suffering He moves every one who has a heart" (*CrD*, 288). Doing literature is only reflective love at best. But by this identification, the psychological withdrawal from normal expressions of love avoids the ascription of fantastic idiosyncracy. His body in his literature, by being unable to do anything but suffer, might move hearts to faith. This is his dream. But it was always disturbed by the self-conscious decisions of doing. At least he can move past the Romantic imitation of the Christian pattern. Rousseau's pretense of historical passivity hides a powerful will, reversing time as it organizes the life into symbolic representation. The presence of Kierkegaard's God renders this pattern agonizing. And Kierkegaard perceives that Rousseau had the movements of the Christian collision ("to do good and suffer for it, to do the good and thereby manage to make oneself and others unhappy," *J/P*, III, 773; n. 3827 [1851]) but was without the Christian dedication. Like Hegel, Kierkegaard would call Rousseau's sacrifice egotism. The presence of Christ allows Kierkegaard to sublimate self-justification and to lobby his audience less crudely than Rousseau.

But in the absence of the demands of tragic drama, suffering as action is vulnerable to charges of arrogance. Many have complained of the exclusivity of Kierkegaard's equation of sickness with Christian health, which, after all, chases all possibility of ethical mediation, the spontaneity of contingent experience, from the religious arena; but no one has complained with such forceful modesty as Dietrich Bonhoeffer.

> You think the Bible hasn't much to say about health, fortune, vigour, etc. I've been thinking over that again. It's certainly not true of the Old Testament. The intermediate theological category between God

and human fortune is, as far as I can see, that of a blessing. In the Old Testament—e.g., among the patriarchs—there's a concern not for fortune, but for God's blessing, which includes in itself all earthly good. In that blessing the whole of the earthly life is claimed for God, and it includes all his promises. It would be natural to suppose that, as usual, the New Testament spiritualizes the teaching of the Old Testament here, and therefore to regard the Old Testament blessing as superseded in the New. But is it an accident that sickness and death are mentioned in connection with the misuse of the Lord's Supper [the cup of blessing, I Cor. 10 : 16, 11 : 30], that Jesus restored people's health, and that while his disciples were with him they "lacked nothing"? Now, is it right to set the Old Testament blessing against the cross? That is what Kierkegaard did. That makes the cross, or at least suffering, an abstract principle; and that is just what gives rise to an unhealthy methodism, which deprives suffering of its element of contingency as a divine ordinance. It's true that in the Old Testament the person who receives the blessing has to endure a great deal of suffering [e.g. Abraham, Isaac, Jacob, and Joseph], but this never leads to the idea that fortune and suffering, blessing and cross are mutually exclusive and contradictory—nor does it in the New Testament.[6]

It is difficult to answer this accusation, for it is certainly true that Kierkegaard seems to split severely the Old Testament blessing from the cross. In a "new" 1853 version of *Fear and Trembling*, projected in a *Journal* entry, he has Isaac actually sacrificed as a prototype of Christ, with a promise only of restoration in eternity. And Kierkegaard then makes this distinction: "This is the relationship between Judaism and Christianity. In the Christian view Isaac actually is sacrificed—but then eternity. In Judaism it is only a test [*Prøvelse*] and Abraham keeps Isaac, but then the whole episode still remains essentially within this life" (*J/P*, II, 508–509; n. 2223 {1853}). This does not mean that it can be understood. When Kierkegaard insists on misrelationship and misun-

---

6. Dietrich Bonhoeffer, Letter to Eberhard Bethge, July 28, 1944, *Prisoner for God: Letters and Papers from Prison*, trans. Reginald Fuller, ed. Eberhard Bethge (New York, 1960), 173.

derstanding as the basis of reality and of faith, he insists, also, that the immediate gladness of Abraham's recovery is still an impossibility for us who are not knights of faith. Therefore, it is fair to assume that recovery of Isaac, like that of Job's losses, actually is a primitive (Old Testament in relation to New Testament) sign that material recovery is, after all, irrelevant to blessing. Because the temptation, demoted in the new version, is still too difficult for us to imagine, we are stopped at that point, and the fairy-tale ending would seem available precisely to indicate that it is a solution incommensurable with faith. The test is an early version of the dialectic of God's love as suffering and blessing. The return must not be construed as a reward for faith instead of as evidence of it. Even this severity does not make of suffering an abstract principle in Kierkegaard. While the complicated patterns and colors of the social world are allegorized and blanched, the presence of Kierkegaard's own anxiety, testing the test as always, precipitates the hidden drama between personal suffering and suffering as example.

This anxiety is the "holy hypochondria" of which Hamann speaks, which invades those heterogeneous with their age. "This impertinent uneasiness, this holy hypochondria, is perhaps the fire whereby we sacrificial animals must be salted and preserved from the decay of the passing age."[7] Before the salt of the New Testament can be used as sacrifice to the age, it must be used against it by those who are "set outside of the universally human. . . . I cannot repeat enough what I so frequently have said: I am a poet, but a very special kind, for I am by nature dialectical, and as a rule dialectic is precisely what is alien to the poet. Assigned from childhood to a life of torment that perhaps few can even conceive of, plunged into the deepest despondency, and from this despondency again into despair, I came to understand myself by writing. It was the ethical that inspired me—alas, me, who was painfully prevented from realizing it fully because I was unhappily set outside of the universally human" (*J/P*, VI, 38–39; n. 6227 [1848]). The dialectical in the poetry is the axis between defense and offense, the literature itself a transition. It cannot be a solution, for like "man regarded as spirit," it must always be "in critical condition" (*SD*, 158). The hyperconscious

7. J. G. Hamann, *Schriften*, ed. Friedrich Roth (8 vols., Berlin, 1821–43), VII, 59. In *CD*, 145*n*, Kierkegaard calls this the high hypochondria of one "educated by possibility." See also Kierkegaard, *J/P*, IV, 519; n. 4906 (1854).

suffering from "hypochondriacal acumen and subtility" (*E/O*, II, 13), the common trait of the nineteenth-century antihero diagnosing the European toothache of an age in which morality had become a problem, is at once the sickness and the medicine.[8] Unlike Kafka's poetry of frustration—which, with neither a God, consciousness, nor will ever free from infantile projection, cannot point beyond ambivalence (except to suicide)—Kierkegaard's dialectical poetry is a diagnostic and prescriptive property, but it also registers the suffering of the physician. Kierkegaard's dialectical structure represents a more aggressive and perverse challenge to desire's ambivalence than does Freud's, for growth of consciousness raises guilt instead of lowering it. To choose guilt is the homeopathic treatment for having it. Most important of all is this paradoxical recognition that is the common ethical bond between Kierkegaard and his reader—that the anxiety which separates man from man can prepare each for the faith that isolates him before God.

With only this as a social buffer, the agent of heterogeneity itself, the dialectical poet, like the sacrificial beast, is both preserved and annihilated. Father Taciturnus speaks for Providence on the subject of Quidam. "What he is capable of he shall never learn to know, but I want to make use of him. He shall not be humbled by any reality . . . but in himself he shall be sensible of annihilation as other men are not sensible of it" (*SLW*, 407). The consciousness addicted to the Speculative System abbreviates "the pathological factors of life," for like undialectical poetry it wants to be rid of repentance. But this man, a blocked repenter yearning for full faith, is "stuck in a dialectic relationship to reality," and this becomes his major ethical value (*SLW*, 404). While sensible of annihilation, Kierkegaard expresses himself in the incognito of polemic and persuasion; he is a sacrificial beast, himself salting Christendom. If the sickness is a passionate ambivalence from the earliest childhood, it could change the dialectical fate into virtue. The dialectical teacher, whether born (Christ) or made (Socrates), engenders out of the human conflict a stimulus to the goal of Paradox (the ambivalent structure both reflected and solved). He who is annihilated takes charge of his annihilation and makes a self of it. Then movingly, he gives himself away to

8. This is a contention of Nietzsche, who with some scorn says in *Twilight of the Idols*, 70: "For the Englishman, morality is not yet a problem." See also Fëdor Dostoevski's *Notes from Underground*.

become nothing before God, and this repeatedly, for even this surrender cannot be abbreviated. The relations are drawn between expression and its atonement, renunciation. Behind every attack is a defense, behind every act of transvaluation a withdrawal, behind every projection a surrender.

The possibility of demonic misuse of the power of expression haunts Kierkegaard and hovers over his literature through every change of style and tone. Judge William speaks of the delight in the heart of the unhappiest man as he appalls the world by reciting his suffering (*E/O*, II, 237, 242), so that the talent is "a snare unto his feet" (*E/O*, II, 302). A demonic author, writes Kierkegaard, "loves his sickness and is afraid of the remedy" (*J/P*, I, 341; n. 733 [1854]). He wonders through Anti-Climacus about the arrogance of cultivating misunderstanding. "Is he the elect, is the thorn in the flesh the expression for the fact that he is to be employed as the extraordinary, is it before God quite as it should be with respect to the extraordinary figure he has become? or is the thorn in the flesh the experience he must humble himself under in order to attain the universal human?" (*SD*, 209). Can the literature's expression as the only means of social service, and even relationship, justify anxiety as a universal value while using it to separate the individual from the common claims of the universal? Can his case be only extraordinary or can it, even in its hyperbole, be normative? "The source of my strength and bold confidence for reaching such a heterogeneity with the universally human is that my strength is my weakness. Practically from childhood I was set outside of the universally human by reason of distinctive sufferings. I am not a capricious experimenter or even perhaps a rash venturer—no, I am a sufferer, constrained in suffering. Without these sufferings I of course would have married long ago, perhaps also have had an appointive position" (*J/P*, VI, 372; n. 6718 [1851]). If he is not to be merely the passive "Alienated Soul which is the consciousness of self as a divided nature, a doubled and merely contradictory being" described by Hegel, he must come to terms with the tortured relation between polemic and annihilation.[9] In the provisional guise of the aesthetic narrator of *Either / Or*, Kierkegaard admits that one reads about Hegel's

9. G. W. F. Hegel, *The Phenomenology of Mind*, trans. J. B. Baillie (New York, 1967), 251.

unhappy consciousness "with an inner restlessness, with a trembling of the heart, with a fear lest one learn too much, or too little" (*E/O*, I, 220). The alienated soul must get past the having as "its only joy, the reflex of its unhappiness." [10] To one who really chooses to see existence as a "separation between subject and object, thought and being" (*CUP*, 112), terms that can never be in any relation to each other but of longing, Hegelian education would not be a remedy.

The poison itself must be the remedy, dialectical expression and withdrawal the preparation for faith. In a moving scene in *Works of Love*, Kierkegaard thinly disguises himself as a child standing apart from the others, unwilling to share in communal mischief. Of course he is misunderstood.

> They do not see that the situation permits a quite different explanation, that the strictly brought-up child, wherever it is, continually has with him the parents' standards for what it may and may not do. If the parents were visibly present so the naughty children could see them, they would better understand the child, especially if the child appeared sad because of having to obey the parents' orders, for then it would be obvious that the child would more than willingly do as the naughty children did, and it would be easy to perceive, in fact, to see, what is holding the child back. (*WL*, 195)

And then Kierkegaard expands the picture to the world stage.

> The world just cannot get into its head (and therefore it cannot be) that a Christian should not have the same inclinations and passions the world has. But if he has them, it can even less get it into its head why, out of fear of the invisible, he wants in this silly way to constrain self-love, which the world not only calls innocent but praiseworthy, why he wants to constrain anger, which the world not only regards as natural but as the mark of a man and a man's honour, why he wants to make himself doubly unhappy: first, by not satisfying his inclinations and, second, by reaping as reward the world's ridicule. (*WL*, 196)

10. This is a phrase of Stephen Crites, *In the Twilight of Christendom*, 97. The temptation to take pleasure in treating offenses aesthetically is a favorite theme of Dostoevski.

Heterogeneity is at once rebellion and withdrawal; a psychological adjustment starts the rhythm both of the ethical building of the self and of its ultimate spiritual surrender. It is no wonder that Kierkegaard so persuasively contends that any notion of reality that does not make the psychological and spiritual intimate is sophistic. The question readers of Kierkegaard must decide is whether the perpetual transition from psychological sickness to spiritual health, repeatedly enacted, is finally a persuasive reality for others. I would agree with the judgment of Louis Dupré, who fully recognizing that Kierkegaard was not, in conventional terms, a healthy man, feels that "his psychology, however one-sided and deformed, transcended its limitations through religion and came to grips with reality."[11] I would add that the anxiety, which breathes through his literature in many forms and tempos, represents us. Psychological atonement must be given over, ultimately, to another power that atones beyond the psychological, but the need for this power is stimulated by the anxious dialectical poetry of attack and defense.

When one is checked by genetics and environment, one must really be checked by Providence, for to isolate the psychological compulsion from the spiritual need is impossible. He who takes charge of his annihilation under those circumstances chooses his Providence, as he is chosen. It is a delicate equipoise. "I therefore asked my physician whether he believed that the structural misrelation between the physical and the psychical could be dispelled so that I could realize the universal. This he doubted. I asked him whether he thought that my spirit could convert or transform this misrelation by willing it. He doubted it; he would not even advise me to set in motion all the powers of my will, of which he had some conception, since I could blow up everything" (*J/P*, V, 335; n. 5913 [1846]). Kierkegaard does transform his misrelation by will, but he cannot transform it for others without the help of Providence. "On the whole, the very mark of my genius is that Governance broadens and radicalizes whatever concerns me personally. I remember what a pseudonymous writer[12] said about Socrates: 'his whole life was personal preoccupation with himself, and then Governance comes and adds world-historical significance to it'" (*J/P*, VI, 144; n. 6388

11. Louis Dupré, *Kierkegaard as Theologian* (London, 1963), 31.
12. Johannes Climacus, in *CUP*, 132.

[1849]). The realization is that until it is transformed for others, the suffering, a symptom of a will so powerful (hence guilty) that it terrifies, cannot be endured.

The dialectical relation between the psychic and physical makeup is the way in which God keeps Kierkegaard in check (*J/P*, V, 336; n. 5913 [1846]). With every expression he must deny his own authority to keep himself in the correct position. He is "continually under orders to annihilate himself so that he does not become an authority to anyone" (*J/P*, VI, 36; n. 6220 [1848]). The anguish and pressure behind this compulsive and obsessive declaration of the motto, "no authority"—a new authorial norm that annihilates the authority of earthly fathers (while preserving the authority of Kierkegaard's own father)—contrasts markedly with the cool play surrounding the motto in contemporary deconstructive thinkers. The bold and guilty checking of his power as a form and theme comes out with particular strength in *The Point of View for My Work as an Author*, in which the dialectical poet is an obedient one.

> It is said of the "poet" that he invokes the muse to supply him with thoughts. This indeed has never been my case, my individuality prohibits me even from understanding it; but on the contrary I have needed God every day to shield me from too great a wealth of thoughts. Give a person such a productive talent, and along with that such feeble health, and verily he will learn to pray. . . . I could sit down and continue to write for a day and a night, and again for a day and a night; for there was wealth sufficient for it. If I had done it, I should have been broken. Oh, even the least dietetic indiscretion, and I am in mortal danger. When I learn obedience, as I have described above, when I do the work as if it were a sternly prescribed task, hold the pen as I ought, write each letter with pains, then I can do it. (*PVA*, 68).

And further on he adds:

> The dialectical factor in this is that whatever extraordinary gift may have been entrusted to me, it was entrusted as a precautionary measure with such elasticity that, if I were to obey, it would strike me dead. It is as if a father were to say to his child: You are allowed to take

the whole thing, it is yours; but if you will not be obedient and use it as I wish—very well, I shall not punish you by taking from you; no, take it as yours . . . it will smash you. Without God I am too strong for myself, and perhaps in the most agonizing of all ways am broken. (*PVA*, 69–70)

The expression of rebellion against his father, of engagement to Regine—these are explosions. There is satisfaction, he admits in a draft of a letter of reconciliation to a married Regine, "to be found in having this powerful personality, but the responsibility becomes all the greater."[13] The torment of that qualification keeps him in bonds (*J/P*, VI, 340; n. 6659 [1850]). He is "constrained in suffering" (*J/P*, VI, 371; n. 6718 [1851]). It is by the repeated awareness and expression of this dialectic between his body and mind, fear and passion, which is never "solved" ethically nor ever fully dissolved spiritually, that he draws us in.

Perhaps the refrain with which Kierkegaard taunts Hegelians, of wanting to go further than faith, is a reflection of his own qualms about going further than the father, usurping him. We are already familiar with these checks and balances in the relation to God, in the venturing past communal universals. "No man has ever lived who has truly done this without discovering with horror the horror of spiritual trial, that he may be venturing too boldly, that the whole thing might be lunacy" (*J/P*, IV, 262; n. 4372 [1849]). Could he dare to imitate Socrates and Christ as one who worked much more self-consciously to "explode existence"? "Outside of Christianity Socrates is the only man of whom it may be said: he explodes existence, which is seen quite simply in his elimination of the separation between poetry and actuality" (*J/P*, IV, 222; n. 4301 [1854]). Here again is the secret check, for Kierkegaard will never be able to feel confident that he has indeed wiped out the line between poetry and actuality; further, unlike Christ and Socrates, he will have to use his literature to work himself through to this possibility. The literature is a symbol of his dialectical "debility," which is why he rarely, indeed, drops the epithet *poet* from his role. It unmakes his body as it

13. Søren Kierkegaard, *Letters and Documents*, trans. and ed. Henrik Rosenmeier (Princeton, 1978), 327.

makes it. It is the necessary medium within which to explode illusion in the highest cause, and this is Kierkegaard's only alternative to exploding himself or the world in the cause of vanity, private retribution.

The choosing of sickness in an age of false faith becomes the only health, a familiar reversal to the twentieth-century reader, but one that allows Kierkegaard to use anxiety, expressed through literary diction, as an explosive corrective, even in the deceptively becalmed medium of the edifying discourses. Deliberately he chooses the term *edifying* to transvaluate its conservative definition. The term will mean *dismaying*, for

> the edifying is not for the healthy-minded but for the sick; to the supposedly healthy and strong it must therefore in the first instance appear as the dismaying. The sick person understands as a matter of course that he is subjected to the treatment of the physician; but for a person in sound health it would be dismaying to discover that he had fallen into the hands of a physician who without more ado was treating him as a sick man. So it is with the edifying, which first is the dismaying—for the non-contrite it is a means to contrition. (*CrD*, 101−102)

Healthy upbuilding must be offended by the shadow of its contrary, for Kierkegaard anticipates Nietzsche and Freud in his conviction that we are sick from too much of the wrong kind of morality. Health cannot be cured except by the consciousness of the offense of the dialectical structure of reality. "There is healing for all pain, victory in all conflict, salvation from all danger—that is edifying; the dismaying thing is that there is pain, conflict, danger; and the degree of the dismaying and of the dismay corresponds to the edifying and to the edification" (*CrD*, 102). The sign of the dialectical turning, the transvaluation that undoes the didactic until it touches dread and then rolls forth doubled into eternity, is a constant in the discourses. The physician transforms medicine into poison before he turns it into medicine again (*CrD*, 102). With this act, the endless suffering of this life is seen as an instant in comparison to the health of eternity, its long day abbreviated to a "once" in order, precisely, to parody those who would attach suffering to misfortune instead of to misunderstanding, and finish it in a plot (*CrD*, 103). Kierkegaard has once again anticipated his critics who, like Bonhoeffer, would suggest that there is a false pride in the glorification of sickness that renders the whole venture private and abstract. But Kierkegaard never does glorify suffering without hounding it by demonic possibilities that check its authority, and he is always aware of the temptation to use suffering as grace itself instead of as passage. "Suffering must never itself be the *telos*—you must not venture in order to get suffering, for this is presumptuously tempting God. To want to lay yourself open to suffering for the sake of suffering is presumptuous personal indiscretion and impertinence toward God, as if you would challenge God to a competition" (*J/P*, IV, 418; n. 4692 [1852]).

The poison of unconditional commands—"Wherefore, if thy hand or thy foot offend thee, cut them off" (Matthew 18:7−9)—is a medicine to the bourgeois rationalizations of Christendom. In the same way, the antidote to Kierkegaard's rationalization, the collision of grammars, is sent down by the Paradox—"Here the possibility of offense consists in the self-contradiction that the remedy appears infinitely worse than the disease" (*TC*, 112). The task of the literature is to present the collision between these two grammars without ever solving them, for the dialectical poet can only lead to the possibility of faith through offense, and prepare the understanding to stumble on contradiction. When Christendom does away with dialectical suffering, it does away with the possibility of offense and then with the possibility of faith.

The dialectical poet is a physician who, in the best Platonic tradition, deceives into the truth (*PVA*, 39). And he can hang upon the long tradition of the church fathers who saw Atonement itself as a remedy that appears as sickness.

> It was by means of a certain amount of deceit that God carried out this scheme on our behalf. For that not by pure Deity alone, but by Deity veiled in human nature, God, without the knowledge of His enemy, got within the lines of him who had man in his power, is in some measure a fraud and a surprise; seeing that it is the peculiar way with those who want to deceive to divert in another direction the expectations of their intended victims, and then to effect something quite different from what these latter expected. . . . Two persons may both mix poison with food, one with the design of taking life, the other

with the design of saving that life; the one using it as a poison, the other only as an antidote to poison.[14]

If this great physician offends with his cure, so should those who write for him. Kierkegaard's literature is surgical and will raise the anger of the patient who winces with the pain of the incision. The physician claims that he brings healing: "Very well then, one has recourse to it as one has recourse to a person with whom one seeks refuge, and one thanks it as one thanks a helper; for by the aid of it or by its aid one expects to be enabled to bear the suffering one sighs under. And then exactly the opposite occurs. One flees to the word in search of help—and then one has to suffer because of the word" (*TC*, 116). So, too, Socrates uses shame as medicine. Why should not Kierkegaard make an insomniac of his reader, who unlike the "Christian" child, is told what the true God will do to him?

> That before God this world is a lost world, where he who is born is by being born lost, that what God wills (out of love) is that a man shall die from the world and that if God is so gracious as to turn His love toward him, that what God then does (out of love) is to torment him with every anguish calculated to take his life; for this is what God wills (yet out of love). He would have the life of everyone that is born, have him transformed into a deceased man, one who lives as though dead. (*AC*, 224)

Otherwise, he will "doze off into secular security" (*J/P*, IV, 506;

---

14. Gregory of Nyssa, "The Great Catechism," trans. William Moore and Henry Austin Wilson, in Philip Schaff and Henry Wace (eds.), *A Select Library of Nicene and Post-Nicene Fathers of the Christian Church*, 2nd ser. (14 vols.; Grand Rapids, Mich., 1892), V, 495. See also Plato's *Republic*, V: 459D. Jacques Derrida's rescue of the ambiguity of writing as both remedy and poison from Platonic hostility in the *Phaedrus* is of interest in assessing Kierkegaard's guilt concerning his literature. Kierkegaard's Socratic preference for speech over writing might also be seen from Derrida's perspective that identifies writing with filial usurpation of the father (hence, Kierkegaard's habitual "apologies" to Providence). The aesthetically and psychologically "healthy" recovery of filial rights to ambiguity and ambivalence obviously could not have satisfied this dialectical poet of Christianity. See Derrida, "Plato's Pharmacy," *Dissémination*, trans. and ed. Barbara Johnson (Chicago, 1981). Also of interest are the many self-references in Nietzsche's work to the author as both patient and physician.

n. 4890 [1851]). Posthumous from childhood, Kierkegaard deceives to become the norm for the true life, his disease a standard for health.

The severity of the clash between the two grammars seems to demand indirect communication. Rousseau, who saw both terms of contradiction as immanent, would never claim to deceive into the truth, especially not by indirect communication. The gradual education into the truth that God practices—"You were too loving and faithful not to deceive me" (*J/P*, IV, 506; n. 4890 [1851]), says Kierkegaard to him— is his form of indirect communication. The literature imitates the gesture of God: "He deceives a man into the truth. He grasps the truth in imagination—it looks so inviting, he cannot escape it, he goes along— and now he stands right in the middle of actuality, and the matter is altogether different" (*J/P*, IV, 9; n. 3839 [1851]). The literature entices the reader, then falls away from him and strands him amid mere possibilities that he must annihilate into actualities. Conventionally, literature gives the comfort of "imitation at a distance" (*J/P*, II, 356; n. 1913 [1852]) so that our reading and hearing are fairy tales: "Once upon a time there was a man who as a child had heard the beautiful story about how God tempted Abraham . . . " (*F/T*, 26). But Kierkegaard, like the sleeping Socrates, gives the reader nothing to hold on to except movements of faith, as protective devices like closure and foreshortening are sabotaged. *Now* the listener must be irritated, frustrated, repelled by the endless beginnings: "It was early in the morning . . ." (*F/T*, 28). The work destroys the possibility of imitation to become an instrument of propulsion into actuality. Christ speaks "about the man who is offended when tribulation and persecution arise because of the word" (Matthew 13:21, and *TC*, 116). Christ would lead past this offense, but Kierkegaard must lead his reader to it:

But if the real difficulty is to become a Christian, this being the absolute decision, the only possible introduction must be a repellent one, thus precisely calling attention to the absolute decision. Even the longest of introductions cannot bring the individual a single step nearer to an absolute decision. For if it could, the decision would not be absolute, would not be a qualitative leap, and the individual would be deceived instead of helped. . . . Philosophy offers an im-

mediate introduction to Christianity, and so do the historical and
rhetorical introductions. These introductions succeed, because they
introduce to a doctrine, but not to becoming a Christian. (*CUP*, 343)

The literature consciously undermines conventional philosophical, historical, and rhetorical modes of persuasion. It must in itself be an
offense, since as in Christianity, consciousness of offense is a defense
against speculation (*SD*, 214). (For once, English has the advantage over
Kierkegaard's punning Danish, for "taking offense" and "to take the
offensive" are quite different expressions in Danish.) Kierkegaard imagines that even if the learner is warned that he is to undergo education by
the "awakening of misunderstanding" (*J/P*, I, 310; n. 662 [1848]), he
will in time regret the pain of getting involved with him. He does not
call himself a teacher without qualifying the term with the epithets poet
and learner, but as these, he has the task of devising "the most irritating
and wounding means" to further Christian consciousness. He is an artist
of offense, one who, as Jean-Paul Sartre puts it, remains the scandal and
stumbling block of subjectivity. [15]

When he gives us hierarchies of talent, genius, and spiritual worth,
he gives, typically, the lowest rank to talent because it receives the
applause of the universal; the second rank to genius because at least it
defines itself in opposition to the world; the highest rank to the religious
character because it causes offense (*J/P*, II, 85; n. 1301 [1854]). Defining himself by opposition may be a kind of defense, but it is paid for by
the active task of giving offense. To compel people to take notice without
using "all the old military science, all the apologetic" demands the
aesthetic incognito (*PVA*, 38–39). But the bringing of offense does not
close the gap between it and the truth. Christ fulfills the law in offend-
ing, because he embodies it and is both its explanation (*Forklaring*) and
its transfiguration (*Forklarelse*). "Our earthly life, which is weak and

---

15. Jean-Paul Sartre, "The Singular Universal," in Thompson (ed.), *Kierkegaard*,
243. Again, Derrida's comments on Rousseau's craving for an innocent language might
be of interest here, though the fact that this craving stays immanent in Rousseau does
create a different kind of pressure from that in Kierkegaard's prose, in which frustration
and guilt in language are recognized as necessary before God. See Jacques Derrida, *Of
Grammatology*, trans. Gayatri Chakravorty Spivak (Baltimore, 1977).

infirm, must distinguish between explaining and being" (*WL*, 108).
How much more agonizing is it to have to exploit this distinction to
compel attention? Although this standpoint goes beyond that of Kierkegaard's early view of Socrates' irony, since the offense serves the Paradox,
still it has something in common with it because it seems "a healthiness
insofar as it rescues the soul from the snares of relativity . . . a sickness
insofar as it is unable to tolerate the absolute except in the form of
nothingness" (*CI*, 113–14). To cause the consciousness of offense that
might precipitate the consciousness of a larger offense and not in itself to
be revelation, to obstruct and stop but to be unable to be a refuge, a
stopping place—this is the torment of the literature. The author cannot
close the gap between the offensive grammars of speech and silence. "If I
were to speak with someone simply about my activity as an author, I
would speak only about big things. I cannot speak directly to another
person of how before God I feel less than a sparrow, or just as insignificant. In conversation among men we use human standards, and by
human standards I have a great superiority. But to speak in this way is
extremely painful to me and afterward it grieves my spirit; it is to me as if
I deceived God" (*J/P*, I, 266; n. 646 [1848]). To be an author before
God is in itself to be in a state of offense. By carrying the burden of
offense without the boon of salvation or revelation, the art is, like
Regine, the determination of a "negative relationship" that "makes a
man idealistically productive" (*SLW*, 70).

Throughout his authorship, Kierkegaard yearns to be free of giving
offense, yearns merely to be; for his task evidences an "unhappy lover"
(*SD*, 209) who as a poet and thinker has "depicted everything in the
medium of imagination" while "living in resignation" (*J/P*, V, 447;
n. 6135 [1848]). He does not have the immediacy of the spontaneous
believer who cannot understand why communication of faith cannot be
direct, who "cannot take himself out of direct continuity with others,
. . . cannot maintain that what for him is the surest thing of all, eternal
salvation, is and must be for others the absurd" (*J/P*, I, 6; n. 8 [1850]).
But Kierkegaard, as a reflective religious poet, has the burden of dialectical tension; as a yearning believer, "dialectically consolidated," he
must not only see but transcribe by his literature the way in which "the
content of faith, seen from the other side, is the negative absurd" (*J/P*, I,

6; n. 8 [1850]). Kierkegaard's last period, with its direct and explosive polemic, testifies belatedly to his passion to make his words be, to be innocent of literature, to raise his offense to that of Christ.

> Christ cries woe to them who give offense, to them by whom offense comes—and yet the possibility of offense is inseparable from every qualification of the essentially Christian, and Christ frequently repeats: "Blessed is he who is not offended in me." The difference is this—the divine truth is "the truth," but in such a way that the world takes offense at it. It cannot be otherwise. But it cannot therefore be said that it gives offense. To give offense is something else, for example, deliberately intending to wrench faith away from the believer. When the possibility of offense is shown in order to strengthen in the faith, this is the truly Christian proclamation of Christianity. (*J/P*, III, 371; n. 3036 [1850])

Could Kierkegaard ever be sure that his mode of displaying the possibility of offense was fully justified? His literature is full of figures in positions of despair continually falling away from the Paradox as "acoustic illusions" (*PF*, 63), boasting rebellion, suffering doubt and anxiety, but always, from the view outside literature, from the view of the Paradox itself, passive in their activity and parasitic in their independence. Is the act of showing faith from the other side, of depicting the offended by merely acoustically imitating Paradox's understanding of him—is this enough to free Kierkegaard's consciousness from the offense of not understanding itself? (*PF*, 63). At least the literature can, by its conscious position of offense, set up a longing for its own abandonment by the reader.

Another dialectical tension in the tormented passage between condition and weapon is that between polemic and compassion. Kierkegaard is, by nature polemical. Yet as a physician of the age he must feel compassion. This is the bond that he forges between the two: "How fundamentally polemic I am by nature I can best see in the fact that the only path by which the attacks of men can affect me is the sadness I feel on their behalf" (*J/P*, V, 321; n. 5891 [1846]). His suffering is to be the source of his compassion. "In regard to this whole side of psychiatry, it is so profoundly true that to be a physician is to be willing oneself to suffer.

He who does not have this humble devotedness, patience, and love to be willing to endure the suffering, serving (like a servant, like the subordinate one, in the form of a servant), putting himself in the other's situation—he heals no one; and if the physician is in this way willing to suffer more than the patient—he heals many" (*J/P*, IV, 353; n. 4552 [1849]). Kierkegaard sees the famous diagnosis of his friend and teacher, Poul Møller, that he is the "most thoroughly polemical of men" (*J/P*, V, 360; n. 5961 [1847]), as an illness brought on by a natural heterogeneity with a world that denies spirit. He is, in fact, only "thoroughly dialectical" (*J/P*, V, 368; n. 5979 [1847]). He is polemical because, being misunderstood, he is compelled to misunderstand. It is a design that has an interesting relation to that of his father who, as his figure is presented in *Johannes Climacus or De Omnibus Dubitandum Est*, "belied his own self-depreciation through the very virtuosity which enabled him to crush every opponent and bring him to silence" (*JC*, 110). Again, assuming the ignorance of Socrates and the humility of Christ as a disguise, Kierkegaard claims that "being regarded as less than I am is my *working capital* (the propelling agent)." And he is sure to add, "but I am also by nature polemical" (*J/P*, VI, 386; n. 6740 [1851]). Then again, he must appear a fool, for it is "the law for the religious . . . to act against sagacity" (*J/P*, VI, 518; n. 6890 [1854]).

On one hand, one makes another suffer from an incognito that "must hide a heart-felt emotion and to seem to be other than one is" (*TC*, 136). On the other, the old anxiety in the public claim of service drives the physician to the hardest of all human sufferings. He suffers not merely from repression of his own love, but from the suspicion that the educational responsibility he assumes might disguise the reality that "he who cannot reveal himself cannot love" (*E/O*, II, 164). Is the extreme economy of Kierkegaard's view of his life as providential in every detail a necessary compensation for the dialectic of incognito that both preserves and exhausts his true feelings, for the necessary playing out of possibilities that might truly torture the self, "like those unhappy demoniacs," into a "legion"? (*E/O*, II, 164). Or worse, the fear might be that the masquerade is the only substantial element in the personality that, otherwise, would be nothing. From the beginning the questions are certainly, what is Kierkegaard guarding and what is he giving, until at last, after the spiritual deepening of 1848, the boil of indirect communication bursts. And even then, Johannes Hohlenberg might be right that in the last polemical battles, the deliberate exposure of the suffering life to ridiculed caricature is an incognito.[16]

Jean Starobinski astutely and persuasively describes the dialectical purpose of the incognito as a cover-up of emptiness and fragmentation on one hand, and as a guard against the world's encroachment on the latency on the other. That is, the emptiness comes into being as fullness *against* the world. The mask, assumes the critic, stimulates the misconstruction, assures the isolation and separation that enables the God-relationship to establish itself on the ruins of all possibility of human relationships.[17] And further, the identity by opposition to the crowd protects innocence as well. If the crowd is untruth, then Kierkegaard, like Socrates, needs to be *thought* a seducer in order not to *be* one. All of these sound, modern psychological suppositions derive from Kierkegaard's own testimony, especially in the *Journal* passages in which he worries about the demonic element in assertion. The mask drops at the end, but even then, polemic and obedience are tensed against each other. The maieutic always envies the witness; the ironist always strives to pass from deceiving into the truth to testifying to it. "Yet the communication of the essentially Christian must end finally in 'witnessing.' The maieutic cannot be the final form, because, Christianly understood, the truth doth not lie in the subject (as Socrates understood it), but in a revelation which must be proclaimed" (*J/P*, II, 383; n. 1957 [1848]). The identity is strong enough, finally, for directness, strong enough to give itself up, but it will never call itself a witness. Even in 1850 Kierkegaard could still be anxious about surrendering the indirection.

> When I look back on my life, I must say that it seems to me not impossible that something higher hid behind me. It was not impossible. I do not say more. What have I done, then? I have said: for the present I use no means which would disturb this possibility, for example, by *premature* direct communication. The situation is like that of a fisherman when he sees the float move—maybe it means a strike, maybe it is due to the motion of the water. But the fisherman

16. Hohlenberg, *Søren Kierkegaard*, 201–202.

17. Jean Starobinski, "Kierkegaard et les masques," *Nouvelle revue française*, XXV (1965), 619, 815, 821.

says: I will not pull up the line; if I do, I indicate that I have
surrendered this possibility; perhaps it will happen again and prove to
be a bite. (*J/P*, II, 384; n. 1959 [1850])

At the same time, he worries that the disguise of indirectness might
protect him from the direct commands of the gospel imperatives to
witness. The task is to force his literature to be as it lures others into
being. Could that literature *be* if it hid his latency, even to emancipate
the latency of others? The anxiety of giving offense in the hope of going
beyond offense is the heart and soul of Kierkegaard's power. His literature must repel him as well as the reader into terrifying freedom.

Wahl contrasts the persistent "sentiment du secret" and the "sentiment de l'existence" in Kierkegaard with the public and open nature of
Hegel's deepest meanings, of his mediation between the internal and
external motive.[18] Kierkegaard's exasperation of Hegel's Pattern, the
qualitative and perpetual strain between the inner and outer versions of
the self and its relation to the world, Hegel would deem an egotistical
romanticism. But Kierkegaard could defend the public meaning of his
tactic, the ceaseless aggravation between form and content, as a refuta-
tion of the Hegelian mediation that he termed fantastic. By keeping the
qualitative gulf open between the subjective and objective, between man
and God, man as possibility and as actuality, the literature could be used
as an agent of existential reality. Hiding the truth, it is also the authentic
dialectical approach to it. The powers of offense used by one "who has not
unconditionally stepped forth as personally being Christian in a decisive
sense" can awaken Christendom if he remembers that "unqualified indirect communication belongs to being more than human, and no man,
therefore, has the right to use it" (*J/P*, II, 383; n. 1958 [1848]). The
use of qualified indirect communication against worldly shrewdness,
Kierkegaard contends, sanctifies ingenuity.

> He must guarantee that he is existentially more advanced than the
> established order. Thereupon he turns aside and makes the admission;
> I feel that I am not a Christian; Christianity is so infinitely elevated
> that I am no Christian.
> At first the established order will perhaps think this wonderful.

18. Wahl, *Etudes kierkegaardiennes*, 162–63.

But it had better look around—It has been tricked. With its claim to being Christian the established order is way behind him, and he who insists that he is not a Christian is ahead.

They will perhaps say: He is a fool. The established order had better look around. In the game *Gnavspil*, when the fool goes he takes only one along with him—here he takes everybody along. (*J/P*, II, 386; n. 1961 [1851])

To make men aware of spirit is "still in the context of the universal" (*J/P*, VI, 281; n. 6577 [1850]), though the plan betrays it. In a particular case as well, that of Regine, the egotistical and frivolous fool who "secretly experienced the Christian collisions" (*J/P*, II, 468; n. 2125 [1850]) led him to something higher and freed her to her possibilities.

But we have seen that the offense was never free from the defense. By 1852, still wondering if perhaps he could have been "secretly proud of having no fellowship with other Christians" (*J/P*, II, 388; n. 1962), he cannot be sure of the justification of declaring himself not a Christian. There is always the envied image of the ease of the hidden inwardness of Abraham (who never had to be a literary offender). Having lived before Christ, he at least *was* his faith, as was Socrates. In *Concluding Unscientific Postscript*, Johannes Climacus teases the question of hidden inwardness through an outing of the religious individual to Deer Park, equivalent, though in a comic cast, to the return of Abraham. Abraham's domestication is displaced onto an imagined modern knight of faith, and the humor of the religious man as a lounging bourgeois might have inspired Kafka's rueful parody of the justification of Kierkegaard's patriarch. "He takes delight in everything he sees, in the human swarm, in the new omnibuses, in the water of the Sound; when one meets him on the Beach Road one might suppose he was a shopkeeper taking his fling, that's just the way he disports himself, for he is not a poet, and I have sought in vain to detect in him the poetic incommensurability. Toward evening he walks home, his gait is as indefatigable as that of the postman. On his way he reflects that his wife has surely a special little warm dish prepared for him: (*F/T*, 50). Unburdened by the social incommensurability of either the genius or the poet, he "smokes his pipe; to look at him one would swear that it was the grocer over the way vegetating in the twilight" (*F/T*, 51). No, this is not Kierkegaard, the anxious offender, who shares the wonder and self-irony of Johannes de Silentio watching this knight and the Abraham who "resigns everything infinitely, and then . . . grasps everything again by virtue of the absurd" (F/T, 51). The knight makes the movements of infinity "with such correctness and assurance that he constantly gets the finite out of it, and there is not a second when one has a notion of anything else" (F/T, 51). In this dialectical concealment there is no demonic anxiety, for faith is full.

Kierkegaard explores his own qualms further through the figure of the merman. This was one of his favorite identifications, for he was fond of seeing himself as a spirit who hears the world through the distorted echoes of his underwater medium.[19] The fairy tale of "Agnes and the Merman" he typically alters, making the exchange between fortune and misfortune a tangle of dialectical possibilities. His literature must torture him so that it does not become a therapeutic solution. The possibility of an absolute relationship to the demoniacal, to the evil motive beneath the blessed act—beneath, for example, renunciation of seduction—gives one version the apparent stature and structure of the hidden inwardness of faith. The silencing of motive causes pain, the noble assumption of the disguise torment, and this would seem to justify the act. Possibilities in patterns of repentance are ushered forth: the Middle Ages would have him "remain in concealment, but not rely upon his shrewdness" for "the deity will save Agnes." Or his love for Agnes might save him from being a deceiver (F/T, 107)—the aesthetic solution. Now the possibilities of hidden inwardness are paraded, impelled by the dearest wish of Kierkegaard that he could have had enough faith to marry Regine's love. How can the merman come back to Agnes after being projected by guilt past the universal? What kind of return can he make by virtue, or not, of the absurd? The old envy of Sarah reappears.

> If he remains hidden and initiates himself into all the torments of repentance, then he becomes a demon and as such is brought to naught. If he remains concealed but does not think cunningly that being himself tormented in the bondage of repentance he could work Agnes loose, then he finds peace indeed but is lost for this world. If he becomes revealed and allows himself to be saved by Agnes, then he is the greatest man I can picture to myself; for it is only the aesthetic

19. See Kierkegaard, Letters, 72.

writer who thinks lightmindedly that he extols the power of love by letting the lost man be loved by an innocent girl and thereby saved, it is only the aesthetic writer who sees amiss and believes that the girl is the heroine, instead of the man being the hero. (*F/T*, 109)

The merman does not have the strength for a return like Abraham's, nor does Kierkegaard, but we could not feel the power of Abraham without the trial and torment of both.

Faust's story is altered as well, and as a noble doubter who remains silent in order to spare the universal, he is subject to demonic motives of hidden pride. He is accused by a jealous universal that wants him to talk in order that he not go beyond it. The only warrant for the silence of the doubter is the choice of becoming the particular individual who "as the individual stands in an absolute relation to the absolute" (*F/T*, 120). In this case, the doubt would change to guilt and he would move within the medium of the Paradox. But the doubt is prematurely cured. The New Testament itself sanctions the silence of hidden holiness, its deceit when it is not demonic; for if "subjectivity is incommensurable with reality," as indicated in Christ's recommendation, "When thou fastest, anoint thy head and wash thy face, that thou be not seen of men to fast," then it "has leave to deceive" (*F/T*, 121).

And it is the leave to deceive that Kierkegaard is searching for, a leave that would put demonic silence, seduction, and disguise all together in the medium of faith. That he never can absolutely have this allows us the identification that we find so powerful in the works. As varieties of despair fall away from the divine Paradox (the real prototype for all earth's metaphors), so, too, varieties of demonic concealment fall away from divine silence and Abraham's perfect hidden inwardness; surging analogies crash back and by this negative action describe the posture of worship and awe. "The examples were simply educed in order that while they were shown in their own proper sphere they might at the moment of variation indicate as it were the boundary of the unknown land" (*F/T*, 121). There would be no literature if the stories of fathers, sons, lovers, completed the returns "by virtue of the absurd" again and again. In a fit of maieutic misunderstanding, Constantine Constantius brings forth the young poet who dialectically "completes" his creator and invents the religious exception who defines the universal by being outside it (*Rep*,

134). "A poet's life," says Constantius, "begins in conflict with the whole of existence. The gist of it is to find an appeasement or a justification." In the first of his collisions with the world, explains Constantine Constantius aphoristically, "he must always be defeated, and if he is bent upon triumphing at once, he is an unjustified exception" (*Rep*, 135). The long and sometimes tedious configuration of concealment and disguise, the fairy-tale versions of his own story—these are the necessary deceits for one like Kierkegaard, who shuttles back and forth between the boundaries of the known and the unknown, whose spiritual gifts are great enough to expose Christendom, but not to live in it in perfect hidden inwardness.

One way that he justifies disguise is to turn it into a cause of suffering. The crowd has "no idea at all of the self-renunciation required to carry through an incognito. It really does not credit Christ with being able to keep quiet. They have no awareness, therefore, that it honors Christ to believe that he succeeded in being neither more nor less than a despised man, an incognito that was open only to faith" (*J/P*, II, 270; n. 1753 [1848]). This is one example, the highest, of course, and the other, predictably, is Socrates. "How many have the slightest idea of what it means to say that for him irony was an impersonation, that it was by no means a matter of trying to become understood but simply of remaining true to character, consequently of being misunderstood. He wanted to be misunderstood, because he wanted to be incognito. It was no holiday charade to entertain the cousins and nephews—and thus he lived day in and day out for many, many years" (*J/P*, II, 271; n. 1753 [1848]). Kierkegaard himself pictures the average man as having no idea of the difference between "assuming this or that guide" and actually carrying out the role, especially one like Christ's, that of willingly taking on "an incognito of such a sort that one seems to be something much lowlier than one is" (*TC*, 129). The incognito is self-abnegation, the atonement for aggressive identity and expression. "He exerts himself to the utmost, employing all his inventiveness and intrepidity to maintain the incognito. This effort is either successful or unsuccessful. If it is successful, then he has, humanly speaking, done himself an injury, he has made everybody think very poorly of him. What self-abnegation! And, on the other hand, what an immense strain upon a man! For he had it in his power every instant to show himself in his real character. What self-

abnegation!" (TC, 129). To remain true to character, asserts Kierkegaard in relation to Socrates and himself, is to be misunderstood. The
incognito frees them from direct instruction into a relationship with the
truth, and this is the relationship that teaches ignorance through irony.
Surely it is his own imitation of these models that makes Kierkegaard so
vehement a protester against the aestheticizing of one's suffering by
typology. "Someone has had a loss, and presto!—the preacher refers to it
as the Isaac whom Abraham *sacrifices*. What nonsense! Is a loss a *sacrifice*?
To sacrifice means voluntarily to bring a loss upon oneself. A man is sick,
presto!—it is the thorn in the flesh. . . . Life is carried on as in
paganism, where they also aspire to a certain external righteousness and
then provided for earthly needs whereby they got consolation. But in
Christendom they immediately talk about Gethsemane" (*J/P*, I, 154;
n. 374 [1848]). Christ's disguise was clearly providential, and history
cannot make his suffering accidental. Kierkegaard chooses his suffering
but can never be free from the possibility that history (the accidents of
psychological patterns) created his Providence.[20] When he then takes the
responsibility of using his history providentially for others, the problems
are even more severe. "Whether a man has a right to employ such
mystification, whether he is able to do it, and if he were able to do it,
whether the maieutical education of another man were not too great a
responsibility, or on the other hand, whether it might not be his duty to
do it, if it were done in self-abnegation and not in pride—I do not
undertake to decide" (*TC*, 130–31). However, when defense and attack
are "together in such a unity that no one can say directly whether one is
attacking or defending" (*TC*, 133), the responsibility for learning is
truly on the listener. Just so, it is fruitless to try to decide where
Kierkegaard's own self-defense and his spiritual purpose divide. That we
cannot do this cleanly allows us to receive more freely the task of inter-
preting the life in the literature according to our spiritual needs and
capacities. That we cannot appropriate the life of another is a firm and
crucial truth for Kierkegaard. His sickness is justified by its service of
liberation. The composer of himself has made himself in the literature an
"interrogation" (*TC*, 141).

The maieutic teacher constructs a dialectical difficulty for the learner

20. See *TC*, 37.

by erasing the line in his own being between seducer and lover, defense and attack (*TC*, 84). This is quite different from the deception of Christ, whose disguise is directness. "One says directly, 'I am God; the Father and I are one,' that is direct communication. But when he who says it is an individual man, quite like other men, then this communication is not just perfectly direct; for it is not just perfectly clear and direct that an individual man should be God—although what he says is perfectly direct" (*TC*, 134). Because the communicator is naught in the first instance, and all in the second, the teacher "without authority" must use his indirection to push the reader toward the offense of the second, an offense that is not constructed but merely *is*. Kierkegaard's body enters into its costume of poetry, a robe like Joseph's of blessing and curse. The strenuousness of the disguise is tenaciously endured, for it exposes the possibility of offense done away with in Christendom, which regularly pretends to hear Christianity as direct communication, and promotes "the false invention of human sympathy which forgets the infinite qualitative difference between God and man" (*TC*, 139). The procedure causes Kierkegaard an "indescribable suffering from inquietude and anxiety," for it involves a binding of "icy indifference" to "intense passion" (*TC*, 142). Even in the edifying discourses, the most passionate need is hidden under a surface quieted by sermonic poise but tenacious still in its rhythm of urgency and transvaluation, of prayer pressing toward the Paradox and petition toward faith.

The dialectical tension between Kierkegaard's body and its literature makes his body in the literature, as Sartre claims, "nearly the perfect *secret place*," a place that shuts him off from being defined as "an object of knowledge."[21] In this place, protection and service to faith can live together. Striving can be defense and attack, for the self and for others. "Every striving which does not apply one-fourth, one-third, two-thirds, etc. of its power to systematically *working against* itself is essentially secular striving, in any case unconditionally not a *reforming* effort. Reduplication means to work against oneself while working; it is like the pressure on the plow-handles, which determines the depth of the furrow—whereas working which does not work against itself is merely a superficial smoothing over" (*J/P*, VI, 294–95; n. 6593 [1850]). The

21. Sartre, "The Singular Universal," in Thompson (ed.), *Kierkegaard*, 259.

countereffort against himself takes this pattern, that "the public's darling introduce the single individual, and finally, that [he] plunge [himself] into all the dangers of insults!" (*J/P*, VI, 294–95; n. 6593 [1850]).[22] The sickness and the remedy, the patient and the physician, defense and offense, dialectically bind personal psychology to public history. The secret place, repelling the petitioner, dialectically lures to revelation and reform. Personal protection and the refusal of authority, the seduction and freeing of the other, become identical enough for endless apologetic resources by metaphor. One of them is metaphysical. Isn't God, after all, an elusive author?

> The immediate relationship to God is paganism, and only after the breach has taken place can there be any question of a true God-relationship. But this breach is precisely the first act of inwardness in the direction of determining the truth as inwardness. Nature is, indeed, the work of God, but only the handiwork is directly present, not God. Is not this to behave, in His relationship to the individual, like an elusive author who nowhere sets down his result in large type, or gives it to the reader beforehand in a preface? And why is God elusive? Precisely because He is the truth, and by being elusive desires to keep men from error. (*CUP*, 218)

All the more that the writer in his service should hide behind his literature, an elusive deceiver into the truth, not the truth itself. His negative body is the secret place that rhetorically reminds the reader of the presence of Christ's body, as the offense negatively reflects the presence of the Paradox.

> To point out how deceptive the rhetorical can be, I shall here show how one might rhetorically perhaps produce an effect upon a listener despite the fact that what was said was dialectically a regress. Let a pagan religious speaker say that here on earth, God's temples are really empty, but (and now begins the rhetorical) in heaven, where all is more perfect, where water is air and air ether, there are also temples and sanctuaries for the gods, but the difference is that the gods really dwell in these temples: then we have here a dialectical regress in the

22. Kierkegaard is referring to the public attention after the interest raised by the publication of *Either / Or*.

proposition that God really dwells in the temple, for the fact that He does not so dwell is an expression for the spiritual relationship to the invisible. But rhetorically it produces an effect. (*CUP*, 219–20*n*.)

A major dialectical metaphor expressing the need for secrecy in a society that is spiritually empty (exile then being the only presence and power) is that of the master thief (*J/P*, V, 10; n. 5074 [1835]) and police spy in the service of God (*Rep*, 37). Kierkegaard probably picked up the image of God's spies from Lear's famous speech and the mirror metaphor from Romantic literature, from Balzac's novels, for example, where it functions as an agent of social protest for his artist heroes who are also heterogeneous with much of their culture. In the best Romantic tradition, Kierkegaard starts as a misunderstood, melancholy, isolated, hidden sufferer and becomes, through his metaphor, a protester. "The master-thief has also been thought of as one endowed with natural goodness, kindness, charitableness, together with extraordinary bearing, cunning, ingenuity, one who really does not steal just to steal . . . but for some other reason. Frequently we may think of him as someone who is displeased with the established order and who now expresses his grievance by violating the rights of others, seeking thereby an occasion to mystify and affront the authorities" (*J/P*, V, 7; n. 5061 [1834]). He is forced into an inverse relation to the world because the dream cannot be fulfilled positively. His virtues, like those of Rousseau and of Nietzsche's "criminal," have been excommunicated by society.[23] As an active agent of arrest instead of crime, he puts himself into the passive position. "My task is to make room—and I am a police detective, if you please. But in this world the police come with force and arrest the others—the higher ranking police come suffering and ask instead to be arrested (*J/P*, VI; 551; n. 6936 [1854])." Power expressed in the active voices might be construed as envy of the social world, guilt in relation to it; so, a secret agent in God's care, he is humbled by "unconditional obedience" (*J/P*, VI, 21; n. 6192 [1848]). The criminal, who is identified with the Christ who comes to "set a fire to the human race" (*J/P*, VI, 534; n. 6916 [1854]) by his heterogeneity, is often indistinguishable from the secret agent, as defense and attack are twinned in Christian

23. See Nietzsche, *Twilight of the Idols*, 98.

education. The important offense that is shared is the secret prowling around the outskirts of the social world, the impossibility of integration. Mediation cannot reveal. As Constantine Constantius declares: "It is often a dreary thing to be an observer, it makes one as melancholy as being a detective on the police force; and when an observer performs well the duties of his calling he is to be regarded as a police spy in a higher service, for the art of the observer is to bring hidden things to light" (*Rep*, 37). Like the elusive author, the spy, the criminal, and like the God of Kierkegaard's "negative theology," Kierkegaard is present "precisely by being invisible." "The relationship between omnipresence and invisibility is like the relation between mystery and revelation. The mystery is the expression for the fact that the revelation is a revelation in the stricter sense, so that the mystery is the only trait by which it is known; for otherwise a revelation would be something very like a policeman's omnipresence" (*CUP*, 219–20).

The Point of View for My Work as an Author, which is so largely a defense of deceit and runs the spy metaphor through its text, can be looked at, despite the directness of Kierkegaard's presence there, as a vessel of negativity, an empty temple, its substance deceit; for "negativity understood in relation to the communication of the truth is precisely the same as deception" (*PVA*, 40). The calculated emptiness traps sophistic fullness.

> Indeed, it is only by this means, i.e. by deceiving him, that it is possible to bring into the truth one who is in an illusion. Whoever rejects this opinion betrays the fact that he is not over-well versed in dialectics, and that is precisely what is especially needed when operating in the field. For there is an immense difference, a dialectical difference, between these two cases: the case of a man who is ignorant and is to have a piece of knowledge imparted to him, so that he is like an empty vessel which is to be filled or a blank sheet of paper upon which something is written; and the case of a man who is under an illusion and must first be delivered from that. (*PVA*, 39–40)

The literature unwrites man so that he can be rewritten by Revelation. Unfit and without authority to assume the reforming incognitos of the Princes of Atonement, Kierkegaard assumes the demonic role of aesthetic seducer.[24] He will not allow his purpose to be free of its demonic possibilities of sexual guilt, but he exploits it for his ethical plan.[25] If the examples of Christ and Socrates give leave to deceive, so does that of the devil. That is why he has Victor Eremita imagine, as he edits the aesthetic seducer's papers, that he comes "like a shadow over the floor as if he fixed his demoniac eye upon me" and warns: "Well, so you are going to publish my papers! It is quite unjustifiable in you; you arouse anxiety in the dear little lassies. Yet obviously, in return you would make me and my kind harmless. There you are mistaken; for I need only change the method, and my circumstances become more favorable than before" (E/O, I, 9). Publication is castration, but Kierkegaard can hide in the literature. The very mark of Kierkegaard's dialectical vision of reality is that there is a great similarity in form between the seduction of the aesthetic, reflective deceiver who stirs counterseduction and conquers by displacing aggression, and that of Socrates who might reply to those who would be his Alcibiades: "My friend, how deceitful a lover you are! You wish to idolize me on account of my wisdom, and then to take your place as the friend who best understands me, from whose admiring embrace I shall never be able to tear myself free—is it not true that you are a seducer?" (PF, 29).

It is the closeness that establishes the vastness of the qualitative difference. Socrates is that perfect teacher, the model of "rare faithfulness, seducing no one, not even him who exercises all the arts of seduction in order to be seduced!" (PF, 30). Repeatedly Kierkegaard will tell us that the Seducer's diary was "intended to repulse" both Regine and the world, to repulse with all his power (J/P, VI, 194, 196; n. 6472 [1849]). But even if the Seducer's design came out of the search for the interesting and Kierkegaard's design came out of passionate infinite interest, the identity must not be forgotten, for it reminds the religious poet that his purpose can never be free from demonic temptations.

24. See Roy W. Battenhouse, "*Measure for Measure* and the Christian Doctrine of Atonement," *PMLA*, LXI (December, 1946), 1032–50.

25. The most thorough discussion of the seducer theme is Walter Rehm's *Kierkegaard und der Verführer* (Munich, 1949), esp. 469ff: "Der Verführer—er war die dämonische 'Möglichkeit' Kierkegaards" ("The Seducer—he was the demonic possibility of Kierkegaard" [author's translation]).

Kierkegaard knew that his books, like the Seducer's diary, were "neither historically exact nor simply fiction, not indicative but subjunctive" (*E/O*, I, 300). And is it not his task and talent, like the Seducer's, to "keep those who listen in suspense, by means of small incidents, of an episodic character, to ascertain what they wish the outcome to be, to trick them in the course of the narration . . . to make use of ambiguities, so that the listeners understand one thing in the saying and then suddenly notice that the words could also be interpreted otherwise?" (*E/O*, I, 365–66). We do not forget that while the Seducer enjoys his aesthetic talents, Kierkegaard is constantly anxious about his. On the aesthetic level, the figure of the Seducer is Kierkegaard's demonic double. Kierkegaard sees himself as a "special" seducer, a reflective, intellectual, "systematic seducer . . . a trained psychologist." (*E/O*, I, 358). He might be the active and negative name called out from the public to shield the pathos and guilt of the frightened lover of Regine, as Denmark is prodded into Athens. On the ethical level, he becomes a teacher who lures to free. If he does not have enough faith to marry Regine, the reader, Kierkegaard can give, at least, an ethical designation to the stranding. On the spiritual level, the savior is the seducer who deceives into the highest truth. The three levels are constantly bound in all of Kierkegaard's major metaphors of disguise.

The common weapon is longing. The Seducer uses the Romantic rhetoric of longing to entrap Cordelia. "My Cordelia! What is longing? Language and the poets rhyme it with the word prison [*Laengsel-Faengsel*]. How absurd! As if only a prisoner could know longing. As if one could not long when one is free" (*E/O*, I, 390). We remember Kierkegaard's recognition that in the *Symposium* Socrates made "love the substantial element in life, but then took it back again with the other hand by conceiving love negatively as longing" (*CI*, 100). Aesthetic longing skips over the present; ethical longing seeks to establish it as a place for the making of the self. In this distinction, Kierkegaard is quite close to Hegel, who severely distinguishes the longing of the unhappy consciousness that swallows itself from the longing that leads to the growth of consciousness.[26] Kierkegaard separates the poetry of Plato

26. Hegel, *Phenomenology*, 257–58.

from the "hungry dialectic" of Socrates (*CI*, 136) by noting that the poet
Plato "dreams into being all that the dialectician Socrates thought to
establish. It is in the world of dreams that irony's unhappy love finds its
object" (*CI*, 139). This would suggest that while the mythical embraces
the Idea, the dialectical represents longing, "a glance which gazes upon
the Idea so as to desire it" (*CI*, 134). In Kierkegaard's literature the
mythical is always qualified by the dialectical, for there are no words past
the Paradox and no embrace before it. Plato's dream, like that of the
mystics, is too close to the aesthetic fulfillment that short-circuits the
consciousness of offense. That Socrates makes his whole body irony
makes him a preliminary model for the movement of faith that is not a
dream. Judge William gives us an important criticism of the aesthetic
mysticism that softens the fierce dialectic between this life and the next,
and this was a criticism Kierkegaard would constantly support. The life
of the mystic "lacks continuity. What really supplies the continuity is a
feeling, the feeling of longing, whether this longing be directed towards
what is past or towards what is to come. But the fact that a feeling fills
the intervening space shows precisely that cohesion is lacking. The life of
the mystic is determined metaphysically and aesthetically to such a
degree that one dare not call it a history except in the sense in which one
speaks of the history of a plant" (*E/O*, II, 247).

The prayer of the mystic is compared to the erotic whisperings of
lovers, "inflamed by a burning love." Every instant it "makes trial of
. . . love." Instead, he hopes for the mystic: "He will have enough
greatness of soul to believe in God's love, and then he will also have the
frank-heartedness to believe in his own love and to continue gladly in the
situation assigned to him, knowing that this continuance is the surest
expression of his love, of his humility" (*E/O*, II, 249). This was an ideal
of hidden inwardness that Kierkegaard passionately yearned to reach.
Primarily, the mystic's problem is that he "chooses himself abstractly.
One can therefore say that he constantly chooses himself out of the
world. But the consequence is that he is unable to choose himself back
again into the world. The truly concrete choice is that wherewith at the
very same instant I choose myself out of the world I am choosing myself
back into the world" (*E/O*, II, 253). Like Hegel, whom he liked to
accuse of being too abstract, the young Kierkegaard insisted on the

concrete binding of the spirit to its suffering as he always would, though later not in such Hegelian rhythms as in this passage: "But this longing must not hollow out actuality; on the contrary, the content of life must become a true and meaningful moment in the higher actuality whose fullness the soul desires. Actuality in this way acquires its validity—not as a purgatory, for the soul is not to be purified in such a way that it flees blank, bare, and stark naked out of life—but as a history wherein consciousness successively outlives itself, though in such a way that happiness consists not in forgetting all this but becomes present in it" (*CI*, 341). Mystical longing is not used as a weapon of offense but as a promise of fulfillment. Nor does Hegel use it as a weapon. But Kierkegaard must anxiously "employ the longing" (*CrD*, 261), and that is why he feels such a strong bond with Socrates. To choose oneself out of the world or to stop at embodiment with it are relatively easy acts. What makes Kierkegaard's pressure seem particularly modern is the passion associated with renunciation. Kierkegaard wonders "if Socrates was that cold," as he appeared to be, "if it did not hurt him that Alcibiades could not understand him" (*J/P*, IV, 209; n. 4262 [1844]), and it seems a crucial distinction that surfaces with this question. No elenctic impasse could save Kierkegaard from his anxious torment about misunderstanding. We do not feel the sorrow in Socrates of Kierkegaard's God, who is imagined experiencing, like Kierkegaard himself, "the deep grief of having to deny the learner what he yearns for with all his heart, of having to deny him precisely because he is the beloved" (*PF*, 37).

If the denial of positive body in the world and in his literature is a protection, the assumption of a negative one is a courageous guarantee of its own suspension. We read in Quidam's diary, "I am far from being paradigmatic, I am rather a sample man" (*SLW*, 334), and we have no trouble imagining Kierkegaard echoing this self-assessment:

> I indicate with fair precision the temperature of every mood and passion, and while I produce my own inwardness, I understand these words: *homo sum, nil humani a me alienum puto*. But in a humane sense no man can fashion himself after me, and least of all in a historical sense am I a prototype for any man. I am rather a man such as might be needed in a crisis, an experiment which existence uses to feel its

way before it. A man half as reflective as I, would be able to acquire significance for many, but precisely because I am wholly reflective through and through I acquire none at all. (*SLW*, 334–35)

The necessary misunderstanding between life and literature which assures that the poet dies as prototype on the page is furthered by the splitting of the poet between experimenter and experiment, between Constantine Constantius and Father Taciturnus on one hand and the spiritual fledglings on the other, between the physicians and the patients, between those who elicit transformation and those who endure it. This is the only way in which the jest of the sample life, the experimental page, can carry "the deepest seriousness" (*SLW*, 335).

Kierkegaard identifies with Paul's self-selected epithet of *aphorismenos* (Romans 1:1, and *J/P*, V, 390; n. 6021 [1847]), but he realizes that as a poet who becomes more and more unhappy, he must still "through imagination continue[s] to relate himself to the world" (*J/P*, I, 63; n. 168 [1849]) while he uses his literature to offend, lest art be considered a higher sphere than faith. While his religious requirement is to learn silence from the lilies and the birds, his task as a religious poet is to lend them words. And these tasks are yoked together so that all metaphor brings guilt. "A Poet's Confession: His suffering is that he continually wants to be a religious individual and continually goes about it wrongly and becomes a poet—consequently an unhappy love affair with God . . ." (*J/P*, I, 58; n. 151 [1845]). It will be the strenuous work of his art to feed the spiritual history in such a way that being a poet and religious comes to be the right way of going about it. The partly unwilling, unconscious sacrifice of the poet to life prepares for the willing sacrifice to the life of faith. As early as 1840 Kierkegaard is able to criticize Goethe for being too self-confident to "be a sacrifice and not profound enough to want to be" (*J/P*, I, 450; n. 1027 [1840]). If expression cannot be renunciation, it can reflect it by its yearning.

In an important distinction between the religious and political perspectives, Kierkegaard speaks of the political passion to seek a fixed point ahead and of the religious passion to start from the fixed point behind. This is a reversal, in some sense, of our most literal expectations of the directions of history and faith; but Kierkegaard, while sharply distinguishing Greek recollection from Christian repentance, still uses

Socrates as a religious hero because he forced the world of sophistic progress to stop and go backward. Only a religious stumbling block, sacrificial salt, can stop the forward momentum of "European confusion,"[27] what Nietzsche would call "herd morality."[28] Socrates is a sacrifice to his age because he had "the fixed point *behind*. His point of departure lay in himself and in the god." And Kierkegaard projects the need in the modern world for such a gadfly to sting into reversal the "whither of modern haste." (He cannot use Luther now because the Reformation, starting out as a religious movement, turned out to be a political one.) Only the man who realizes that his victory will mean his sacrifice will leave the world a legacy of spiritual worth. "He conquers as the dead man who returns. The dead Socrates stopped the vortex, something the living Socrates was unable to do. But the living Socrates understood intellectually that only a dead man could conquer, as a sacrifice—and he understood ethically how to direct his whole life to becoming just that."[29] With all the vivacity of a passionate fashioner of faith, Kierkegaard directed himself, too, with more and more ardor, as salt and fire, to the sacrificial altar.

A NEGATIVE AGE

Every profound spirit needs a mask: even more, around every profound spirit a mask is growing continually, owing to the constantly false, namely *shallow*, interpretation of every word, every step, every sign of life he gives.
NIETZSCHE
"Beyond Good and Evil"

To be sure, our age is positive and understands what is positive; Socrates on the other hand was negative.
Philosophical Fragments

One of Kierkegaard's most persistent ways of viewing his role is as a corrective to an age that was positive in the wrong way, hence negative; reflective in the wrong way, hence passive; and ironic in the

27. See Kierkegaard, *Letters*, 262.
28. Friedrich Nietzsche, "Beyond Good and Evil," in *Basic Writings of Nietzsche*, trans. and ed. Walter Kaufmann (New York, 1968), 304.
29. Kierkegaard, *Letters*, 263.

wrong way, as a crowd, hence without spiritual passion. Of his contemporaries he writes, "They proudly imagine that their attitude is ironical—as though real irony were not essentially a concealed enthusiasm in a negative age (just as the hero is enthusiasm made manifest in a positive age), as though irony did not involve sacrifice, when its greatest master was put to death" (*PA*, 47). As the Paradox stops the offended in his tracks, so the corrective stops the age by a sacrifice that dismays its understanding. In his earliest judgment of Socrates, Kierkegaard remarks that "trust demanded a silence before again lifting up its voice, and it was Socrates who should occasion this silence" (*CI*, 232). And in the last of his judgments, the notion of silencing the age by becoming salt, its burnt offering, is virtually obsessive. This identification becomes quite insistent as a "political" category after the historical disturbances of 1848, if we accept Kierkegaard's assumption that, "from a religious point of view, the greatest impotence is the greatest power" (*J/P*, IV, 184; n. 4214 [1851]). The entry has as much psychological as political interest for us, for we see how much Kierkegaard needed to make expression out of social and sexual repression, and how much the Christian example helped him to do this. In a *Journal* entry marked by sarcasm directed against the tendency to displace blame for the spiritual mediocrity of this age from Denmark onto Germany, its enemy, Kierkegaard speaks of a people "who must either be saved by a tyrant or by a few martyrs" (*J/P*, IV, 146; n. 4127 [1848]). The tyrant is, of course, the potent and perverted expression of individuality, and the martyr the impotent one, but it is clear that the tyrant gains by contrast with the mob. We see here and in many other references that Kierkegaard's religious sensibility is not indifferent to political power but in direct competition with it. If he scolded Luther for his political bent, he also recognized a common bond with the courage, tenacity, and patience of his polemic (*J/P*, IV, 269; n. 4379 [1851]). It was really the fault of the clergy that character had crumbled and power was courted, for it promoted the age. So, if "a people's government will at most only be able to create a few martyrs, from whom it profits as Joseph's brothers profited from Joseph" (*J/P*, IV, 152; n. 4144 [1848]), then he would be the Joseph.

The extremism of his last years makes the contrast with Hegel vivid, but it is important to remember that the same contrast has been there throughout the authorship. Direct communication is a symptom of the desire to close in on being, to sacrifice literature to act, so that we should not imagine that the final polemic is antipodal to Socratic dialectic. In either case, the unconditional requirement of the spiritual forces a collision with the world that is, precisely, the conditioned (*J/P*, III, 118; n. 2571 [1854]). For Kierkegaard there never would be social morality adequate to bring the age back from its fantastic constitution in which smug notions of grace dim the need for striving and the individual is absorbed by the crowd. Christianity's eagerness to break with the world, says Kierkegaard in a late *Journal* entry, accounts for the constant use in the New Testament of words that "imply stopping, words such as: to be salt, to be sacrificed, etc." (*J/P*, III, 137; n. 2620 [1854]). From this perspective, the inability to marry becomes providential for Kierkegaard. "Every time the single state, motivated by love to God, makes its appearance, this is a move in the direction of complying with God's intention. But I almost shudder when I think how far I went in this direction and how amazingly I was halted and turned back to the single state" (*J/P*, III, 143; n. 2624 [1854]). The subjunctive has become fully indicative. Instead of communal marriages with the individual, Hegel's *Sittlichkeit* with *Moralität*, we have the unconditional break with the world (not to be confused with existence). "Christianity is simply this—the qualitative break of the divine with the human in the breakthrough which constitutes becoming a Christian, becoming salt—and then they want to bring up Christians from childhood—that is, they want to avoid the break with this existence, the break with this world" (*J/P*, III, 348; n. 2995 [1854]). The break (*Brudet*) is a staple of Kierkegaard's diction, and he puns on it mercilessly. The Seducer in *Stages on Life's Way* speaks cynically of the value of seduction that teaches a bride (*en Brud*) that a breach (*et Brud*) is to her as a male is to a female (*SLW*, 87). Kierkegaard gives the Christian counterpart of this design that, typically, transvaluates the aesthetic correspondence. "With a quite different meaning, Christianity says (when one reflects on its calling the believer a bride and Christ the bridegroom): A breach [*et Brud*] and a bride [*en Brud*]—that is, in order to become a bride you must make a breach between the world and everything and yourself. Consequently, not a [*en*] bride and a [*et*] breach but a [*et*] breach and a [*en*] bride" (*J/P*, III, 756; n. 3778 [1854]). Jacob P. Mynster's preaching, like his life, is characterized by its lack of breaching, "a breach, the very deepest and most incurable breach with this world" (*AC*, 17), and this breach is what distinguishes the New Testament Christianity from Epicureanism.[30] "I am," says Kierkegaard of himself, because of this, "a constant attack upon the Mynsterish preaching of Christianity" (*AC*, 15).

We might use English to extend his pun by allying his break with the world with the role of being a brake to the age. Against bourgeois Protestant eudaemonia, which understands itself as innocent and wants to comprehend more and more (as Hegel goes further than faith, and H. C. Martensen further than Hegel), Kierkegaard sets up the ideal of ignorance.[31] "The majority of men in any generation . . . live on and die in the illusion of a continuous process, that if they were granted a longer life the process would be a continued direct ascent of comprehending more and more. How many ever arrive at the maturity of discovering that a critical point comes where it reverses, where from now on the ascending comprehension is to comprehend more and more that there is something which cannot be comprehended" (*J/P*, III, 636; n. 3567 [1849]). This is, of course, the role of Socratic "silence," to act as a brake on progress. It is not the age of the Old Testament in which prophets and judges were needed to lead us forward to Christianity. Now, now that Christianity has been thoroughly "understood," he must force the generation back into unknowing and the intensity of inwardness. "With the help of this human going-further, everything merely becomes thinner and thinner—with the help of God's governance everything becomes more and more inward" (*J/P*, III, 152; n. 2640 [1848]). In some way or another, the forms of all the works of Kierkegaard reflect this movement of working back from the full System to the individual, from historical approximation posing as objective knowledge to subjective inwardness, that is, objective ignorance. The movement of Christianity, imitated in *Concluding Unscientific Postscript*, says Kierkegaard in *The Point of View for My Work as an Author*, is *back*, and "although it is all done without

30. Bishop J. P. Mynster was primate of the Church of Denmark. He had been Kierkegaard's pastor and a friend of his father. For an important historical perspective on Kierkegaard's relation to Mynster, Grundtvig, and Martensen, see Elrod, "The Modernization of Denmark," in *Kierkegaard and Christendom* esp. 3–46 and 75, 78.

31. Professor H. C. Martensen was Kierkegaard's tutor at the university, where he absorbed the influence of Hegel that marked his theological writings. After Mynster's death, he himself became bishop primate of the Danish church.

'authority,' there is, nevertheless, something in the accent which recalls a policeman when he faces a riot and says, Back!" (*PVA*, 75). As his literature acts as a brake on him, itself pressed back by pseudonyms and positions of possibility which interrupt momentum, so too can he push back the age. Although in his own time Kierkegaard thought Luther's emphasis on faith (really, the qualitative breach between God and man) had become an excuse for not striving, nevertheless, he greatly admired Luther's act of "express[ing] a halt" (*J/P*, III, 286; n. 2898 [1853]). All the more to be regretted is his favoring of Paul over Christ, of marrying over burning, and his acceptance of apostolic compromises (*J/P*, III, 480; n. 3213 [1855]). With this kind of commerce with the world, the fact that Christianity is "intrinsically" a religion of suffering and not just an opposition to a political world, is lost, and Christianity itself uses political tactics (*J/P*, III, 482; n. 3213 [1855]). The task of the believer is not to make Christians of others, to catch Christians, but in isolated earnestness to become himself, day after day, in faith, as the task of the religious poet is to repel disciples while stirring movements of faith.

To Kierkegaard, no one represented established eudaemonism in the contemporary Danish church more than the highly respected Bishop Mynster. His symbolic import was doubtlessly magnified because he was, as a friend of Kierkegaard's father, a father image. "I ought not to get into a struggle with one who reminds me of my father" (*J/P*, VI, 208; n. 6477 [1849]). The struggle broke out into full polemic after Mynster's death when his eulogist, Bishop Martensen, Kierkegaard's former teacher, called Mynster a witness. It enraged Kierkegaard that "a worldly shrewd eudaemonist" (*J/P*, VI, 546, n. 6927 [1854]), who had replaced the terms "either / or" with "both / and" (*J/P*, VI, 557; n. 6947 [1854]), should be called a witness to the truth, while his own standards were deemed too high. The indirect communication that bound us to the poet is exchanged for a higher one, that of the gospel's requirements, stated to the world and disguised by directness. "Then this poet suddenly transformed himself, threw away the guitar, if I may speak thus, brought out a book which is called *The New Testament of Our Lord and Saviour Jesus Christ*, and . . . put it up to these good perjured teachers whether this is not the book to which they were bound by an oath, this book whose standard is a good deal higher than that which the 'poet' had employed" (*AC*, 118). His task, to reveal that "the Christian-

ity of the New Testament does not exist at all" (*J/P*, VI, 554; n. 6943
[1854]), is more difficult than Luther's, though the latter had ninety-five
theses and he but one. The polemic flattens the metaphors and turns
them outward, away from himself.[32] The seducer becomes the forger.
Kierkegaard rails against the counterfeit banking of Mynster's Christianity: "On the whole, when it comes to scope and size, there is absolutely
nothing analogous to the crimes practiced in the realm of the religious.
Even the most experienced and most undaunted secret police agent
anywhere in the world will shudder at taking on this case, which involves using false bank notes on eternity to defraud a whole generation
throughout its whole life and to defraud them for eternity" (*J/P*, VI,
572; n. 6967 [1855]). The Mynsters are not missing out on the world.
"The fact is that people are very well informed about the creaturely
definition of what it is to be a virgin and the like. But they know nothing
at all about what a witness to the truth is, simply because they have
managed to make Christianity and the world coincide, whereas the
'witness to the truth' is related to Christianity's heterogeneity with this
world, and therefore always suffers, renounces, and misses out in this
world" (*J/P*, VI, 552; n. 6938 [1854]). They are at home in an age of
"sudden enthusiasms followed by apathy and indolence" (*PA*, 39), of
advertisement and publicity instead of passion and value; they transform
ideality into "representational ideas" (*PA*, 40).[33]

Mynster's age, and Christianity with it, has "become a committee"
(*PA*, 44), so that individuals can be related to it only inversely. This
inversion consciously preserves the dialectical relation between form and
content that reflects the true nature of our reality. Mynster, like Hegel, a
negative figure in Kierkegaard's literature who achieves body by the
passion of Kierkegaard's opposition, conflates form and content and lets
"the ideal vanish" (*J/P*, VI, 242; n. 6521 [1849]); for without dialectical stimulation, the ideal passes out of reality into poetry. In Mynster's
age, "people are quite prepared to leave the Christian terminology un-

32. On this point see Kresten Nordentoft, *Hvad Siger Brand-Majoren? Kierkegaard
Opgør med sin Samtid* (Copenhagen, 1973), 113. Nordentoft ascribes the strength of this
turning largely to Kierkegaard's reaction to the political turmoil of 1848.

33. For a good discussion of Kierkegaard's distinctions between true and false passions in mid-century Denmark, see Johannes Sløk, *Kierkegaard-Humanismens Taenker*
(Copenhagen, 1978), 19–22.

touched, but they can surreptitiously interpolate that it involves no decisive thought" (*PA*, 47). The crowd cannot endure dialectic. That is why the crowd is untruth (*PVA*, 110) and promotes the category *genera-tion* over the category *individuality* (*PA*, 52). Highly visible, Mynster allows the ideal to vanish in the crowd. The inverse leader dialectically related to the age (Kierkegaard himself), however, "will be without authority because he will have divinely understood the diabolical prin-ciple of the levelling process; he will be *unrecognizable*; he will keep his distinction hidden like a plainclothes policeman, and his support will only be negative, i.e., repelling people" (*PA*, 80). True irony is "un-social" (*PVA*, 54).

If the dialectical relation of the hidden self to a negative age is a guarantor of reality (for the only reality for Kierkegaard comes from the religious position of the individual, living among men but standing before God); if, on the other hand, assimilation to the age is equivalent to unending abstraction; if this is an unconditional, unqualified differ-ence—then we come back once again to the problem of trying to imag-ine what to Kierkegaard would be a *reformed* age. Could it be filled with spiritual tax collectors of hidden inwardness, as rare in life as they are in his literature? Is the tension within us between the infinite and finite enough to keep the Christian realist defined, or must he not always have against him the age? Is not God's secret agent dependent for his identity on what he spies on and hopes to arrest? Except for Abraham, is anyone's confidence sufficient to do without this antagonism? It would seem that it is, rather, Hegel's Abraham who is the pattern for Kierkegaard's own vision of the inevitable disjunction between the religious, the natural, and the larger social world. Even though one learns to love one's neigh-bor, Christianity needs the opposition of men: "As soon as the opposition is taken away, the thing of being a Christian is twaddle—as it is in "Christendom," which has slyly done away with Christianity by the affirmation that we are all Christians" (*AC*, 127). Although this is an affirmation of his last years, it is a constant understanding in the work of Kierkegaard, not persuasively qualified by his own town walks and Deer Park excursions. Hegel's Abraham chose this opposition. In "The Spirit of Christianity," Hegel contends, "The same spirit which had carried Abraham away from his kin led him through his encounters with foreign peoples during the rest of his life; this was the spirit of self-maintenance in strict opposition to everything—the product of his thought raised to be the unity dominant over the nature which he regarded as infinite and hostile."[34] He struggled against the fate that could have rooted him in a firm communal life with others, "steadily persist[ing] in cutting himself off from the others." And now comes the crucial identification: "The whole world Abraham regarded as simply his opposite." He subjugated the world, mastered it by exclusion. Subsequently, his God is also alien to the world that is alien to Abraham. The Love that Christ would bring was beyond him; even, we remember, the love for Isaac was not strong enough to prevent Abraham from slaying him.

Like Kierkegaard, Abraham lived for the Ideal and used it to help him master the world. Hegel contrasts Abraham's jealous God with the pagan Lares and the national gods that, while representing a form of separation from others, concede "the existence of other shares." The pagans recognize "the Lares and gods of others as Lares and gods."[35] The *Trennung* between Abraham and the world is certainly suggestive of Kierkegaard's breach, though the first supposedly assures survival, the second, sacrifice.[36] Abraham left an indelible mark on his descendants, who without "the soul and the spontaneous need of freedom," passively allowed themselves to be liberated by Moses.[37] The content of their lives is entirely made by the positive relation to God and by opposition to others. They are, in turn, slavishly dependent on the Other.

Mosaic Judaism becomes positive religion in its studied subjection to the command of God. In contrast to the spirit of Deucalion and Pyrrha, who made peace again with nature and friendship with men after the flood, Abraham becomes a progenitor of a nation by snapping "the bonds of communal life and love." Hegel's Abraham "wanted *not* to love, wanted to be free by not loving." This voluntary severance leads his descendants to the fate of Macbeth, "who stepped out of nature itself,

34. Hegel, "The Spirit of Christianity and Its Fate," *Early Theological Writings*, 185–86.

35. *Ibid.*, 186–88. Mark C. Taylor's book on the relation between the thought of Hegel and Kierkegaard, *Journeys to Selfhood: Hegel and Kierkegaard* (Berkeley, Calif., 1980), is of particular relevance in this section.

36. Harris, *Hegel's Development*, 284. For a discussion of the debate in *Fear and Trembling* between Kierkegaard's Abraham and Hegel, see Merald Westphal, "Abraham and Hegel," in Perkins (ed.), *Kierkegaard's "Fear and Trembling,"* 62–80.

37. Hegel, "The Spirit of Christianity and Its Fate," *Early Theological Writings*, 190.

clung to alien Beings, and so in their service had to trample and slay everything holy in human nature, had at last to be forsaken by his gods (since these were objects and he their slave) and be dashed to pieces on his faith itself." Hegel's note that "the sons of Jacob avenged with satanic atrocity the outraging of their sister even though the Shechemites had tried to make amends with unexampled generosity" would seem to indicate that the sacrifice of Isaac may have been a forerunner of this merciless need to subject the alien to atrocious domination. Everything outside the intimate order of the domination is "a stuff, loveless, with no rights, something accursed" which, as soon as the subjugators have power enough, "they treat as accursed and then assign to its proper place (death) if it attempts to stir."[38]

Now what seems interesting here, in thinking of Kierkegaard's Abraham, is that that knight of faith's hidden inwardness did not, as we would expect, isolate him from the finite that he grasps again by virtue of the absurd; nor does his deep faith eliminate pain in the test, in the love. On this last point he is as far as possible from Hegel's Abraham, who does not love enough to make the test agonizing. In his own form and away from his literature, Kierkegaard takes on the shape of an Abraham who *suffers* from his hidden inwardness, from his heterogeneity with his age. "Abraham is an eternal prototype [*Forbillede*] of the religious man. Just as he had to leave the land of his fathers for a strange land, so the religious man must willingly leave, that is, forsake a whole generation of his contemporaries even though he remains among them, but isolated, *alien* to them. To be an alien, to be in exile, is precisely the characteristic suffering of the religious man" (*J/P*, IV, 394; n. 4650 [1850]). We might note that the voluntary choosing of the fate that gave satisfaction to Hegel's Abraham is here attached to intense suffering. The exile from love is "perhaps eased by the wilderness where nothing reminds him of his home," but it is "a bitter consolation for one who is filled with longing" (*PH*, 152). Kierkegaard calls himself alien, even superfluous, to his age, but not to coming generations, for his exiled body will be seen as positive against a negative age such as his (*J/P*, VI, 538; n. 6918 [1854]). Only as a sacrifice does he have social identity. To his contemporaries, to Mynster, his position would seem "pitched altogether too

38. *Ibid.*, 185, 188, 205.

high," but he must offend them by withdrawing "so as not to indulge in their nonchalant point of view" of him. In his earnestness, he would "inevitably . . . seem an exaggeration" (*J/P*, VI, 540; n. 6919 [1854]).

He pictures himself, some years removed from *Fear and Trembling*, waking one morning with this thought: "What you are experiencing is similar to the story of Abraham." But when he adds, "But he did not understand Abraham or himself" (*J/P*, VI, 433; n. 6791 [1852]), we realize that, for this very reason, the most moving identification with Abraham is in the thick of the literature, in the position of Johannes de Silentio straining after him. As Abraham achieves his body through the difficulties experienced by his poet in understanding him, so Kierkegaard achieves his body through the difficulties of his "objective" self struggling to understand the relations between his psychological and spiritual desires. It is the longing of Kierkegaard for Abraham's full faith that frees the patriarch from the exclusivity of jealous national and historical confinement. And because concentration is not upon his character but upon his position, faith is liberated from possessive idiosyncracy. Literature can protect that faith from restrictive accidents of interpretation because it admits, as philosophy cannot, that Abraham's life is "so paradoxical that it cannot be thought at all" (*F/T*, 67). The body of longing usurps the place of character by its passion and persistence.

No one could project better than Luther the bodied nature of his faith, and readers have been tempted to contrast his plump earthiness with Kierkegaard's apparently abstract negative body. But it is illuminating to compare their remarkably similar versions of the body of Abraham, their rhythm and structure. We might juxtapose, for instance, this presentation of Luther with the scene set by Johannes de Silentio: "I have said . . . that we cannot comprehend this trial; but we can observe and imagine it from afar, so to speak. Moreover you see that the passage does not deal with a work, as James says in his letter (2 : 21), since as yet no work has occurred. It is the faith we admire and praise."[39] Luther asks his audience:

39. Martin Luther, in Jaroslav Peliken and Helmut T. Lehmann (eds.), *Luther's Works*, trans. George V. Schick (55 vols.; St. Louis, 1964), IV, 96.

What do you suppose the sentiments of Abraham's heart were in this situation? He was a human being, and, as I have stated repeatedly, he was not without natural affection. Besides, the fact that he did not dare divulge to anyone what was happening made his grief greater. Otherwise all would have advised against it, and the large number of those who advised against it would perhaps have influenced him. Therefore he sets out on the journey alone with young slaves and his son. It is a momentous command and far harsher than we are able to imagine. Yet the fact that the text clearly states that God was doing this to test him is full of comfort. If Abraham had known this he would have had fewer worries.

Luther's present tense is mixed, now, with the subjunctive and is set off from Abraham's decisive past definite, and the scene sounds more and more like that in *Fear and Trembling*. "This account deserves to have each word carefully examined. Abraham rose early in the morning. He did not delay; he did not argue. . . . I could not have been an onlooker, much less the performer and slayer. It is an astounding situation that the dearly beloved father moves his knife close to the throat of the dearly beloved son, and I surely admit that I cannot attain to these thoughts and sentiments either by means of words or by reflecting on them."[40] This is the style that Kierkegaard terms the style of "personal appropriation": "Open to any page of his writings, and note in every line the strong pulse-beat of personal appropriation. Note it in the entire trembling propulsive movement of his style which is as if it were driven from behind by the terrible thunderstorm that killed Alexius and created Luther" (*CUP*, 327). This is the beat we feel in the rhythms of Kierkegaard, who counts Christianity on his pulses.

The pressure of the onlooking is what gives body, then, to the scene. In Kierkegaard's account, which stresses an aspect absent in Luther's—Abraham's receiving of Isaac again without resentment, guilt, or anger—the primitive gladness is fed by the author's yearning for undemonic faith. Through the poet-watchers of knights of faith, experimenters and their subjects, lovers, Kierkegaard fulfills in literature the Socratic ideal of "subjectivity raised to the second power." "His rela-

40. *Ibid.*, 98, 102, 114.

tionship is one of objectivity just like that of a true poet in relation to his poetic production; with this objectivity he relates to his own subjectivity" (*J/P*, IV, 364; n. 4571 [1854]). And it is important to see this doubling as antithetical to Hegel's mediation between the objective and subjective terms. The love of Hegel's Jesus, which transforms positive religion, pits against the empty formalism of the laws "the whole subjectivity of man." This Jesus, "above bondage to a command, above the purity or impurity of an object . . . puts purity or impurity of heart. He made undetermined subjectivity, character, a totally different sphere, one which was to have nothing in common with the punctilious following of objective commands."[41] If we imagine Kierkegaard's assent to the most general distinction in the passage above, we might be right. But if we let Hegel widen the historical perspective around it, we see that the subjective for Hegel is not a function of the Kierkegaard particular. It is instead a fuller claim on the immanent universal, a claim that establishes it as the reserve for pragmatic worth, satisfaction, and fulfillment for men within the community. For Hegel it was a historical pity, albeit necessity, for Christ to have to express his morality at the cost of his full development in a community, as he was "sacrificed to the rising hatred of the priesthood and the mortified national vanity of the Jews." He was doomed to a "life undeveloped and without pleasure in itself."[42] Can we possibly imagine Kierkegaard viewing Christ's life as a historical pity?

Hegel consistently brings the Incarnation back into the world to rescue, at least, the dead Christ from his positive worshippers. But for Kierkegaard, the Incarnation must remain a stumbling block for the world and draw the world past itself.[43] Hegel laments the loss of an inherited folk imagery for Germany and the adoption, instead, of biblical (alien) stories. And H. S. Harris' suggestion that "it is not really the *foreign* character of Christianity that troubles him . . . so much as its authoritarian character and its emphasis on human helplessness" seems

41. Hegel, "The Spirit of Christianity and Its Fate," *Early Theological Writings*, 209.
42. *Ibid.*, 181, 285.
43. See Wahl, *Etudes kierkegaardiennes*, 134: "L'incarnation chez Hegel est le symbole de l'homogénéité entre l'humain et le divin; chez Kierkegaard, elle est marque de l'hétérogénéité; elle n'est pas symbole, mais scandale." (The incarnation for Hegel is the symbol of homogeneity between the human and the divine; for Kierkegaard, it is the sign of heterogeneity; it is not symbol, but scandal [author's translation].) And see Bohlin, *Kierkegaards dogmatische Anschauung*, 481ff.

sound.[44] In his *Lectures on the Philosophy of Religion*, Hegel recommends a closing of the ghostly gap between the finite and the infinite. "The man who does not rid himself of this phantom steeps himself in vanity, for he posits the Divine as something which is powerless to come to itself, while he clings to his own subjectivity, and, taking his stand on this, asserts the impotence of his knowledge."[45] He is ambivalent about a Luther who, though a national hero by his break with the past, furthered private and joyless religion by emphasizing authority.[46] With these emphases, we can clearly see the enormous gulf between Hegel and Kierkegaard. Instead of understanding or a higher Reason, the will in Kierkegaard drives the subject to offense, and past it with its surrender. Human helplessness is the most powerful stimulus to faith, and faith the only reality for consciousness. Always to be in the wrong before God is not an accidental situation. Breaches, gulfs, gaps, between finite and infinite, particular and universal, being and thought, are the given landscape of the world before God, and Kierkegaard would not patronize the "cost of a life undeveloped and unenjoyed" as the price for a full vision and recognition of the qualitative divisions and divorces, dialectically bound in existential pathos but entirely indifferent to world-historical progress.

Hegel sees Abraham, Moses, Jesus, and Socrates as, in one way or another, ahead of their people, as sacrifices to their historical moments. Either they are wrenched away from their natural fate or they must renounce personal fulfillment for the sake of their vision. And most of the time, for all his admiration, Hegel cannot hide his irritation at these "necessary" distortions of natural harmony between man and his community, man and nature, man's finite and infinite directions. Suggestively like Kierkegaard's again, Hegel's Moses is forced to transform

---

44. Harris, *Hegel's Development*, 235n.

45. Hegel, *Lectures on the Philosophy of Religion*, I, 200.

46. See E. M. Butler, *The Tyranny of Greece over Germany* (Cambridge, England, 1935), 4–5. Butler contends that it is partly Luther's fault that German art depends on philosophy, for Luther "destroyed the mythological element of Christianity, that poetical combination of beauty and truth for which [it has] ever since been seeking in Greek or Nordic mythologies or by reverting to the Catholic faith." The German poets found the Christianity he left "barren of beauty and also lacking in the mystical profundity which philosophy supplied instead." Compare Hegel's ambivalence to Luther, in Harris, *Hegel's Development*, 235–36, *n.* 4.

his vision of liberation into one of lawgiving, because he was ahead of his people. Kierkegaard's martyred Moses is also one who "set a *slave-minded people free.*" But even in the *Journals*, his Moses, like Abraham, has his watchers, who imagine his torment.

> Let us take a look at it! Moses is commanded by God to be an instrument by which a miracle is to be performed. (We only imagine the torture, what a maiming it must be for an individual to be used in that way—we imagine it but we do not grasp it.) Moses is willing, he strikes the rock, but doubtingly, and as punishment—we imagine it, as punishment he does not get to enter the promised land.
>
> And this terribly strenuous life! What a scale it is on, this life that overwhelms me and makes me a nothing beside a Moses. (*J/P*, VI, 3; n. 6141 [1848])

The Moses-watcher sees his own suffering stretched to its farthest typological boundaries, though he cannot enter the Promised Land of embodiment. While Hegel complains that "Christianity has emptied Valhalla," Kierkegaard passionately raids biblical legends for his most intimate national identification.[47] For he really did see a justification of his hidden and isolated posture in those exiles from the Promised Land who were leaders, through sacrifice, of a negative age. They second Socrates, who emptied his body through irony as a sacrifice to his age. And they all prefigure Christ. What makes these figures literary rather than philosophical is that they can never be free of Kierkegaard's negative body, while Hegel's had only the burden of carrying his mind.

In an interesting section of *The Concept of Anxiety*, Kierkegaard discusses the relation of the religious genius to his outward fate. In the historical hierarchy of cultures from pagan to Christian, fate becomes more and more interiorized until it is seen as Providence. There is no accident when one becomes what one already is, the ethical ideal of the Christian. "As soon as spirit is posited, anxiety is canceled, but so also is fate, for thereby Providence is also posited" (*CA*, 97). Immediate genius is still involved in fate; but the reflective religious genius understands that he must "turn inward into himself," or his life is either a fairy tale

---

47. Hegel, "The Positivity of the Christian Religion," *Early Theological Writings*, 146.

(*CA*, 99) or world-historical. From his own perspective, Kierkegaard not surprisingly affirms: "Only through a religious reflection can genius and talent in the deepest sense be justified. Take a genius like Talleyrand. There was in him the possibility of a much deeper reflection upon life. This he shunned. He followed that constituent in him that turned him outward" (*CA*, 102). As the Hegelian movement turns subjects toward history and immanently sanctions fate as a moment in the evolution of consciousness up to *Geist*, the Kierkegaard movement turns them inward to the task of their making and transcendently meets Providence as it pushes the self toward the Christian Paradox. Here is the trajectory of the religious genius: "The first thing he does is to turn toward himself. Just as the immediate genius has fate as the figure that follows him, so he has guilt. In turning toward himself, he *eo ipso* turns toward God" (*CA*, 107). By making the movements of faith instead of fate, the religious genius, says Vigilius Haufniensis, finds the "freedom to know of himself that he is freedom" (*CA*, 108). With the positing of guilt, freedom becomes repentance.

In this entire discussion, often in Hegelian cadence and terminology, Kierkegaard emphasizes tenaciously the inward movement of the journey of consciousness, just as Hegel, while paying respect to the inward movement as a major term in his dialectical design, emphasizes its outward movement into universal history. In distinguishing the immediate genius of history from the religious genius of existence (who is by no means finished), Kierkegaard writes:

> Just as fate at last captures the immediate genius, and this is indeed his moment of culmination, not the glittering outward realization that amazes men and even calls the artisan from his daily work to stop and take notice, but the moment when by himself he collapses for himself by fate, guilt likewise captures the genius who is religious, and this is the moment of culmination, the moment when he is greatest, not the moment when the sight of his piety is like the festivity of a special holiday, but when by himself he sinks before himself in the depth of sin-consciousness. (*CA*, 110)

Kierkegaard is willing to concede the Hegelian recognition of danger in "abstract subjectivity, arbitrariness, the single individual's [*den Enkeltes*] encroachment upon the universal," of egotism. But the problem in his dialectic is that "the universal, which Hegelianism considers the truth (and the single individual to be the truth by being swallowed up in it) is an abstraction—the state, etc. He does not come to God, the subjective in the absolute sense, or to the truth—that ultimately the single individual is really higher than the universal, namely, the single individual in his God-relationship" (*J/P*, II, 224; n. 1614 [1850]). And he adds, "How frequently have I sworn that Hegel basically regards men, paganly, as an animal-race endowed with reason," a hyperbole tempered by Hegel's own fluctuating pessimism in the *Phenomenology*, concerning the difficult education to consciousness past the "Kingdom of Animals." It is the major design of *Fear and Trembling* that the particular, rising through the universal, breaks the ceiling of conventional wisdom, re-opens the curtain after the fifth act to reappear, in defiance of reconciliations, as the single survivor before God. Abraham does not prepare the sacrifice "for the sake of saving a people, not to maintain the idea of the state . . . and not in order to reconcile angry deities" like the tragic heroes Agamemnon, Brutus, Jephtha (*F/T*, 70).

The same urging that drives Kierkegaard's figures to solitary Mount Moriahs, high above the meadows of mediation, dislodges his Socrates from the Hegelian fields of the world-historical in which he appeared as a rebel in the name of *Moralität*, a tragic hero embodying one term of a future mediation, a perilous enemy of the political world. In 1850 Kierkegaard looked back on his dissertation and rebuked its Hegelianism. "Influenced as I was by Hegel and whatever was modern, without the maturity really to comprehend greatness, I could not resist pointing out somewhere in my dissertation that it was a defect on the part of Socrates to disregard the whole and only consider numerically the individuals. What a Hegelian fool I was! It is precisely this that powerfully demonstrates what a great ethicist Socrates was" (*J/P*, IV, 214; n. 4281 [1850]). Actually, Kierkegaard had almost always in the dissertation consciously qualified his general agreement, and when he takes away the Hegelian ascription of tragedy from Socrates' case, saying, "The Greek state comes too late with its death sentence" (*CI*, 288), we see clearly that in Kierkegaard's mind, from the beginning, Socrates' ignorance and his easy binding of thinking and dying are becoming permanent values tested against the state, not just historical moments. Thus he can easily lift Socrates out of history to chastise the positive understanding of his age. "The only analogy I have before me is Socrates. My task is a Socratic task, to revise the definition of what it is to be a Christian. For my part I do not call myself a 'Christian' (thus keeping the ideal free), but I am able to make it evident that the others are that still less than I" (AC, 283). While he longs to talk with Socrates, he frequently amuses his imagination with a scene in Hell in which the System is humiliated by the wise old man's dialectic. "My wish, although I do not know whether or not it can be fulfilled, is that Socrates, who, according to his own statement wanted to ask the wise in the underworld whether they know something or not, may get hold of Hegel in order to question him about the absolute method" (J/P, II, 219; n. 1606 [1844]).

Since history is but a moment in hell, it quickly separates, like Kierkegaard's literature, the individual from the race. All Kierkegaard's figures are separated as far as possible from the historical, cultural, and social conditions we expect to find in the novel, so that they can be thoroughly exposed to the demands of the unconditional; "for the numerical is the very thing which tramples upon the unconditioned" (J/P, II, 421; n. 2046 [1853]). Offering no fig leaf of the word, the literature scatters the herd and strips it, sabotaging the already "imperfect reconciliation with life" through poetry and art (E/O, II, 277). Unlike the individual listener, figure of despair, of faith, the crowd is ruthlessly allegorized into untruth. Again, the religious poet would imitate the divine example (though he cannot be the Truth). "The crowd is untruth. Therefore was Christ crucified, because, although he addressed himself to all, He would have no dealings with the crowd, because He would not permit the crowd to aid him in any way, because in this regard He repelled people absolutely, would not found a party, did not permit balloting, but would be what He is, the Truth, which relates itself to the individual" (PVA, 114). This leads him to wonder why God, in an "annoying caprice" perhaps, "put us together in this way, or cut us off in this way from what we animals regard as the true well-being, from coalescing with the herd, everyone just like the others" (AC, 167). Spirit, the individuating quality, has "gone out of the race entirely" (J/P, III, 168; n. 2666 [1854]). As usual, the childhood of Kierkegaard looms behind this kind of generalization. In childhood one "stand[s] in a close relation to the generic qualification expressed in the species, the race" (PVA, 81). This accounts for the torment of not being like the others. Eventually, this torment becomes the very definition of spirit ("A spirit can very well put up with not being like the others—indeed that is precisely the negative definition of spirit" [PVA, 81]). The literature then becomes a carrier of the individual; it becomes the "category of spirit, of spiritual awakening, a thing as opposite to politics as well could be thought of" (PVA, 132). Unlike the press, it sees the crowd as untruth, and like God and Christ, it is a wedge between terms bound in the wrong kind of passion. It exposes by its interference the love of neighbor, in the crowd, as fear of the neighbor, a task taken on by the literature of Nietzsche too (PVA, 118).[48] And like Christ, it uses its "incendiarism with the intention of tearing apart 'the generation' in order to reach 'the individual'" (J/P, VI, 549; n. 6932 [1854]).

The crowd is not interested in dialectical reality; it is fantastic. The individual is dialectical not only in his isolation before God but as he is doubled with the universally human. "'The single individual' can mean the one and only, and 'the single individual' can mean every man" (PVA, 124). The literature, then, is dialectical in its function, as the poet uses an aesthetics that works against illusions and his own glory. He is denied the role of fantastic spellbinder (PVA, 147), and because of this his art is able to serve as an instrument of reality to existential man, putting before us types that resist allegory and single individuals that resist full embodiment. The life of the religious poet cannot hide behind the aesthetic autonomy of its fairy tales, not because it is that of an apostle, but precisely because it, too, has from time to time been taken in by their illusions. Literature must stay in the world; it cannot be the Archimedean point of faith outside the world to which Kierkegaard is so drawn (J/P, III, 166; n. 2665 [1854]). Because of this, it can work as a force against the press and repel the crowd. Perhaps since it cannot be confused with faith, the literature can better work for it.

This is not true of the Grundtvig movement, which, like the System, once again mediates the individual out of his essential dialectical torment. By turning from apostolic authority to the living word in the Church, Nikolai Grundtvig substitutes the notion of one objective standard for another, ignorant of "the subtle little Socratic secret: that the point is precisely the relationship of the subject" (CUP, 37). Again we

48. Nietzsche, "Beyond Good and Evil," 201.

see how the impossibility of taking literature as an object of faith has its advantages. For it can free the individual to a transformation away from it. The Grundtvig reform still points the subject away from himself, away from the concentration on the "subject's transformation in himself" (*CUP*, 38). Contemporaneous existence, not a contemporaneous Church, is the true enemy of historical proofs, of the scholastic itch to demonstrate and document the divine. Against the speciously subjective correction, Kierkegaard sets his notion of the contemporaneity of each life with the historical Christ. Socrates' skepticism is a better basis for faith than Grundtvig's "living word," for by routing objective certainty, it leaves the way clear for the only objective truth, the Revelation, and Lessing's doubts are more to be honored than this reform.[49] The folk church is another abstraction, like the state church and Christian countries. "They are the featherbeds and blankets that help smother the fire still more. But efforts of the kind that aims at dispersing, aims at 'the individual,' are the solution" (*J/P*, VI, 550; n. 6932 [1854]). The literature had aimed at dispersing and, by its negative body, had *prevented* solutions before that of true faith. We can imagine Kierkegaard's horror at Hegel's notion that, while art and religion are the business of a whole society, philosophy is not; for it is then given an authority that denies its abstraction.[50]

The unconditional qualitative chasm between God and man, between the individual and the generation, between one man's faith and another's, has been narrowed by domestic and political adjustments. The "characterless" age is compared to a closet in which men's and women's garments are hung indiscriminately (much to the dismay of Herr Zierlich, a character in a play by Heiberg), except that this age hangs together the infinite with the finite (*AC*, 144). Kierkegaard's diatribes against his age, the distinctions he makes between the historical climate of Luther and his own in determining the nature of correction—these certainly tell us, as do his comments on the European political and social turmoils of 1848 and his identification of that year as one of subsequent personal turning, that Kierkegaard was an astute observer of his contem-

49. On the relationship between the philosophical skeptical tradition and Kierkegaard's faith, see Richard H. Popkin, "Kierkegaard and Scepticism," in Thompson (ed.), *Kierkegaard*, 342–72.

50. Charles Taylor, *Hegel* (Cambridge, England, 1975), 512.

porary situation. Yet there is always an element of the speciously historical in his major complaints, for the pattern of heterogeneity between
Christianity and the world (*always* sinful) is a constant base of his
reality.[51] "Yes, humanly speaking, there is something cruel about Christianity. But this is not due to Christianity; it is due to the fact that it has
to exist [*existere*] in a sinful world, manifest itself and expand in a sinful
world. The cruelty is not Christianity but what happens to Christianity"
(*J/P*, I, 194; n. 489 [1848]). Whatever the relative situation, it will
clash with the absolute, not just now, for "it was this way in the year 1,
the year 335, and the year 1848—and it will be just the same in the year
10,008" (*J/P*, I, 197; n. 492 [1848]).

To Hegel, both Socrates and Jesus are necessary heroes of the history
of moral thought; they had to explode common ethics of the age for the
sake of a better society. That the ethical movement of faith in Socrates
could not, as John Gould points out, be achieved by society, since "its
characteristic features, particularity and inwardness, cannot be those of
whatever moral virtue society as a whole might be said to possess," is
what obviously endears him to Kierkegaard.[52] Kierkegaard's own task,
to "put the established order in suspense" like the God-relationship (*TC*,
92) by his literature (his obedience, persecution, suffering, and death), is
not a task for one age, any more than Abraham's teleological suspension
of the ethical is an act of faith for one age. The singleness and integrity of
the concentration on the unconditional largely humiliates the bourgeois
busyness of multifarious ethical duties, and we feel Kierkegaard's presence strongly in the boy that Judge William describes, who memorized
his lessons with exaggerated ardor, an ardor turned ultimately to the
eternal (*E/O*, II, 270–71).

This passion, if it is to last, must not couple with the world but
correct it with irony and polemic and climax in personal renunciation.
Typically, Kierkegaard is aware of the demonic possibilities of this
correction. "When from generation to generation these thousands and
millions have been permitted unchallenged to diminish and to diminish
[Christianity]—well, then the reversal certainly must appear to be a

---

51. Hence, it is not too surprising to have F. J. Billeskov Jansen remind us that
Kierkegaard's age was not culturally mediocre, but of high quality. See "Colloque
Kierkegaard: Groupe de discussion," in *Kierkegaard vivant*, 216.
52. John Gould, *The Development of Plato's Ethics* (Cambridge, England, 1955), 146.

frightful exaggeration, especially since (for the simple reason that the error has been continued for such a long time) it must be taken, if possible, to a qualitative extreme so that the reversal itself does not finally become conformed to the error" (*J/P*, I, 213; n. 520 [1850]). Furthermore, he could not offer the promise of great historical progress, even of consciousness, sometimes a satisfying outlet to the frustrated Romantic sensibility, nor the kind of psychological regeneration Rousseau thought possible, for our deepest sin is not social; our natural, unreflective being is merely unconsciously sinful. One of the jobs of the literature is to keep the passion open and unfulfilled as it sifts out the individual and strands him for faith. The works activate a counterliterary movement by doubling the personal act of withholding, itself in attendance on the great embodiment outside of literature and the secular world but not out of time, the Incarnation. The passion in Kierkegaard's illustrations and proclamations are inevitable by-products of the act of withholding. And the act itself, which accompanies the vision of the world as "a loose aggregation of millions of individuals each of which severally has his own God-relationship" (*TC*, 92), is to paralyze the established order.

It does this in at least two ways. In the best parabolic tradition, the literature features fairy tales that, by setting up huge distances of rank between kings and commoners, only emphasize the democracy of faith. On the aesthetic level, poetry democratizes the distance in the fairy tale, putting it ultimately at naught, but Kierkegaard will not allow art to do what only Christ can do to the world by his love. Since no politics, no worldliness, can "think through or realize to its last consequences the thought of human equality" (*PVA*, 107), the religious vision alone carries it "to the utmost limit" (*PVA*, 108). Worldliness would die with complete equality, but it stubbornly wants to try to enforce it "by worldly means." It forgets that it thrives on false differences and comparisons. Only the religious man, "unpractical as he is," can actually be the "transfigured rendering of the politician's fairest dream," and he is, therefore, the "true humanity" (*PVA*, 108). If the communist agitations of 1848 made doctrinal conflicts about Christianity anachronistic, instead concentrating attention on "the problem of Christianity as an existence, they might seem to have done religion a favor" (*J/P*, IV, 172; n. 4185 [1850]). But the communist ideal of equality is a parody of religious love as it is defined in *Works of Love*. Kierkegaard makes this crucial judgment: "But the most dreadful hoax of modern times is that egotism passes itself off as love, so that love becomes the demander instead of the giver. It is love if someone says: If everyone else has this or that advantage and I am the only one who does not have it, then I rejoice that the others have it. It is egotism to say: If I do not have this advantage, then no one else ought to have it either" (*J/P*, IV, 181; n. 4206 [1851]). This modern version of love is "a disastrous caricature of religiousness—it is politics," for politics is, after all, "egotism dressed up as love" (*J/P*, IV, 181; n. 4206 [1851]). For this reason, Kierkegaard speaks as scathingly as Flaubert about the communist "tyranny of the fear of men," which, as it already manifests itself in France, is another version of bourgeois leveling (*J/P*, IV, 148; n. 4131 [1848]).

Kierkegaard's literature is a special stage, not that of an enchanted world but rather one that, calling attention to itself as only fiction, sets up an anxious relation between the aesthetic and ethical life. The habit of breaking illusion, a staple of the self-irony of the novels of Fielding, Sterne, Austen, was traditionally used as a way of testifying to the integrity of the social world and the intimate relationship to it of the novel. However, modern experimentation is more often a sign of a desperate testimony to the world's ghostly insecurity. In this respect Kierkegaard can be said to have moved closer to the modern meaning of self-conscious fictive exposure, for while the modern emphasis seems distant from Kierkegaard's vision by implying that art is the only value in a fantastic universe, it effects, by its moral helplessness, the impression that art is cast adrift from life. It negatively signals the world's ethical needs by its bravado of autonomy. The break between the two worlds is comic on the surface, but a matter of life and death. For Kierkegaard, the distinctions of the aesthetic world, like those of the social and political world, mask the equality fostered by the religious perspective, and his art must reflect the discomfort, the incommensurability, between the two visions. It can reveal that "the individual is tragic on account of his passion, and comical because he attaches it to an approximation" (*CUP*, 42). Here is the stage for the realization:

> Just suppose that some evening a common absent-mindedness confused all the actors so they thought they really were what they were

representing. Would this not be, in contrast to the enchantment of art, what one might call the enchantment of an evil spirit, a bewitchment? And likewise suppose, that in the enchantment of actuality (for we are, indeed, all enchanted, each one bewitched by his own distinctions) our fundamental ideas became confused so that we thought ourselves essentially to be the roles we play. Alas, but is this not the case? It seems to be forgotten that the distinctions of earthly existence are only like an actor's costume or like a travelling cloak and that every individual should watchfully and carefully keep the fastening cords of this outer garment loosely tied, never in obstinate knots, so that in the moment of transformation the garment can easily be cast off, and yet we all have enough knowledge of art to be offended if an actor, when he is supposed to cast off his disguise in the moment of transformation, runs out on the stage before getting the cords loose. (*WL*, 95–96)

Kierkegaard's figures, living in the medium of his dominating and manipulating voice, do come running out with their cords loose to remind us that "in actual life one laces the outer garment of distinction so tightly that it completely conceals the external character of this garment of distinction, and the inner glory of equality never, or very rarely, shines through, something it should do and ought to do constantly" (*WL*, 96).

The religious poet, like Christianity itself, does not want to abolish worldly distinctions, but "wills that differences shall hang loosely about the individual, loosely as the cloak the king casts off in order to show who he is, loosely as the ragged costume in which a supernatural being has disguised himself" (*WL*, 96).

Then, too, while politics wants to change possibility into actuality and to usurp what can be real only on the ethical and religious level, literature deliberately tries to block a collective appropriation of possibility to put into relief the singularity of the transformation of the individual life into actuality. Since no man can impart to another his actuality, no author should try to impart the actuality of a hero to his reader. "When reality is apprehended by an outsider it can be understood only as possibility. Everyone who makes a communication, in so far as he becomes conscious of this fact, will therefore be careful to give his existential communication the form of a possibility" (*CUP*, 320). Only with this recognition can the ethical become a requirement instead of an object of admiration. The literature that reminds us of its possibility by continually breaking its illusions of actuality is a literature of withholding. That one cannot get hold of Kierkegaard's characters might be deemed his aesthetic weakness, but it works as an ethical strength and justification for the absence of social communion, for the necessary inducement of spiritual insomnia. "When Themistocles was rendered sleepless by thinking about the exploits of Miltiades, it was his apprehension of their reality as a possibility that made him sleepless. Had he plunged into inquiries as to whether Miltiades really had accomplished the great things attributed to him, had he contented himself with knowing that Miltiades had actually done them, he would scarcely have been rendered sleepless" (*CUP*, 321–22).[53]

By the negative body, the negative age is to be drawn out. When the crowd is brought to a stop, it breaks into individuals. Kierkegaard's suffering, the isolation of his body, are at last the perfect weapons, though they are sheathed in literature. "The reformer who, as they say, fights a power (a pope, an emperor, in short, an individual man) has to bring about the downfall of the mighty one; but he who with justice alone confronts 'the crowd,' from which comes all corruption, must see to it that he himself falls" (*J/P*, V, 369; n. 5979 [1847]). It is difficult not to see Luther as one of the reformers; while recognizing the specific historical pressure on Luther and prizing insights in the sermons (he seizes upon Luther's emphasis on the subjective *for you* in Christ's address to each listener (*J/P*, III, 64; n. 2463 [1847]), Kierkegaard is consistently hard on the Luther who marries the world in political verve. "A reform which amounts to casting off burdens and making life easy is appreciated—and one can easily get friends to cooperate. True reforming always makes life difficult, lays on burdens, and therefore the true reformer is always slain, as if it were enmity toward mankind" (*J/P*, III, 69; n. 2481 [1849]). What now is needed is the reentry of Christ as prototype, of imitation and striving, of the law; for Luther's emphasis on Christ as gift, itself a corrective, has mitigated the strenuousness of

---

53. See Edith Kern, *Existential Thought and Fictional Technique: Kierkegaard, Sartre, Beckett* (New Haven: 1970), 54.

inward deepening, has become "a fig leaf for the most unchristian shirk-ing" (*J/P*, III, 70; n. 2481 [1849]), the favorite metaphor for consoling literature. That Luther urged faith against a background of high as-ceticism was his historical task. Yet, when Kierkegaard has paid his historical tribute, he often compensates with an ahistorical criticism that is more powerful—that Luther was not dialectical enough, but sorted the world out politically, even in the metaphysical sphere. "Do good and suffer for it" is the equation he loosens by too often separating the rhetorical from the existential (*J/P*, III, 88; n. 2531 [1850]). The man who "sometimes has one thought, then again another" (*J/P*, III, 66; n. 2467 [1848]), who is politically jubilant (*J/P*, III, 80; n. 2514 [1850]) instead of strenuously dialectical, cannot compete with Socra-tes. "I have the deepest respect for Luther—but was he a Socrates? No, no, far from that. When I talk purely and simply about man I say: Of all men old Socrates is the greatest—Socrates, the hero and martyr of intellectuality. Only you understood what it is to be a reformer, under-stood what it meant for you yourself to be that, and were that" (*J/P*, III, 80; n. 2514 [1850]). The dialectical courage of disguise, of deliberate misunderstanding, the truest imitation of Paradox—this is the martyr-dom. Luther undoes the doubling. "He distributes: the good is credited to Christianity; all sufferings, spiritual trial, etc., come from the devil. Dialectically one must say: both the consolation and the suffering come with Christianity, for this is the dialectic of the absolute, and Christian-ity is the absolute" (*J/P*, I, 192; n. 486 [1848]). At least Luther's life expressed his convictions. But not so the life of Martensen, which Kier-kegaard also calls undialectical.

> Martensen, whose activity is to find half-terms and definitions, also says that Christianity must be a life, an actual life—and now come the assertions—a genuinely actual life, a completely genuine, actual life in us; one must not relate to Christianity by way of imagination. Good. But Martensen's own existence—what does this express? It expresses that he wants to be a success in the world, have great honor and regard, be in a high office, etc.—is this the actualization of Christianity?
>
> As a philosopher, Martensen makes assertions and is not at all dialectical, and as a Christian, he also merely makes assertions. Gen-

erally the categories are purely rhetorical—which can very well be-
guile a person. (*J/P*, I, 203; n. 508 [1849])[54]

Kierkegaard's ethical resistance to spending himself in history is
balanced by his passion to be spent by history, a maneuver with which we
are familiar. Johannes Climacus imagines that God might speak this way
to the exception, as to Abraham, in a solitary place, far from the "world-
historical entrepreneurs": "Do you now live through and experience the
human in unparalleled intensity; labor so that half the effort might
suffice to transform an entire contemporary generation. But you and I,
we are to be alone about all this; your efforts are to have no significance
whatever for any other human being. And yet, you understand, you are
to will the ethical, and you are to be enthusiastic in your striving,
because this is the highest" (*CUP*, 123). The ethical is defined at the end
of this scene (Kierkegaard's definitions of categories are parts of scenes
and do not rise above the medium) as the "true hypertension (*Over-
spaendthed*) of the infinite in the spirit of man" (*CUP*, 123), which must
persist without the relief of world-historical significance, always eager to
ease the burden of the subjective (*CUP*, 124). In contrast to history's
rewards are those of God, harsh and hidden. "The earnestness of it all is
his own inner life; the jest is, that it pleases God to attach this significance to his striving, he who is nothing but an unprofitable servant"
(*CUP*, 125). Besides Hegel, only God can recite the line of Schiller,
"*Weltgeschichte ist das Weltgericht*," because "he has in his eternal consciousness the medium which alone provides the needed commensurability between outer and inner" (*CUP*, 126). The philosopher who
"seeks to occupy this standpoint . . . is a fool" (*CUP*, 126). The quantitative consolations of the world-historical promoter are, once again,
"the fig-leaf" to the "sophistical man" (*CUP*, 127).

It is not by historical knowledge of the dead that we come to know our
actuality, but precisely the reverse. It is by one's self-knowledge that the
dead can be raised past their caricature by history back into their own
possibilities. This is a process that clearly anticipates the act of "raising"
Christ to contemporaneity in the individual's life. In an amusing foot-

---

54. For a review of the relationship between the thought of Martensen and Kierkegaard, see Arild Christensen, "Efterskriften Opgør med Martensen," *Kierkegaardiana*,
IV (1962), 45–62.

note in *Concluding Unscientific Postscript*, Johannes Climacus speaks of the Socrates who, wearing a mere pelt in the marketplace (Xantippe having taken his clothes and left the house), is less ridiculous than the Socrates costumed by the System, "where he appears fantastically draped in the rich systematic trappings of a paragraph. Did Socrates go about talking of what the age demands, did he apprehend the ethical as something to be discovered, or which had been discovered by a prophet with a world-historical outlook, or as something to be determined by an appeal to the ballot box? No, Socrates was concerned only with himself. . . . He attended to himself—and then Providence proceeds to add world-historical significance to his ironical self-contentment" (*CUP*, 132). When Hegel puts his Jesus in a world-historical perspective, Jesus becomes a world-historical prophet. And this history has nothing what-soever to do with the historical moment in which he entered the world; for that moment is Paradox, resistant to speculative understanding that summons the dead "to a fantastic-objective life, and God becomes in a fantastic sense the soul in a process" (*CUP*, 140). So Hegel can cross the ditch between the historical and the eternal that Lessing refused to cross. The terrifying gulfs and thrilling boundaries of Kierkegaard's landscape are trespassed, the offense of misrelationship neutralized in the absence of repentance and grace.

The understanding must be crucified, for "Christianity is not content to be an evolution within the total definition of human nature" (*CUP*, 496). For all Hegel's claims for the freedom and self-sufficiency of his God, its own object and end, there are many readers besides Kierkegaard who have felt the interdependence of man and God in his system as a fatality.[55] Lamenting the imprisonment of the Hegelian God in the dialectical method and of his self-movement in the movement of man, Karl Barth contends, "In making the dialectical method of logic the essential nature of God, he made impossible the knowledge of the actual dialectic of grace, which has its foundation in the freedom of God." Kierkegaard would certainly second Barth's complaint against the deter-minism (however mobile) of Hegel's spiritualized universe, pictured in this way: "Creation is necessary, and reconciliation too is necessary. The Church is necessary to God . . . for in it he can be the mind of the

55. Hegel, *Lectures on the Philosophy of Religion*, I, 2.

Church; and it is this alone which first makes it possible for him to be mind and God."[56] For Kierkegaard there can be no genuine ethics in a world-historical universe where subject is type, choice is necessity, and the finite is compelled by a relentless dialectic to be a vehicle for *Geist* and by *Geist* to have a vehicle. Since he insists that "the fact that God's will is the possible makes it possible for me to pray" and that "if God's will is only the necessary, man is essentially as speechless as the brutes" (*SD*, 174), he might be pleased to ponder with one of Hegel's best commentators how, in all this immanent necessity, "does a Hegelian philosopher *pray*? Certainly the prayer of petition has no meaning for him. Nor can he really thank God. What he does is to contemplate his identity with cosmic spirit which is something quite different."[57]

In his struggle against Hegelian mediations, Kierkegaard had behind, beside, and in front of him a long line of thinkers as allies—his teachers Frederik Sibbern and Møller, Friedrich von Schelling and Immanuel von Fichte, Hamann, Jacobi, Friedrich Schleiermacher, and thinkers as different from each other as Franz von Baader and Friedrich Trendelenburg, and as different from him as Feuerbach and Marx.[58] In his *Journals*, Kierkegaard speaks of the exciting moment in which he heard Schelling, lecturing about the relationship of philosophy to reality, refer to "actuality." Schelling stirred in his listener an excitement that testified to the direction Kierkegaard's passionate thought would take (*J/P*, V, 181; n. 5535 [1841]). The younger Fichte had helped him

56. Karl Barth, *Protestant Thought: Rousseau to Ritschl* (New York, 1959), 303–304.
57. Taylor, *Hegel*, 494.
58. Good discussions of these sources can be found in Walter Ruttenbeck, *Søren Kierkegaard: Der Christliche Denker und Sein Werk* (Berlin, 1929); Bohlin, *Kierkegaards dogmatische Anschauung*; Emanuel Hirsch, *Kierkegaard-Studien* (2 vols., Gütersloh, West Germany, 1933); James Collins, *The Mind of Kierkegaard* (Chicago, 1953); George Price, *The Narrow Pass: A Study of Kierkegaard's Concept of Man* (New York, 1963); Gregor Malantschuk, *Kierkegaard's Thought*, trans. H. V. Hong and E. H. Hong (Princeton, 1971), Niels Thulstrup, *Kierkegaard's Relation to Hegel*, trans. George L. Stengren (Princeton, 1980). Thulstrup maintains that Kierkegaard's understanding of Hegel in his formative period was marked by spotty concentration and that it "continued to bear the mark of the interpretations of right-wing Hegelians" to whom he had been exposed as a student (13). On Feuerbach and Marx in relation to Hegel, see Karl Löwith, *From Hegel to Nietzsche: The Revolution in Nineteenth-Century Thought*, trans. David E. Green (New York, 1964). Jerry H. Gill discusses Kierkegaard's debt to Kant, in "Kant, Kierkegaard and Religious Knowledge," in Jerry H. Gill (ed.), *Essays on Kierkegaard* (Minneapolis, 1969). And see Bohlin, *Kierkegaards dogmatische Anschauung*, 481ff.

by advancing "beyond Hegel's abstraction to intuition" (*J/P*, II, 39; n. 1190 [1837]). Von Baader's mysticism had the muscle to strike at the supernaturalism of Hegel's (the negation of nature by the Idea): if Schelling's nature was too high for the spirit, Hegel's was too low.[59] In 1847, Kierkegaard is sorry that he had not heard Trendelenburg earlier at the university (*J/P*, V, 367–68; n. 5978). Trendelenburg thought it "impossible to find a place for experience without making holes in the internal connection of the self-productive Concept."[60] But it is, oddly, Feuerbach, from whose attacks theology has never recovered, with whom Kierkegaard perversely identifies himself as a traitor to Christendom (*J/P*, VI, 243; n. 6523 [1849]). It is he who most pointedly complements Kierkegaard's ethical complaints against Hegel when he writes, "The philosopher must insert into the text of philosophy what Hegel put in a footnote: that part of man which does not philosophize, which is against philosophy and opposed to abstract thought."[61] Sibbern and Møller carped at the design of Hegel's psychology, the predominance in his view of thought over feeling and thinking, and Hamann, Jacobi, and Schleiermacher all contributed emphases on subjectivity and inwardness in their discussions on faith. Although Kierkegaard protested against the static nature of Schleiermacher's notion of dependence as a basis of faith, dependence "merely as a condition," and was himself suspicious of the religion of the heart in contrast to the religion of striving, still these thinkers helped to restore the sense of wonder to faith, a wonder immune to the deliberations of speculation.[62]

Hamann was Kierkegaard's particular favorite,[63] and we can imagine what his interest would be in passages like this in one of his letters to Jacobi in 1785: "I have repeated *ad nauseam* that the philosophers are just

---

59. Eugène Susini, *Franz von Baader et le romantisme mystique* (2 vols.; Paris, 1942), I, 347.

60. See translations from Trendelenburg called "The Logical Question in Hegel's System," by Thomas Davidson, in two issues of *Journal of Speculative Philosophy*, V (1871), 349–59, and VI (1872), 82–93, 163–75, 350–61. This passage appears on page 85 of VI.

61. Quoted in Löwith, *From Hegel to Nietzsche*, 78.

62. See, for example, Kierkegaard, *J/P*, IV, 15; n. 3853 (n.d.).

63. For a full discussion of this relationship see Stephen N. Dunning, "Kierkegaard's 'Hegelian' Response to Hamann," *Thought: A Review of Culture and Ideas*, LV (September, 1980), 259–70.

like the Jews: neither of them knows what reason or the law is, or what they are given for—for the recognition of sin and of ignorance, not of grace and truth, which must be historically revealed, and cannot be attained by thinking, or by inheritance, or by working for it." [64] After his Christian humor and love for the ignorance of Socrates, perhaps what was most to be cherished in Hamann was the term *Missverhältnis* as a description of the gapped relationship between God and man that cannot be mediated by speculation. [65] As for Jacobi and Schleiermacher, Hegel was as critical as Kierkegaard of the religion of feeling that fostered dependency, concentrated on the worshiper too emphatically; but Hegel deviated from him in his anger at the assumption that God was unknowable. [66] (Charles Taylor suggests that he might have been particularly harsh because it was so close to his own early religion of love.) [67] Kierkegaard feared most the tempering of the requirements, of the will's striving, and of the hardness of the commands of love and suffering. The immanent dialectic of Hegel, subordinating Religion to Philosophy, made of Evil (sin) only a relative opposite of the Good, a moment in the development of consciousness rather than a positive category, and contributed as much as the religion of the heart to the pantheistic sapping of the strenuousness of Christianity. But in splitting off dogmatics from speculative metaphysics, Schleiermacher could give this support to Kierkegaard: "Dogmatic propositions never make their original appearance except in trains of thought which have received their impulse from religious moods of mind; whereas, not only do speculative propositions about the Supreme Being appear for the most part in purely logical or natural-scientific trains of thought but even when they come in as ethical presuppositions or corollaries, they show an unmistakable leaning towards one or other of those two directions." [68] For all the qualifications of his theology, Kierkegaard is happy to pit Schleiermacher against the System, rubbing salt in the attack by comparing him to the well-

64. Quoted in R. G. Smith, *J. G. Hamann: A Study in Christian Existence* (New York, 1960), 251.

65. See Hamann, *Schriften*, VII, 59.

66. See Hegel, *Lectures on the Philosophy of Religion*, I, 14–18.

67. Taylor, *Hegel*, 508.

68. Friedrich Schleiermacher, *The Christian Faith*, ed. H. R. Mackintosh and J. S. Stewart (Edinburgh, 1948), 82.

balanced Greek thinker. "He was left behind long ago when men chose Hegel. Yet Schleiermacher was a thinker in the beautiful Greek sense, a thinker who spoke only of what he knew. Hegel, on the contrary, despite all his outstanding ability and stupendous learning, reminds us again and again by his performance that he was in the German sense a professor of philosophy on a large scale, because he *à tout prix* must explain all things" (*CA*, 20).[69] Schleiermacher refuses the world-historical consciousness of the philosophical hero and is therefore timeless.

A primary aim of Hegel's spirit is to find an adequate expression in history. "World history is the expression of the divine process which is graduated progression in which the spirit comes to know and realize itself and its own truth."[70] The spirit comes to know itself only in the history of the world. And if the Church, with the rise of Christianity, is at first exiled from the political reality of the community, it must, like all heroes of *Moralität*, be ultimately reconciled with external history. The task of bringing together this new Christian *Sittlichkeit* and *Moralität* will fall to the Germanic nations. Nowhere better than in the *Lectures on the Philosophy of World History* can be seen the opposition of the directions of Hegel and Kierkegaard. That the state should be viewed as an arena for the realization of the Idea is anathema to Kierkegaard. The individual life in Hegel's plan, especially as it yearns for fulfillment in its Ideals, becomes accident, to be changed into purpose by Reason's cunning, history's rational rhythms. Kierkegaard will entirely reverse this relation. It is precisely what is recorded by history's cunning that is accident, and only the individual who defines himself in opposition to it can be spirit, purpose. If philosophy helps us to understand "that the actual world is as it ought to be," then it can be valuable only if it is seen as permanently inverse to spiritual order. Philosophy, for Hegel, "transfigures reality with all its apparent injustices and reconciles it with the rational"; faith, for Kierkegaard, transfigures suffering into fulfillment.[71]

Nothing could be more opposed than what seems allied—the

69. For an interesting view on Kierkegaard as a classicist in opposition to modern speculative philosophy, see John Wild, "Søren Kierkegaard and Classical Philosophy." *Philosophical Review*, XLIX (1940), 536–51, esp. 548.

70. Hegel, *Lectures on the Philosophy of World History*, 64.

71. *Ibid.*, 66–67.

imperative in both thinkers for the realization of the ethical idea into the actual. In the best reality of one, the community publicly receives and helps to express the individual; in the other, the individual lives in secret revolt against the community or else has his chosen life in ethical hidden inwardness of faith, and his necessary life in the disguise of misunderstanding. In Kierkegaard's view, Hegel conflated the absolute and the relative, but for Kierkegaard the realms of accident and providence had to be kept severely separated. The principle of mediation remains outside a genuine ethical life (*CUP*, 366). "The relative relationship belongs to the world, the absolute relationship to the individual himself; and it is not an easy thing to maintain an absolute relationship to the absolute *telos* and at the same time participate like other men in this and that" (*CUP*, 365). If one manages to live with the concentration on relative and absolute in this fashion, this is not the same as mediation "any more than it is a mediation between heaven and hell to say that there is a wide gulf fixed between them. And in the respect which the individual entertains for the absolute *telos* there is a yawning chasm fixed between it and the relative ends" (*CUP*, 366). It is, instead, the deep and strenuous pathos of the religious life. What could be of less interest to Hegelian Reason's cunning sums of world-historical order than this retreat from the monastery to the stillness of solitude, where superfluous to history, one can analyze every ethical shade of guilt and sin, a practice Hegel would call "psychological pedantry,"[72] "where the least loss is an absolute loss and the least retreat is utter ruin; where the mind is not diverted by distractions, but the memory of ever so slight an infidelity is a fire that burns and from which there is no escape, paralyzing the individual like a sunstroke; where every weakness, every faint moment, every disinclination, is as if it were a mortal sin, and every such hour is like an eternity, because time will not pass" (*CUP*, 373). The public ethical example of bearing one's sorrows like a man is humbled in the religious life by the harder psychological task of "feeling sorrow like a man" (*CUP*, 372). Mediation is, in effect, jealousy of the absolute, of its majesty; it is "an attempt to bring the absolute down to the level of everything else, an attack upon the dignity of human life, seeking to make man a mere servant of relative ends" (*CUP*, 375).

72. *Ibid.*, 87.

Of course, no one thinks so persistently about another's intellectual designs without testifying to a deep influence, and we hardly have to prove this. Hegel had ardently desired to come to terms with the subjective aspect of man's morality and psychology, whether speaking of the modern or classical world he so admired for its integrity. It seems ironic to many commentators that Kierkegaard maligned the philosopher who, in the preface to the *Phenomenology*, complained of the abstraction and formalism of the modern mind.[73] With important qualifications, Kierkegaard was willing to follow, in *Either/Or*, Hegel's contrast between the "vexation" of the modern world and the sorrow of the ancient. He gives, however, to his modern Antigone the poignant dimension and depth of his own Christian pathos (*E/O*, 153–54). Here is Hegel's distinction in the *Lectures on the Philosophy of Religion*, which, despite its qualification of the ancient subject's freedom as abstract because it does not internalize its fate, still reflects his admiration:

Vexation is the sentiment of the modern world; the feeling of vexation or annoyance presupposes an end, a demand on the part of modern free will, which considers itself warranted and justified in indulging this feeling if any such end should not be realized. Thus the modern man easily gets into the mood in which he loses heart with regard to everything else, and does not even seek to reach other things he might quite well have made his aim if otherwise unsuccessful. All else that belongs to his nature and destiny he abandons, and in order to revenge himself destroys his own courage, his power of action, all those ends of destiny to which he might otherwise have quite well attained. This is vexation; it could not possibly have formed part of the character of the Greeks or of the ancients, the truth being that their grief regarding what is necessary is of a purely simple kind. The Greeks did not set before themselves any end as absolute, as essential, any end the attainment of which ought to be warranted; their grief is therefore a grief of resignation. It is simple sorrow, simple grief which has for this reason the element of serenity in it. No absolute end is lost

73. And see Harris, *Hegel's Development*, 38. Hegel did, in his mature philosophy, see Christianity as an advance in subjectivity and, hence, a progressive contribution to the history of consciousness.

for the individual; here, too, he continues to be at home with himself, he can renounce that which is not realised. *It is so*; and this means that he has not set his own Being in opposition to what is. The liberation here is the identity of the subjective will with that which *is*. The subject is free, but only in an abstract fashion.[74]

The forms of sorrow that Hegel traces in the *Phenomenology*, the grief deriving from an imbalance between objective and subjective worlds, certainly anticipate the forms of anxiety and despair in *The Sickness Unto Death*. But, while Kierkegaard would be willing to finger vexation as an attribute of living in the condition of offense, he would certainly not see the solution as anything short of trying even harder for the purity to will one thing; he would shatter with the spirited will the notion of peace between fate and man that is an adjustment to accident. Hegel's view of the subjective dimension brought into history by Christianity as an enrichment, a progressive growth of consciousness, seems often a compensatory adaptation, altogether opposed in spirit to Kierkegaard's fierce convictions.

Hegel's spiraling rational economy of world-historical passions and his ardent struggle for freedom might seem at times to resemble more than a little the providential and subjective designs of the Kierkegaard universe, but as with so much of the shared vocabulary and rhythm, Kierkegaard turns his pattern to antithetical directions. Full "freedom" to Hegel means mediation between the subject and the objective universe of nature and laws, and between the finite and infinite; to Kierkegaard it means an obedience to misrelationship between the infinite and finite, an obedience that rests upon will and choice. The providence of Hegel's cunning Reason is accident to Kierkegaard. He felt that Hegel, for all his protests against fideistic dependence, gave to an unpsychological and ethically neutralized Reason working through history the will and faith that he himself gave only to the individual struggling toward God.[75] By doing this, Hegel recommended resignation to the sacrifices history demands and faith in the universal roll of dialectical progress.

74. Hegel, *Lectures on the Philosophy of Religion*, II, 263, 266.
75. Mark C. Taylor provocatively suggests, in *Kierkegaard's Pseudonymous Authorship: A Study of Time and the Self* (Princeton, 1975), 102, that much of Kierkegaard's argument

Kierkegaard, however, who pretended to quarantine the world of personal accident from Providence by paganizing fortune, actually raised the individual above history, the particular above the universal, by giving the individual the power to see misfortune as trial, suffering as the sign of God's love. All personal accident is rescued by the individual who rises to his Providence. Surrender, then, replaces adjustment—surrender to God, not the world. History is then sacrificed to the individual. Kierkegaard can agree with the philosopher that "life must be understood backwards" (*J/P*, I, 450; n. 1030 [1843]); however, the speculative philosopher has never felt the existential torment of simultaneously living it forward, which can be done only by existing in time, but rising above history.

Kierkegaard's choice of thought-experiment over system deliberately withholds fulfillment as a sign of his refusal to adjust to history's demands. By being an experimenter, Socrates rose out of history as a "Christian" educator; and Hegel could have been a noble teacher, for if he had "written his whole logic and had written in the preface that it was only a thought-experiment, in which at many points he still steered clear of some things, he undoubtedly would have been the greatest thinker who has ever lived" (*J/P*, II, 217; n. 1605 [1844]). But Kierkegaard calls Hegel "comic" because he refused the incommensurability between the finite and the infinite, constantly mixing the relative and absolute measures. Kierkegaard's pairs—Alcibiades and Socrates, Isaac and Abraham, experimenters and subjects—through which he expiates the narcissism of demonic doubling and its history, are withheld in some way from normal marriage with the world and its history. From this perspective, it does not seem that Lev Shestov's view, which has often been called hyperbolic, is distorted. "If what he said had any meaning whatever, then we must admit that such an insignificant, everyday occurrence as Kierkegaard's break with Regina Olsen was indeed an event of universally historic importance, more momentous than the discovery of America or the invention of gunpowder. For if it turns out that, from a standpoint invisible and immaterial to anyone else, Kierke-

---

can be seen as a displacement of Hegel's comments about the Absolute Self to individual selves.

gaard maintained his rights to Regina Olsen in the face of self-evidency, then every basis of our "thinking" is shaken. Philosophy is forced to turn from Hegel to Job."[76] In Kierkegaard's fiercely typological universe in which the absolute is a choice, not a necessity, the individual can achieve lordship over history.[77] We can see why Kierkegaard so tenaciously opposed to the notion of the Hegelian "moment" that of the "stand-point" in his discussions of Socrates' irony and elsewhere. What could be more horrible to the promoter of ethical and spiritual contemporaneity than to imagine his passions used by Reason in history as a mere moment in the System?

Once again, the extreme expression of the constant justification in his last period retrospectively clarifies the divorce. The individual who strives to become a Christian "stops with himself," does not marry, and opposes the progress of the race by "coming to a stop" (AC, 214). The Christianity of Christendom arranges "family festivities, beautiful, splendid family festivities, e.g. infant baptism and confirmation" and calls them religious, while it is busy "cementing families more and more egoistically together" (AC, 222). The Church sponsors extroverted, world-historical picnics, when "the first condition for becoming a Chris-tian is to be absolutely introverted (indadvendt)" (TC, 219). To show how constant this sense was, however the expression might be modified, we have only to turn to a passage like this:

> When an existence [Existents] is genuinely considered under the aspect of the eternal, the result is, eo ipso, isolation. The desperate thing about it is that one never gets to know anything concerning this among the thinkers; they leap over such things. But take for example . . . that on the last day Adam will shout: Oh Lord, just save my soul, I'm not concerned about either Eve or Abel; all of Christ's utterances about the fall of Jerusalem, where the meaning is precisely that the God-

76. Lev Shestov, *Kierkegaard and the Existential Philosophy*, trans. Elinor Hewitt (Athens, Ohio, 1969), 239.

77. See Enzo Paci, "Su due significati del concetto dell'angoscia in Kierkegaard," *Orbis Litterarium*, X (1955), 201: "Non si deve mai dimenticare che in Kierkegaard, proprio perchè l'assoluto non è una necessità ma una possibilità, il processo storico non è deterministico" (It ought never to be forgotten that in Kierkegaard, precisely because the absolute is not a necessity but a possibility, historical process is not deterministic [author's translation]).

relationship in its eternal validity will neutralize every relationship, where he says (Mark 13:9): But take heed to yourselves—then what becomes of all the busy world-historical social categories? (*J/P*, I, 451; n. 1034 [1845])

From another perspective Hegel, too, in Kierkegaard's view, sacrifices his primitivity, his "original impression of existence" (*J/P*, I, 292; n. 654 [1847]), to the generation. No better than the caterers of Christendom, "he discovered the historicizing method, which completely abolished all primitivity and actually merely arranges" (*J/P*, I, 292; n. 654 [1847]). Although the observing subject is apparently included in the dialectical process of the education of consciousness—"duality between observer and reality overcome"—he is so wrapped in contemplation and reflection of moments that he assumes an ethical neutrality.[78] "The absolute method explains all world-history; the science which is to explain the single human being is ethics" (*J/P*, II, 292; n. 654 [1847]). True ethics dares us to "renounce everything, including this loftily pretentious and yet delusive intercourse with world-historical contemplation"; it dares us to "become nothing at all, to become a particular individual, of whom God requires everything" (*CUP*, 133).

But to be a truly ethical man, paradoxically, means for Kierkegaard to dare to let go of the world. So he anxiously ponders, "Is it at all possible for a man, without in one way or another failing, to endure the act of separation which is the condition for becoming Christian according to the understanding of the New Testament; is it possible for a man, without failing in one way or another, to be separated even more violently than death separates, to be separated by dying-away and then to live; is it possible to endure being at every moment before God?" (*J/P*, I, 230; n. 562 [1854]). Then he adds sarcastically, "And then there are Christians by the millions." And still thinking of Regine at the end, he writes, "The Christianity of the New Testament would be: in case that man were really able to love in such a way that the girl was the only one he loved and one whom he loved with the whole passion of a soul (yet men as this are no longer to be found), then, hating himself and the loved one, to let her go in order to love God" (*AC*, 163).

This is the ethical problem for Kierkegaard—his highest ethics re-

78. Taylor, *Hegel*, 282.

jects marriage with the world but will not let go of it as a test. It repeatedly presses him to spiritual transformation of relationships—an act he calls *Repetition*—a word that keeps hold of its first stage while it indicates a higher one. The literature is the agency of this repetition, but as it abandons the reader and the writer, it does not take over the task of the self. It is meant to precipitate, explore, work through, not to protect. It testifies to the impurity in every move toward faith, for it is not Archimedes' point outside the world. "He who in the transition to becoming a Christian takes with him his beloved," writes Kierkegaard, carries with him "what for him amounts to the species" (*J/P*, II, 444; n. 2080 [1854]). That the beloved can be spiritually translated into Idea loosens him from the species, but the Idea cannot make him free from the need for continual expiation in relation to this earth. Literature's impurity is an apt medium for the difficult, and never completely innocent, drama of repetition. The God-relationship does not free the religious poet from his tormented position while he lives. "I see only one way out: if a person is going to cling to God in this way, it must not be in the direct super-excellence of humanness but inversely through the misery of being subordinated under the universally human, put outside it, and thus as a sufferer constrained to relate himself absolutely to God as his only possibility" (*J/P*, I, 313; n. 666 [1849]). That all spiritual transformations are bound to the humiliation of literature allows him to demand the superhuman, of himself and others, as a universal ethic.

If anyone were to say . . . that all I have at my disposal
is a little irony, a little pathos, a little dialectics, my
reply would be: "What else should anyone have who
proposes to set forth the ethical?"
Concluding Unscientific Postscript

3 · *The Literature of Unfulfilled Possibilities*

EGEL'S basic vocabulary and his essential
movements were to be prodded into a new pur-
pose by the literature of the religious poet who
would force them to undergo a process like the
spiritual transformation he called "Repetition."
Kierkegaard recovered his father and Regine by
this operation, which was the only way to lose
Hegel. Hegel had to be transposed, a humiliation more terrible than
direct assaults upon Speculation, the allegorization of the System. If the
Danish Hegelians had appropriated "the entire Christian terminology"
for "speculative thought," making "speculative thought and Christianity . . . identical" (*CUP*, 324–25), why could not Christianity, in a
countermove, force Speculation's terminology to go further toward
faith, as it had pretended to go further *than* faith (*CUP*, 321)? In any
case, the maieutic poet must start where men are, in the sphere of
speculation, of "first reflection . . . outside the immediate relationship
to God" (*J/P*, III, 718; n. 3708 [1849]). A second reflection can disori-
ent the first into a new need, its diction into prayer.

It has generally been thought that reflection is the natural enemy of
Christianity and would destroy it. With God's help I hope to show
that God-fearing reflection can tie knots again which a shallow,
superficial reflection has toyed with so long. The divine authority of

131

the Bible and everything related to it has been abolished; it looks as if one final unit of reflection is expected to finish the whole thing. But look, reflection is on the way to do a counterservice, to reset the trigger springs for the essentially Christian so that it may stand its ground—against reflection. . . . Now it becomes a battle between reflection and simplicity armed with reflection. (*J/P*, III, 715; n. 3704 [1848])

As economical in this regard as in all others, the transvaluator seeks, not extension of designation, but common coin, the "language already at hand" (*WL*, 199), for he is interested in depth, not variety. The entire Hegelian diction of "interest"—pathos, passion, collision, dialectical movement, possibility, subject, universal—is played backward to break the magic spell of speculation (one reason, perhaps, why Kierkegaard is so intent on proving that he structures texts backwards), in protest against Hegel's attempt to "reduce 'vertical transcendence' to a 'horizontal transcendence.'" [1] All who are fully conscious of the tension between the finite and the infinite within us and outside of us, all who refuse to mitigate or to mediate, are natural perpetrators of transvaluated language. Socrates talked, Kierkegaard reminds us, "only about food and drink—but basically he was always talking and always thinking about the infinite." His hidden design is a trap for those who always "talk about the infinite . . . but basically are always talking and always thinking about food and drink, money, profit" (*J/P*, IV, 218; n. 4290 [1852]). Christ's parables, too, use the world's business to express the spirit's values. "So infinitely elevated is the divine language of Christianity—but . . . it is nevertheless the same language which we human beings use. Just as Socrates is said to have talked continually only about pack asses and leather tanners, etc., but always with another meaning, so Christianity uses the same words and expressions we human beings use and yet says something entirely different from what we say" (*J/P*, III, 615–16; n. 3532 [1854]). We see why misunderstanding is the basis for acceptance of grace, and psychological misrelationship the basis for acceptance of the Paradox, the God-relationship. Only by this technique

---

1. This is a phrase of Jean Hyppolite, *Genesis and Structure of Hegel's Phenomenology of Spirit*, trans. Samuel Cherniak and John Heckman (Evanston, Ill., 1974), 544, *n.* 18.

can the difference between knowing and knowing come to light, can man understand how dangerous it is to know in both worlds. To know in the transvaluated way, one must achieve ignorance.

Kierkegaard gives us an extensive discussion of this process in *Works of Love*: "All human language about the spiritual, yes, even the divine language of Holy Scriptures, is essentially transferred [*overførte*] or metaphorical language" (199). The spiritual man and the "sensuous-psychic" man use the same vocabulary, but the former uses his entirely metaphorically. The spiritual man, says Kierkegaard, "remains in the language, except that it is transferred" (*WL*, 199). Is not this the process Kierkegaard consistently plied in his "corrections" of those who influenced him but who "do not suspect the secret of transferred language?" Since it has only one foot on the ground, transferred language is intensely dialectical. The language of Speculation and Romanticism flies above the ground. Although Kierkegaard followed Hegel in criticizing the penchant of the Romantic sensibility to dissolve limits ("the romantic lies essentially in flowing over all boundaries" (*J/P*, III, 765; n. 3796 [1836]) to shape its aesthetic vision into Hegelian "bad infinities," he was just as hard on Hegel himself, whom he allegorized as "pure Reason" (*J/P*, I, 5; n. 7 [1850]), as "something fantastical" that "understands everything like the sorcerer who ended by eating his own stomach" (*J/P*, I, 5; n. 7 [1850]).

Neither the Romantic nor the Speculator uses transferred language. But Kierkegaard transforms their words in his literature, relentlessly doubling them into dialectic ("inverted dialectic," *J/P*, I, 352; n. 760 [1847]), so that they furnish the diction of the aesthetic sphere as stuff for spiritual parody. Inferior to the Apostle and his artless immediacy of faith, Kierkegaard nevertheless imitates his act. "The martyr speaks with God, he thanks God that he has been counted worthy of this suffering. And this speech accomplishes the miracle; he does not descend from the cross, but he does the even more miraculous, through courage he transforms the language" (*GS*, 158). Kierkegaard presses Hegel's language into the service of Paradox, as the martyr thanks God "for the favor of being crucified!" (*GS*, 131). And he exclaims in envy of the martyr's bodily integrity: "Marvelous language! Marvelous exaltation!" Steadily he turns the uncrucified vocabulary of the Speculators and Romantics to spiritual coin and humiliates it, as he humiliates his own, by showing its helplessness in the face of what is beyond understanding.[2]

Particularly poignant for the spiritual recovery of Regine is this illustration of transvaluation: "The saying puts it well: out of sight, out of mind. And one can always be sure that a proverb speaks accurately of how things go in the world; it is quite another matter that every proverb, Christianly understood, is untrue" (WL, 324). The gap in the level of diction between Job's counselors and that between Job and God is symptomatic of the way in which proverbs of justice are reversed in inverted dialectic, where all loss is gain (J/P, I, 352–53; n. 760 [1847]). Essentially, transferred language is a sign that the particular is higher than the universal, that "from behind the ethical emerges the religious again" (J/P, VI, 160; n. 6410 [1849]). If transferred language is a secret vengeance against the babble of the mob, for the religious poet (and for most transvaluators) it is also a fate, since it points beyond his literature to silence, "to a place where he no longer hears the earthly mother-tongue of the worldly mind" (ED, 145).[3] For God, who is outside literature, is the source of transferred language, which, like all metaphor in Kierkegaard, works from the top down. Moved by the wretchedness of man, God says, "I shall have compassion on you and make your thinking about death the most precious of thoughts—the outcome, of course, will be that this life becomes more painful than ever." As always, the sign of misunderstanding is there, "always, if you please, this misrelation between God and man, something which cannot be avoided; what God calls consolation becomes in another sense a seriousness" (J/P, IV, 315; n. 4484 [1854]). This is the way God "covers up the understanding with the beloved" (J/P, III, 53; n. 2446 [1854]).

When Hegel speaks of the moments of motivation in the world-historical figures, he assumes that the passion to perform is derived from "the universal principle whose realisation they accomplish from within

2. Stanley Cavell indicates clearly and well the relation between the qualitative gulf and transferred language, in "Kierkegaard's On Authority and Revelation," in Thompson (ed.), Kierkegaard, 382.

3. This is even true of writers like Nietzsche and D. H. Lawrence, whom Kierkegaard would call immanent transvaluators; they are hounded by the secret passion to get beyond words, beyond the bourgeois morality of good and evil.

themselves."[4] He elaborates: "It is not, however, their own invention, but is eternally present and is merely put into practice by them and honoured in their persons. But since they draw it from within themselves, from a source which was not previously available, they appear to derive it from themselves alone." The mediation between the universal and the individual is a continual ideal marked by this reciprocal direction. In Kierkegaard's view it clearly resembles recollection, which he naturally assigns to the immanent Socratic memory of divinity. To break with this prototypical but abortive spiritual notion, Kierkegaard develops the transcendent and transvaluating process of Repetition, his most important category. There are abundant definitions of Repetition, as of all Kierkegaard's categories, but they are always qualified in one sense or another by the need of the perspective, figure, medium. A minimal definition, because it does not go all the way to the religious, appears in a *Journal* entry of 1844: "The threshold of consciousness or, as it were, the key, is continually being raised but within each key the same thing is repeated" (*J/P*, IV 98; n. 3980). This definition might easily be taken for Hegelian if we do not remember that for Hegel it is the process, not the content, that remains the same. As Kierkegaard puts it: "Hegel's subsequent position swallows up the previous one, not as one stage of life swallows another, with each still retaining its validity, but as a higher title or rank swallows up a lower title" (*J/P*, II, 208–209; n. 1569 {1837}). In Kierkegaard's plan, the Hegelian moment and the aesthetic moment, like all his world-historical terms, are "repeated" all the way up to the Moment in which Christ comes into history, when the eternal hits time. The disciple experiences this moment as his conversion: "Such a moment has a peculiar character. It is brief and temporal indeed, like every moment; it is transient as all moments are; it is past, like every moment in the next moment. And yet it is decisive and filled with the Eternal" (*PF*, 22).[5]

The new man has left behind the Socratic direction of recollection and assumed the forward direction of repentance that, looking backward, nevertheless points ahead. "Repetition and recollection are the same

4. Hegel, *Lectures on the Philosophy of World History*, 83.

5. This moment can be distinguished, too, from the romantic moments of mediation between natural and divine. See M. H. Abrams, *Natural Supernaturalism: Tradition and Revolution in Romantic Literature* (New York, 1971), 355–90.

movement, only in opposite directions; for what is recollected has been, is repeated backwards, whereas repetition properly so called is recollected forwards" (*Rep*, 33). And now Kierkegaard converts the Hegelian mediation by stressing the heterogeneity of the Incarnation to man's historical consciousness. The God, as Kierkegaard calls Christ in the pagan context of *Philosophical Fragments*, comes into history out of a resolve "which stands in no equal reciprocal relation to the occasion . . . for when the occasion and the occasioned correspond, and are commensurable as the answer of the desert with the cry that evokes it, the Moment does not appear, but is lost in the eternity of Recollection. The Moment makes its appearance when an eternal resolve comes into relation with an incommensurable occasion. Unless this is realized we shall be thrown back on Socrates, and shall then have neither the God as Teacher, nor an Eternal Purpose, nor the Moment" (*PF*, 30).

Obviously, the psychological compulsion to recover losses and the religious will to transform spiritless reality ardently seek to break through the immanent rhythms of Hegel's conceptual thought, about which Hegel had warned: "We must abstain from interrupting the immanent rhythm of the movement of conceptual thought; we must refrain from arbitrarily interfering with it, and introducing ideas and reflections that have been obtained elsewhere."[6] But Kierkegaard does not raid the System with spontaneous and arbitrary invasions. On the contrary, he opens it by deliberately narrowing the field of reality and education in order, ultimately, to find freedom in depth, not breadth. The pinched motions of anxiety give some sense of this constriction and mark all the movements of ascent in Kierkegaard, even as they undergo metamorphosis. The Repetition that turns losses into gains begins in the life that is unfurled in the literature "with the passionate eloquence of . . . anxious freedom" (*Rep*, 13), on the aesthetic level of quantitative compulsion. This rhythm, which rolls always through the literature, alternates with the rhythms of two higher and stronger waves of repetition. It is marked by an obsessive retelling, governed primarily by the passion for expiation and justification. Its anxiety, like that of the inhabitants of Dante's *Inferno*, desires what it fears, is a "sympathetic antipathy" (*E/O*, I, 152; *CA*, 42), and is unable to move toward the God-

6. Hegel, Preface to *Phenomenology*, 117.

relationship.[7] For Kierkegaard, the figures of aesthetic despair help to carry this rhythm, which always begins with his personal case. A poet like Johannes de Silentio, following a hero of faith, is stuck on a higher level of anxiety, near resignation, but he is still unable to speak the "language of resolution" (*ED*, 202); he might be seen as a transition between seducers and heroes. Kierkegaard, we recall, has Constantine Constantius remind us: "A poet's life begins in conflict with the whole of existence. The gist of it is to find an appeasement or a justification; for in the first conflict he must always be defeated, and if he is bent upon triumphing at once, he is an unjustified exception" (*Rep*, 135). Anxiety forces the poet to seek repeatedly for justification, and if he does not succeed in developing his loss spiritually, beyond resignation, he will not be able to move forward to the next wave of repetition (*F/T*, 60).

The actress in *Crisis in the Life of an Actress* shows us, like the poet, the aesthetic repetition working its way up to the ethical. For, like the poet, she is able to raise the first experience to an idea. The loss of the original role to time is recovered by the older actress with the loss of time itself. The second time around she directs the role beyond time, clearly an important ascent in the history of Repetition. The actress raises the loss to the second power, "or more precisely expressed, precisely because it is the second time does she come to relate herself to the idea in a purely ideal way. . . . for what is ideality but precisely: the second time" (*CrA*, 86). The idea, then, can stand opposed to time (which will not altogether free it) and can dominate it. The consciousness of loss in time becomes a gain, just as the consciousness of suffering leads to faith.

The second wave carries the anxiety forward to ethical choice: one chooses one's despair, in Kierkegaard's famous formula, and works it through, in much the same way the patient works through obsessions in modern therapeutic processes, by repeating them upward. Sartre's definition of the operation of psychoanalysis, which like Kierkegaard's Repetition goes backward to go forward, as a movement instead of knowl-

---

7. See Dante's *Inferno*, III, 126: "Si che la tema si volve in disio." Cf. Otto Rank's definition, in "Life Fear and Death Fear," in *The Myth of the Birth of the Hero and Other Writings* (New York, 1959), 271ff. Northrop Frye's claim that the pattern of Kierkegaard's "Repetition" is modeled on the progressive, typological movement of the Bible is clearly valid. See Frye, *The Great Code: The Bible and Literature* (New York, 1982), 82. But the psychological need compulsively drives the transposition.

edge, suggests why so many have seen Kierkegaard as a precursor of modern therapists of anxiety. "Indeed, psychoanalysis is not knowledge nor does it pretend to be, except when it risks hypotheses about the dead. . . . It is a movement, an interior labor which all at once uncovers it and progressively renders the subject capable of withstanding it."[8] This work is both psychological and ethical, and is preliminary to the spiritual leap. We feel something of this rhythm in Kierkegaard's re-capitulated versions of himself, as in the anxious passing back and forth in Quidam's diary between the past and the present, between the experi-ence and the idea, and then between the verdicts of guilty or not guilty. The intense anxiety in Kierkegaard himself between telling and being testifies, too, to the presence of this pacing between psychological and ethical consciousness and choice.

As penitent, a favorite epithet for himself, Kierkegaard wants, through Repetition, to enter eternity forwards (CA, 90n). He accom-panies his struggling knight of resignation in Fear and Trembling, who, rising to faith, practiced the passionate movement, "the continual leap in existence" (F/T, 53), so that his love for his princess, a love re-nounced, became "for him the expression for an eternal love, assumed a religious character, was transfigured into a love for the Eternal Being, which did to be sure deny him the fulfillment of his love, yet reconciled him again by the eternal consciousness of its validity in the form of eternity, which no reality can take from him" (F/T, 53). Between the first loss and the last gain, the deepening ethical and psychological consciousness has interposed ignorance; for ignorance is the dissolving of knowledge into movement, and chosen instead of imposed, it is the need that finds faith. With this choice, true reality transforms the false one. And it does this, not by broadening the stage of world history and philosophy, but by raising the level of narrowness. The compulsive narrow-mindedness of the first obsessive stage of justification metamor-phoses into the chosen narrow-mindedness of the ethical stage and, finally, into the narrowness of Christ as the way, the gate.

It is easy to come to a stop too soon, before the individual "after having begun religious reflection" can "succeed in returning to himself again, whole in every respect" (CA, 106). After all, it is difficult to keep

8. Sartre, "The Singular Universal," in Thompson (ed.), Kierkegaard, 236.

constricting the "broad way" in pain, anxiety, and distress (*CA*, 107). Coming back to the self is a Christian version of the repetition primitively described in the Old Testament returns of Isaac and Job. There, quantity is a symbol for quality, not a substitution, and the Old Testament's narrowness—one man in relation to one God—is the proper field for the process of Repetition, though it cannot reach its highest circle without Christ, without the Christian consciousness of sin. Christian Repetition makes spiritual compensation out of lost flesh (II Cor. 5 : 17). But even Job's case can stand for the qualitative difference in Repetition, marked by a change in position. "Did Job lose his case? Yes, eternally; for he can appeal to no higher court than that which judged him. Did Job gain his case? Yes, eternally . . . for the fact that he lost his case *before* God" (*Rep*, 117). Immediacy, lost from childhood, yearned for, can be attained again, but only by Repetition (*J/P*, II, 377; n. 1942 [1848]). The loss, the choosing of the self, the giving of the self to God—these are the stages of recovery that attend a second immediacy, against time, a state that the System thinks can be gained again without a break. Kierkegaard's Repetition crashes and crosses the immanent rhythm of the mediation on which rides Hegel's absolute knowledge, which patiently brings together the objective form of truth and the knowing self in "immediate unity." The mind, willing to undergo the negative movement, weds subject to substance in Hegel's dialectic and "cancels abstract immediacy, i.e. immediacy which merely *is*, and by so doing becomes the true substance, becomes being or immediacy that does not have mediation outside it, but is this mediation itself." [9] Once again Hegel's process and diction are repeated into Kierkegaard's revision.

Kierkegaard continually breaches the immanent dialectical vocabulary and movement of Hegel. [10] The collisions we see so forcefully underlined in Hegel's *Aesthetics*, most dramatically in the discussions of Antig-

9. Hegel, *Phenomenology*, 805, 93.

10. Hirsch's description, supported by Wahl, of the relation between contradiction in Hegel and Kierkegaard is too tame and mediating. See Wahl, *Etudes kierkegaardiennes*, 345, n. 1: "Le paradox kierkegaardien n'est qu'une exaspération de l'attrait hégélien pour la contradiction" (The Kierkegaardian paradox is only an exacerbation of the Hegelian attraction for contradiction [author's translation]). It might be interesting to compare the swerving of Kierkegaard from Hegel with the designs of revolt charted by Harold Bloom in *The Anxiety of Influence: A Theory of Poetry* (New York, 1973).

one, are overcome in great art, as in the System.[11] But in Kierkegaard's universe a man who relates himself to God and who if he does not, is only fantastic, "will experience almost insane collisions . . . in even the least thing he does" (*J/P*, I, 309; n. 660 [1848])—this existential shock cannot be tempered in this world, nor in a literature that serves faith. This is the premise for the corrective Repetition of Hegel's movement. The trick is, by parody, to lose Hegel in the flesh so that he can be repeated into a new man. If Socrates is honored by his inclusion as a character in Kierkegaard's literature, Hegel is humiliated by his, for Hegel's participation is a demotion from his role in the System. The Hegel who had to be seriously dealt with is the one who had the same enemies as Kierkegaard, who complained about abstract thought and insisted upon the reflection in philosophy of a full and mobile experience of life. Formal systems that are without this life are viewed by Hegel as a "synoptic index, like a skeleton with tickets stuck all over it, or like the rows of boxes kept shut and labelled in a grocer's stall; and is as intelligible as either the one or the other. It has lost hold of the living nature of concrete fact."[12] This is strikingly close to the spirit of the aphorism of "A" in the "Diapsalmata." "What the philosophers say about Reality is often as disappointing as a sign you see in a shop window, which reads: Pressing Done Here. If you brought your clothes to be pressed, you would be fooled; for the sign is only for sale" (*E/O*, I, 31). Then Hegel constructs passages of great pathos, even if disembodied, concerning the brave dialectic of mind that has the courage not to be that which "shuns death, and keeps clear of destruction; it endures death and in death maintains its being. It only wins to truth when it finds itself utterly torn asunder. It is this mighty power, not by being a positive which turns away from the negative, as when we say of anything it is nothing or it is false, and, being then done with it, pass off to something else: on the contrary, mind is this power only by looking the negative in the face, and dwelling with it."[13]

In the *Phenomenology*, Hegel, the staunch enemy of positive religion, sees the life of God fall into edification (*Erbaulichkeit*), a term that

11. Hegel, *Hegel's Aesthetics*, I, 205.
12. Hegel, Preface to *Phenomenology*, 110.
13. *Ibid.*, 93.

Kierkegaard gleefully retrieves and transforms (*Opbyggelse*) for humble service to faith (*J/P*, II, 214; n. 1588 [1840]), if it "lacks the seriousness, the suffering, the patience, and the labour of the negative."[14] The drifts into alienation and fear resemble markedly the stages of dread and despair in *The Concept of Anxiety* and *The Sickness Unto Death*. "When the condition is that of separation, in which the Universal is the Substantial in relation to which the empirical consciousness feels that it exists, and at the same time feels its essential nothingness, but desires still to cling to its positive existence and remain what it is, we have the feeling of fear. When we realise that our own inner existence and feeling are null, and when self-consciousness is at the same time on the side of the Universal and condemns that existence, we get the feeling of contrition, of sorrow on account of ourselves."[15] But the chosen form of Kierkegaard that "reflects the elusiveness of existence and the possibility of death at any moment" (*CUP*, 76) we feel to be qualitatively different from that of Hegel. Perhaps this is because Kierkegaard, insisting upon the ultimate separation between the individual and the Hegelian universal, rejects the common antidote to isolation. When the System's designs and diction seem echoed in Kierkegaard, they are, in truth, being lost for the sake of Repetition; they are really in the same relationship to the spiritual as the aesthetic pattern, "tautology" signifying inversion (*J/P*, IV, 511; n. 4898 [1852])—one meaning pointing outward to social mediation, the other inward to spiritual distinction. What to Hegel was fantastic, the breach between the subject and the universal sanction of community, was to Kierkegaard the groundwork of reality; but the refusal of the God-relationship elicited the same censorious vocabulary as that of Hegel relentlessly tracking bad infinities of the alienated soul. Despair, guilt, and sin-consciousness are moments of ignorance in Hegel, while they are positive stations of faith in Kierkegaard.

Then, too, the System, which Hegel thought public, was, in Kierkegaard's view, busy with secret shuttling agents closing existential gaps with logic—agents named negation, transition, mediation—making a metaphysic out of our physic. While Hegel sees static contradiction (either/or) as a paradoxical promoter of false identity that must be broken

14. *Ibid.*, 81.
15. Hegel, *Lectures on the Philosophy of Religion*, I, 129.

by his dialectical process, Kierkegaard, making his either/or undergo continual dialectical maneuvers, can claim that the Hegelian system supports false identities of subject and object, thought and being. But existence itself is necessarily the comedy of their perpetual incommensurability (*CA*, 78*n*.; *CUP*, 112). It is for the comic undoing of the closed design that Kierkegaard establishes the necessity for his "experiments," a form that without the System might have had to defend itself as evasive. It is worthwhile noting that in *Works of Love*, which is virtually free of Hegel's breath, the experimenter is pejoratively contrasted to the lover (*WL*, 176), and in *Repetition* and *Stages on Life's Way*, the experimenters reveal their limitations at the same time that they set off their superior suffering subjects. Dismissing the possibility of direct ethical criticism of Hegel (because ethics has nothing to do with the System), Kierkegaard uses comic asides. "Let us therefore not deal unjustly with the objective tendency, by calling it an ungodly and pantheistic self-deification" (*CUP*, 112). By humorously "remaining in the metaphysical sphere," he can expose the professor of concrete life very much as Aristophanes hangs Socrates on the crane.

> If a dancer could leap very high, we would admire him. But if he tried to give the impression that he could fly, let laughter single him out for suitable punishment; even though it might be true that he could leap as high as any dancer ever had done. Leaping is the accomplishment of a being essentially earthly, one who respects the earth's gravitational force, since the leaping is only momentary. But flying carries a suggestion of being emancipated from telluric conditions, a privilege reserved for winged creatures, and perhaps also shared by the inhabitants of the moon—and there perhaps the System will first find its true readers. (*CUP*, 113)

We remember that Kierkegaard had also backed the assertion that, if Hegel had called himself an experimenter, we might have been able to take him more seriously. Or perhaps he would have been satisfied if he had called himself an impressionist, the name William James gives him, insisting that Hegel was not primarily a reasoner: "He is in reality a naively observant man, only beset with a perverse preference for the use of technical and logical jargon. He plants himself in the empirical flux of things and gets the impression of what happens. His mind is in very truth impressionistic." [16]

But Kierkegaard was not willing just to sport with the consequences of making logic out of leaps. Against the mediation that is necessary in a system he pits contrast, which is inherent to experiment. [17] Certainly Kierkegaard's universe is closed at the top, but there are no ladders across the final space, and infinite ways to fall back from leaps. It is not merely the self-conscious announcement of experimental form that persuades us of Kierkegaard's antisystematic intention, but the pervasive sabotage of all attempts to define reality in categories that fly over the leap. Henry E. Allison contends, for example (and at least part of his argument must be accepted because it is experienced by all readers), that "the doctrinal content of *Concluding Unscientific Postscript* must be regarded as an ironical jest, which essentially takes the form of a carefully constructed parody of the *Phenomenology*." [18] Certainly the itch to get one's hands on a fixed and final definition of faith, free of medium and mouth, is mocked as we "arrive repeatedly" (*CUP*, 75) at the relationship between inwardness and Paradox.

All the definitions of faith qualify those of truth, as they struggle likewise toward each other, and the "formula of faith fits only the believer" (*CUP*, 540, and see 182); the definitions are truth or faith, not dogma, for this individual or that at some stage on the way to the truth of the Paradox. For example, we might compare this definition of truth— "an objective uncertainty held fast in an appropriation-process of the most passionate inwardness" (*CUP*, 182)—with this definition of faith many pages later—"Faith is the objective uncertainty due to the repul-

---

16. William James, "Hegel and His Method," in Ralph Barton Perry (ed.), *Essays in Radical Empiricism and a Pluralistic Universe* (New York, 1971), 173.

17. See comments of Malantschuk, *Kierkegaard's Thought*, 359.

18. Henry E. Allison, "Christianity and Nonsense," in Gill (ed.), *Essays on Kierkegaard*, 127. See also Louis Mackey, "The Poetry of Inwardness," in Thompson (ed.), *Kierkegaard*, 73: "Read as a philosophical treatise it is nonsense; but the sense of the nonsense is to strip away every veil that covers the gravity of the human condition and thereby to force the reader back on his own resources." See also p. 61: "It is important, when reading Kierkegaard's 'philosophical' works, to respect their avowed fragmentary and unscientific character." Noting the poetic nature of Kierkegaard's structures, he says on p. 96: "Poems like jokes may be refused; they are never refuted."

sion of the absurd held fast by the passion of inwardness, which in this instance is intensified to the utmost degree" (*CUP*, 540). We are instantly made aware of the changes that hold these two definitions apart and mobile, however obviously they are related; the shifts in expectation and possibility are determined by the stage and sphere of perception. As Gregor Malantschuk puts it cogently: "In the esthetic stage a person relates to the probable, in the ethical stage to the uncertain, since the ethical as the eternal cannot be given ocular proof, and in the religious stage to the improbable (the absurd)." [19] Definitions are also unmoored by the closeness of the dialectical to the pathetic experience.

The spiritual individual who reflects about the ethical and spiritual life reflects passionately. The pathos which stays outside the life, like the dialectic that also stays outside, is aesthetic. "In relation to an eternal happiness as the absolute good, pathos is not a matter of words, but of permitting this conception to transform the entire existence of the individual" (*CUP*, 347). Pathos carries the suffering of resignation, of dying away. But it is doubled by the dialectical helper "which discovers and assists in finding where the absolute object of faith and worship is— there, namely, where the difference between knowledge and ignorance collapses in absolute worship with a consciousness of ignorance, there where the resistance of an objective uncertainty tortures forth the passionate certainty of faith" (*CUP*, 438–39). The Mosaic dialectic cannot enter the Promised Land, but it leads us to the border. The constant in all these "definitions" is the pairing in them, on whatever level, of dialectical thought and pathos in a movement that itself is repeated up the scale of faith. The refusal to uncouple the pair, which had so often in the history of philosophy been separated, is another act that gives Kierkegaard's thought such literary texture. And once more, it is really from the top that this coupling has worked down, for it is Christianity itself which "requires that the individual should existentially venture all" in pathos, but also requires that he "risk his thought, venturing to believe against the understanding" (*CUP*, 384).

The passion of inwardness, by its nature, cannot be universalized from one man to another. We can only suggest the experience by modifying defining predicates with sharpened pathos (*skaerpet Pathos* [*CUP*,

19. Malantschuk, *Kierkegaard's Thought*, 287, *n*. 1.

517–18]). The believer must repeatedly arrive at Deer Park through pages of hypothetical hesitations and settings forth before he walks there in hidden inwardness. The progress of man toward *Geist* in Hegel's immanently sphered education of consciousness is checked by Kierkegaard's "moated" Paradox, which forces things to go backward. In Hegelian manner, Johannes Climacus reasons: "To suffer guiltily is a lower expression than to suffer innocently, and yet it is a higher expression because the negative is the mark of a higher positive. An exister who suffers innocently is *eo ipso* not related to an eternal happiness, unless it be that the exister himself is the Paradox, with which definition we are in another sphere" (*CUP*, 475).[20] Kierkegaard's negative is not a Hegelian term of dialectic but his strongest positive standard, forced by this world into inversion. In the religious sphere, the "positive is the index of the negative," Johannes Climacus reminds us (*CUP*, 387), as "revelation is signalized by mystery, happiness by suffering, the certainty of faith by uncertainty, the ease of the paradoxical-religious life by its difficulty, the truth by absurdity." Without this in mind, it is easy to confuse the aesthetic with the religious act—one directed outwardly, the other inwardly.

The presence of the Paradox "mediates" misunderstanding by aggravating it, forcing Hegelian ascents to be repeated into repentance. As Father Taciturnus reminds us: "The System takes pains to be rid of repentance in order to be finished. An experimenter has more time" (*SLW*, 404). The experimenter's progress reverses Hegel's "going farther," for in the end we are all equally far from understanding. He turns around Hegel's "culture." "Let others extol culture unreservedly—let it then be extolled, but I would rather extol it because it makes it so difficult to become a Christian. For I am a friend of difficulties, especially of such as possess the humoristic quality that the most cultured person, after having endured the greatest exertions, has got no farther than the simplest man can get" (*CUP*, 537). Thus, Speculation is humiliated by a

20. Allison, "Christianity and Nonsense," in Gill (ed.), *Essays on Kierkegaard*, 127–49, contends that Kierkegaard is mocking Johannes Climacus' attempt to locate paradox on a scale of subjectivity. This is not a consistent limitation, since Johannes Climacus has the honorable and protective title of "experimental humorist" and leads us to the objectivity of Paradox with *suppose* clauses—signs of an existential thinker who disarms mocking with self-irony.

mere "experimental humorist" (*CUP*, 546).[21] Although the high humorist cannot go forward like Christianity, he can master the backward movement, for "humor is always a recalling (existence within the eternal by means of recollecting what is behind, manhood's recollection of childhood, etc.), it is the backward perspective" (*CUP*, 533).

From the earliest of his *Journal* entries, Kierkegaard built up the distinction between systematizer and humorist. He speaks in one passage of the desire of every system to "blow up the world with a single syllogism" and of the humorist's conscious attraction to the incommensurable—the measure of reality tensed between the finite and infinite, which the philosopher ignores because he can never solve it. The humorist "lives in abundance and is therefore sensitive to how much is always left over, even if he has expressed himself with all felicity (therefore the disinclination to write). The systematizer believes that he can say everything, and that whatever cannot be said is erroneous and secondary" (*J/P*, II, 259; n. 1702 {n.d.}). From the beginning, too, the powerful guilt of the language yearning for silence, somewhat appeased by the experimental form, is the strongest movement in Kierkegaard's literature. To write, he says in the early literature and constantly thereafter, is to be conciliatory toward the world (*J/P*, II, 258; n. 1700 [1837]). Those humorists he most admired, Socrates and Hamann, left either nothing or aphorisms and cryptic fragments. But Hegel left paragraphs, for "insofar as Hegel was fructified by Christianity, he sought to eliminate the humorous element which is in Christianity . . . and consequently reconciled himself completely with the world, with quietism as the result" (*J/P*, II, 208; n. 1568 [1837]). He has the same complaint about Goethe's concession in the second part of *Faust*, as Hegel and Goethe have by now been paired as mediators.[22] If the humorist, suggests Kierkegaard in *The Point of View for My Work as an Author*, could not lead to Christianity, he could at least, after having shown the way

21. See Malantschuk, *Kierkegaard's Thought*, 170ff., for a discussion on why Kierkegaard's thought is not in itself a system.

22. Fenger, (*Kierkegaard: Myths and Origins*, 137–38), disagrees with Thulstrup's claim that the earliest Kierkegaard was already separating from Hegel, contending that Kierkegaard courted the Hegel and Goethe beloved of the Heiberg circle until Heiberg's review of *Either / Or* in 1843. The reaction was strengthened with Heiberg's review of *Repetition*, which was "corrected" by Kierkegaard because he was anxious to free "repetition" from aesthetic and Hegelian contexts.

"*from* the aesthetical," in *Concluding Unscientific Postscript*, describe the "other way" (namely, *away* from the System, from Speculation . . . in order to become a Christian [*CUP*, 42]).

Kierkegaard's literature punctures the System with pricks of experimental humor, secure in its mischief because Paradox fastens the end of the thread (*SD*, 224). Even literary structures that are closed at the top, like religious allegories, everywhere particularize motion and attribute in order to move parody down as well as up. The high color and contrast of rebellion in Dante's doomed set their artistic vividness and realization against their fixed fate, itself a parodic reflection of the perpetual and just motions and measures of the blessed. The hyperboles of rebellion pit the noisy hierarchy of this life's values against the bright obedience of hymned eternity. We are continually to feel the sharp severance between the spheres, forced by distortions of will and crossed only by ferries of faith. The self, in a universe like Dante's, becomes ever smaller as it climbs ever higher. But in the immanent design of Hegel, which despite literary movements and pathos refuses specificity of attribute in feature, motion, and word, the self grows ever larger in its rise to full consciousness. To be sure, the mature observer, the philosopher himself, can mock the self-satisfaction of bad infinities, but he does not stand by the side of his subjects, noting the resemblance between their scorched pride and his, their doom and fear and his, as do Dante and Kierkegaard. Their parody includes them because, as poets ancillary to the divine creator, they cannot dominate the scene. In its relentless philosophical movement (it seems that history and the history of thought, not God, sent down Christ), Hegel's *Geist* cannot stimulate man's demonic distortion of divine gesture. Kierkegaard's God puts man through trials because he has "one passion"—to love and to be loved. It has pleased him, therefore, to go through existentially with men the various ways of being loved and of loving, "to endure and allow their perversions" (*J/P*, II, 146–47; n. 1445 [1854]). Parody thrives on the double direction of the demonic and the divine, one spinning in slavery and one rising or descending in freedom; their resemblance reminds us of their unconditional incommensurability. It is no wonder the demonic is absent in the *Phenomenology*, for evil is still "pagan" ignorance, not the crippling of spiritual will or the absence of faith. Guilt is philosophical inadequacy, and the fullest philosophical understanding is innocent.

The intense collisions of comedy and tragedy in Dante and Kierkegaard are, in Hegel, muted to a philosophical confidence sensitive to
pathos. The seducer, poet, experimenter, are, in various forms, present
everywhere in Kierkegaard's universe, and this presence makes the parodic structure crackle with the dialectical tension between actuality and
possibility. This strategy assumes the falseness of the formula "the actual
is true" (Kierkegaard pounces upon these stripped Hegelian mottoes for
mediation between history and reason). God, like the poet himself,
allows possibilities, but he is personal in "establishing the most terrible
distinctions—such as between good and evil, between willing according
to his will and not willing according to his will" (*J/P*, II, 147; n. 1445
[1854]).

The provisional pairing of such antithetical temperaments as those of
Dante and Kierkegaard allows us to see how much Kierkegaard's use of
literary forms and processes was a philosophical protest against the
speculation of the individual out of history, and out of his personal
history. One can see how powerfully he contributed to the literature of
doubles coming into the modern world from the Romantic elevation and
isolation of the self, with its "death of God," its insecure relationship
between psychology and morality, its subsequent anxiety and narcissism. That Kierkegaard anticipates Dostoevski has been frequently
noted, but this seems to be especially true when he charts the journey
from doubling as a demonic sign to doubling as a spiritual action,
between repetitions and Repetition. We see this even in the friendly split
between experimenter and subject in *Repetition* and in "Guilty/Not
Guilty" of *Stages on Life's Way*. Constantine Constantius' advice to his
own poet seems to correspond with Kierkegaard's own actions in his
engagement, yet we note later and more dramatically in *Stages on Life's
Way* that the experimenter is demonically motivated by the "interesting," not by maieutic spiritual direction, and that he wants to experience "repetition" for himself with no suffering (*J/P*, III, 764; n. 3794
[1844]). The stories and legends are fixed, like Dante's damned, in
narcissistic reflection until they can be loosed into a movement of ascent
by the rising rhythm of Repetition. The most exciting and successful of
Kierkegaard's literary movements is that which carries his own journey
from the doubling of justification to that of repentance (the acceptance of
guilt in a "silent daily anxiety," [*PH*, 45]). Demonic repetitions of body

and soul are taken up by spirit, which spins them up to the God-relationship. The self becomes more and more real, while the despairing double is fantastic, abstracted from the God-relationship.[23] He is, before God, "not willing to be [him]self or in despair at willing to be [him]-self," for sin is "potentiated defiance or potentiated weakness" (SD, 208). When the will is fantastic, the self is volatilized (SD, 164).

Most fantastic is the Hegelian philosopher, swallowed up in his own immanent speculation, who doubles himself in a whirl of sophistic rhythm. A question one might well ask is whether the philosophical ideal, supposed possible, of a community of interest between the subjective and the objective passion and morality, even when it is illustrated by history, the history of thought, and by literature itself, does not father a less bodied world than does the spiritual ideal of Kierkegaard, which is beyond the reach of this world, assuming isolation, and loss, and is psychologically specified by his own participation. If the reader often feels irritated by Kierkegaard's anxiety, does he not also hunger for Hegel to show it? Although Hegel talks, in his introduction to the *Phenomenology*, about consciousness itself suffering fear and anxiety for the truth, unsatisfied with only a barren ego (*das trockene Ich*), we feel that no version of the journey from demonic double to Repetition is undergone by Hegel's body, so that the moments of compassionate registering of the pathos of false leads seem often patronizing.[24] The inability to let go of the world while spiritually desiring to, notes Kierkegaard, is still "more forgivable than that unashamed brashness of mediation" (*J/P*, III, 48; n. 2437 [1852]). The sparrow and the lily, which seem naturally to enjoy the world, are not, like man, "double essences"; with their help Kierkegaard, in some of his most lyrical and charming recapitulations, tirelessly sets forth the agony and blessedness of man's doubleness. The birds are excused from the tempting grammars of both Kierkegaard and Hegel. "There is no either/or for the sparrow, and consequently no arrogant 'also' is possible for it either" (*J/P*, III, 48; n. 2437 [1852]).

The double nature of man is courted on each side by mediation and Repetition, because both processes seem to take account of it. Perhaps

23. For the clearest and most dependable mapping of the making of the self, see John W. Elrod, *Being and Existence in Kierkegaard's Pseudonymous Works* (Princeton, 1975).

24. Hegel, *Phenomenology*, 139.

Speculation is higher than the thought of the heathen, who on the other side of the bird, is double-minded, masterless, and besieged by alternation and contraries. But there is something in common between the patterns of speculation and those of the double-mindedness featured in Kierkegaard's favorite text, James 1:8, and exposed in *Purity of Heart is to Will One Thing*. Speculation demonically conducts "deceptive transactions in the 'big'" (*PH*, 104) while it speaks the conditional language of approximation, of "to a certain degree"; Repetition is lured on by the language of the absolute, "without condition and without qualification, without preface and without compromise" (*PH*, 54). It is this command, the divine imperative which meets the rising subjunctive, that checks the legends of self-justification and historical rationalization.[25] Despair, then, is flanked by the possibilities of mediation or Repetition, for it can continue negotiating in double-mindedness or become "the first factor of faith" (*SD*, 247n).

The languages of repetition and Repetition are easily confused because alternation and dialectic resemble each other, though they are antithetical. "In the life of the spirit everything is dialectical. Offense is thus, as a possibility annulled, a factor in faith; but offense with a direction away from faith is sin" (*SD*, 247n). So, too, the "question whether despair is conscious or not" is the only thing determining the "qualitative difference between despair and despair" (*SD*, 162). Kierkegaard always reminds us that "spiritlessness can say exactly the same thing, that the richest spirit has said, but it does not say it by virtue of spirit" (*CA*, 95) and that at the same time "silence is the snare of the demon . . . but silence is also the mutual understanding between the Deity and the individual" (*F/T*, 97). The closer the language of demonic and divine, the stronger the testimony to the "yawning qualitative abyss" between man and God. The dialectical nature of identity in the two languages shocks us into the realization of separation, so that the "differences display themselves all the more strikingly, as when one speaks of holding colors together" (*SD*, 252). It is clear that the spheres and stages can be seen in this light and that a word is qualitatively changed when its sphere changes.

25. See Malantschuk, *Kierkegaard's Thought*, 323–24. He traces the movement of "the purity to will one thing" in the lower discourse to the higher *thou shalt* of *Works of Love*.

Father Taciturnus asserts what Kierkegaard has shown again and again, that "the religious . . . plays, though in a higher sphere, the same role as the aesthetic; it spaces out the infinite swiftness of the ethical, and development can take place" (*SLW*, 400). In both God and art all things are possible, and it is the atheist who is enslaved by the formulas of ethical sanction: if God did not exist, all would be permitted. There is all the difference in the world between the outward scene of the aesthetic drama and the inward one of the spiritual. Nevertheless, the structure of parody prevents the ethical from seizing the world didactically or from confusing, in Hegel's manner, the actual with the true. Parody and Repetition are seen as complimentary too. "Esthetically (taking here only the relation to a human prototype) admiration is the highest; wanting to imitate has no place in the esthetic. Then along comes the ethical and says: as a matter of fact, wanting to imitate is decisive; admiration has no place or is an evasion. Then comes the paradox-prototype (the God-man). Here we have the esthetic paradox again. If I want to proceed directly to be ethical about this, I take this prototype in vain. Here it is a matter of worship and adoration first and foremost— and only through worship and adoration can there be any question of wanting to imitate" (*J/P*, IV, 295; n. 4454 [1849]). Although the aesthetic sphere is the inverse of the spiritual, it is obviously also a preparation. The reflective aesthetic narrator of *Either/Or*, Volume I, qualifies William, as he is corrected by him, and when William reappears in *Stages on Life's Way*, he is allowed to rise above his formerly smug ethical appropriation of the aesthetic. However, it is obvious that the repetition of aesthetic love cannot be transformed without rising through the ethical; otherwise, it is a sterile dialectic. "Love still has its own dialectic. I was once in love with a young girl. Last summer in the theater in Dresden, I saw an actress who strikingly resembled her. Because of that I desired the pleasure of her acquaintance; then I discovered there was really not a very great resemblance. Today I met a lady on the street who reminded me of that actress. This story can go on as long as you like" (*E/O*, I, 405).[26] "A" admits that "remembering poetically is

26. The nineteenth-century postromantic novel often exhibits this structure as a way of exposing the dissipation of the moral will in the modern world. Flaubert is, of course, its master. Deconstructive attraction to Kierkegaard's ironic renderings of the aesthetic mentality, particularly its designs of repetition, is not surprising and is of interest in

really only another expression for forgetting" (E/O, I, 289), a parody of repentance.

The perfectly related double is the Christian Paradox, for neither half is torturing the other. While Hegel, going further, has his dialectical movement outside himself, and Kierkegaard corrects him by going backward, pushing the age back (J/P, III, 152; n. 2640 [1848]), working his dialectical movement inwardly, only Christ himself can draw dialectic to the Paradox, using his double nature as the lure to doubleness in man. "The choice is not between lowliness and exaltation; no, the choice is Christ; but Christ is composite, though one and the same. . . . There is nothing, no power of nature, nothing in all the world that can thus draw to itself through a doubleness; only spirit can do that and can thus in turn draw spirit unto itself" (TC, 160). This redoubling, says Kierkegaard in an interesting Journal entry, is difficult for us to understand, for its language is poised between sentence and countersentence, and speaks both to striving and grace. "We have no criterion for the 'I-ness' [Egoitet] which is always just as great in affirmations as it is in denials, just as great in divine prodigality as it is in divine economy, just as great in giving as it is in holding back" (J/P, III, 291; n. 2906 [1854]). The divine invites, but also requires, receives, but is an offense: "Come hither" is also an obstacle (TC, 22–23). Because the world tries to ease the requirement and difficulty of the divine dialectic, the religious poet calls attention to the divine economy by acting as an agent of Christ's humiliation by words ("every word He has uttered was uttered in His humiliation" [TC, 161]). He must hold back, become a countersentence to the promises of grace. Like Johannes de Silentio, he must find the motions, the rhythms, that release the savior into an ascent of silence where he cannot follow. The movement, most patent in Training in Christianity, is like that described in Crisis in the Life of an Actress: "One becomes light by means of heaviness. One swings up high and free by means of—a pressure. Thus the celestial bodies soar through space by

---

relation to this subject. More often, however, these discussions truncate, maim, and impoverish the larger Kierkegaardian vision that depends so heavily on ethical and spiritual transvaluation, to which the deconstructive mind is allergic. See, for example, Edward W. Said, Beginnings: Intentions and Methods (New York, 1975), 85–88, and J. Hillis Miller, Fiction and Repetition: Seven English Novels (Cambridge, Mass., 1982), 105.

means of a great weight; birds fly with the help of tremendous pressure: the light soaring of faith is aided by a prodigious heaviness; the highest upswinging of hope is aided precisely by hardship and the pressure of adversity" (77). Until she assumes the role on stage, the actress suffers the anxiety of the absence of counterweight, as grace becomes aesthetic without ethical striving. The body of Kierkegaard in his literature acts as the counterweight to the reader's aesthetic expectations, and it is only by his drawing back that he can legitimately describe Christ's drawing up. This dramatic presence of his own weight is precisely what distinguishes Kierkegaard's rendering of divine motions, which otherwise would go very little beyond conventional sermonic description. Checked by Providence that forces his talent into counterweight, Kierkegaard binds the reader to his body. His task, and that of the reader, is the utilization of anxiety as a stimulus to a conscious need for weight. "One of the greatest torments a human being can suffer is to have too great an elasticity in proportion to the tension of the little world in which he lives; such an unhappy person can never come to feel entirely free, just because he cannot get enough weight on him" (CA, 78).

The major movement of Christ's words and acts in the literature, as in life, of "building up" (opbygge, which also means edify) and "drawing up" (opdrage, which also means educate [WL, 200ff.]), affects us more powerfully because Kierkegaard's body is hanging upon it. Between the world that drags us back (drage os tilbage) and Christ's promise to draw all up to him (drage Alle til) is set the poet of faith who homeopathically imitates the drag of the world in order to propel Christ's invitation. Identities are constantly colliding and pushing off from one another in pun after pun, an extreme economy, as in "Hope against Hope," against becoming a word of advancement (SE/JY, 2). If we do not feel the torques and drags of Kierkegaard's repetitions and resistance, we do not feel the power of his appeal, or its meaning. We may read, again and again, his diatribes against the easy grace of his age. "'Man' is shrewd; he does not let himself get involved in redoubling. For a time he chose the prototype and cast grace aside, replaced it with meritoriousness, and became, in supposed striving after likeness to the prototype, as impertinent as possible toward God. . . . Then man changed—and now he omitted the prototype, but stole 'grace'" (J/P, II, 358–59; n. 1917 [1852]). We hear him link Protestantism to Speculation as it loosens dialectic into alternation. But unless we *feel* Kierkegaard's body itself, torn between striving and grace in the literature itself, his words are stillborn sermons.

The constant movements of ascent and descent, inside and outside man and over qualitative gulfs, may seem at times to characterize a mystical design that also favors the close verbal play of parody (*Leben ist Leiben*), and we can readily understand why the rabidly punning and fermenting universe of von Baader had such an influence on Kierkegaard.[27] In criticizing Hegel for substituting the draw of necessity for the draw of love between divine and human, von Baader distinguishes his sense of the spiritual movement from sentimental mysticism.[28] Nevertheless, it becomes clear that for Kierkegaard there is too much interpenetration here between divine and human. The movements have a dialectical tension, but essentially the lyricism of mysticism (contrasted to the lurching leaps of Kierkegaard's texture) carries us toward identity and absorption, soothing the stark, elbowed contrasts, boundaries, and barriers of Kierkegaard's cosmology. Perhaps the mystics themselves would accuse Kierkegaard of struggling too much against forgiveness, the cleansing of guilt, and of clinging too tenaciously to his demonic psychology.

With the sensation of God's majesty, man's striving seems childishness, for "with every forward step man makes, God becomes infinitely more sublime—and thereby man decreases, even if this happens through a step forward" (*J/P*, II, 136; n. 1431 [1852]). But we must not be stupefied by this vision lest grace have "a paralyzing, soporific effect." Even if the human effort seems "fool's play," one must push on "just like one who soberly and seriously believed that by his efforts he could earn salvation" (*J/P*, II, 136; n. 1431 [1852]).[29] One needs grace even in

27. Susini, *Franz von Baader*, I, 360.

28. Ruttenbeck, *Der Christliche Denker*, 275 ff., discusses the relationship between mysticism and dialectic in Kierkegaard.

29. Paul Sponheim, *Kierkegaard on Christ*, 91–93, describes these rhythms, but he is so concerned with correcting the severity of those readers who feel most strongly the diastatic push rather than the synthetic draw of Kierkegaard's movement that he really freezes them once again into philosophical positions. Malantschuk's attention to Kierkegaard's collateral design (probably absorbed from Sibbern), against Hegel's linear design, has the advantage of revealing that no conceptual definition in Kierkegaard is free from its immediate perspective (*Kierkegaard's Thought*, 126–31). I endorse the healthy view of

relation to grace. "The easiest thing of all is to die; the difficult thing is to live. In grace everything is intensively compressed—the situation of death is still a factor. But when I have to keep on living, the infinite decision continues to be dialectical, as in this relationship: that grace is needed in relation to grace. This means that life is a striving" (*J/P*, II, 165; n. 1472 [1849]). The pressure we feel between Kierkegaard's literature as justification and maieutic service, a pressure that will never be entirely released, is the means by which we come to feel the general dialectic of striving and grace that must consciously afflict everyman who would have faith. Only in this way can striving truly "express the existing subject's ethical view of life" without resorting to a metaphysical formula, a metaphysical life (*CUP*, 110). Under pressure, Kierkegaard's word would like to annihilate itself in silent prayer, but it is bound to the task of luring and teasing, of frustrating into a need for faith. While it expands in figure after figure, story after story, fairy tale after fairy tale, it also decreases, drawing nearer to God. Maieutically, such a humiliation enables him to find us exactly where we are, in varieties of aesthetic and speculative sloth.

Perhaps this is the most important of all Kierkegaard's literary purposes that serve the existential impression, that the writer in the service of God must start by getting "in touch with men" who wait in the world before choice. "He must have everything in readiness, though without impatience, with a view to bringing forward the religious promptly as soon as he perceives that he has his readers with him, so that with the momentum gained by devotion to the aesthetic they rush headlong into contact with the religious" (*PVA*, 26). The maieutic poet must steer between patronizing and being patronized. If he appears to be one who "would have preferred to remain in the enjoyment" of the aesthetic life, but who, as he got older, "took refuge in religion" (*PVA*, 31), he must turn this to ethical advantage with a "simultaneous achievement of aesthetic and religious production." In this way religion cannot be seen as a mere compensation for lost youth. If one appears interesting, a scoundrel, one has the advantage of beginning with the attraction of the crowd and can turn seduction to a higher purpose; "for in the age of

Paul L. Holmer in "On Understanding Kierkegaard," in Howard A. Johnson and Niels Thulstrup (ed.), *A Kierkegaard Critique* (Chicago, 1972), 40–53.

reflection in which we live people are prompt to parry, and even the death of the saint is of no avail" (*PVA*, 94). The novel readers and clever wits must be lured by their own language. "If you are capable of it, present the aesthetic with all its fascinating magic, enthral if possible the other man, present it with the sort of passion which exactly suits him, merrily for the merry, in a minor key for the melancholy, wittily for the witty, etc." (*PVA*, 29). In this way the religious can be brought forward. The second front is speculation, and his language must beckon and tease into elenctic impasses.[30]

Kierkegaard was scrupulous about suiting tone and form to their maieutic purpose. In distinguishing, for example, between upbuilding discourses and reflections, like *Works of Love*, he writes:

> Reflections [*Overveielse*] do not presuppose the qualifying concepts as given and understood; therefore, they must not so much move, mollify, reassure, persuade as *awaken* and provoke men and sharpen thought. The time for reflections is indeed before action, and their purpose therefore is to rightly set all the elements in motion. Reflections ought to be a "gadfly"; therefore their tone ought to be quite different from that of upbuilding [*opbyggelige*] or edifying discourse, which rests in mood, but reflections ought in the good sense to be impatient, highspirited in mood. Irony is necessary here and the even more significant ingredient of the comic. One may very well even laugh once in a while, if only to make the thought clearer and more striking. An upbuilding discourse about love presupposes that men know essentially what love is and seeks to win them to it, to move

---

30. I entirely agree with Vernard Eller, *Kierkegaard and Radical Discipleship* (Princeton, 1968), 132.

S. K.'s contention against reason was a purely and thoroughly *religious* one. S. K. was *not* a philosopher who through his philosophic-rational investigations of reason discovered and gave rational definition to the limits of reason—as though reason were capable of mapping the territory into which it cannot go and then denying itself entry. S. K. was not a philosopher-theologian graciously "leaving room" for faith; he was a man of faith "making room" for faith against the incursions of intellectualism. If at times some of the pseudonymous works give this other impression, it is not because S. K. himself actually was operating out of a philosophic stance; rather, the religious maieuticer had "gone back" in the guise of a pseudonym to interest "philosophers" and entice them forward into religion.

them. But this is in fact not the case. Therefore the "reflections" must first fetch them up out of the cellar, call to them, turn their comfortable way of thinking topsy-turvy with the dialectic of truth. (*J/P*, I, 263; n. 641 [1847])

The edifying discourses are, according to Johannes Climacus, "humoristically revoked" (*CUP*, 244), for unlike sermons, they are not ordained by authority. They start where the reader finds himself, in immanent ethical possibilities, aesthetic repetitions, and are themselves vulnerable to the lure of poetic sirens. They force the dialectical movements of the making and unmaking of the self before God to undergo lyrical imitations of mediation while the clefts, rifts, abysses, are everywhere to be seen. We might be lulled into the sense of mystic absorption with this sentence: "It is in this sense that man is great; and he arrives at the highest pitch of perfection when he becomes suited to God through becoming absolutely nothing in himself" (*ED*, 155). But the waves of repetition crash against the tenacious stability of the repeated assurances, so that we experience the incommensurability of rhythms through the pressing forward and falling back of need.

The fairy tale is a major maieutic form for Kierkegaard for several reasons. As we noted in speaking earlier of the persistent working through of the broken engagement, the social difference between kings and commoners, princesses and peasants, is an ideal design to illustrate misunderstanding between different levels of spiritual development and a negative reminder of the democracy of God's grace. "Since there is this absolute difference between God and man, how does the principle of equality in love express itself?" (*CUP*, 439–40). The analogy between the internal fairy-tale hierarchy and the relation of human to divine also has the advantage of reinstating love as the major motive for elevation, instead of compassion or necessity. "The more superior one person is to another whom he loves, the more he will feel tempted (humanly speaking) to draw the other up to himself, but (divinely speaking) the more he will feel moved to come down to him. This is the dialectic of love. Strange that people have not seen this in Christianity but always speak of Christ's becoming man as compassion or necessity" (*J/P*, I, 128; n. 301 [1843]). The fairy tale is a form that hosts the mystical hierarchies attached to religious poetry, in which, as Kenneth Burke suggests, mystery itself is communication over a vast abyss.[31] It is thus a structure that can register misunderstanding and misrelationship through indirect communication. But if it is the poet's task to "find a solution, some point of union, where love's understanding may be realized in truth" (*PF*, 35), Kierkegaard will suspend the possibility, for such a solution belongs only to the Paradox. He leaves his mermen and kings, maidens and princesses, stranded in the anxiety of possibility. What could better show up the endless striving of the existential venture into faith than the refusal to close the most traditionally closed of all literary forms? Putting the fairy tale through the paces of possibility repeatedly, as in the story of Abraham, is the movement that in itself *becomes* the tale by making "unintelligibility . . . more desultory" (*F/T*, 121). Aesthetic expectation yearns for the happy ending, but this is a "faithless" desire; for those who love it are inevitably made unhappy by the distance between the ideal and the real. But, adds Kierkegaard in a typical reminder of the relationship between aesthetic and spiritual structures, "he who has never loved it is and remains a *pecus*" (*F/T*, 107).

Because no character is allowed to carry the full quality of the Christian vision, position is crucially emphasized. Here, too, literary genres like fable and fairy tale, which are forms of position, not character, are obviously of use. In a *Journal* entry concerning the first discourse of *The Gospel of Suffering*, Kierkegaard speaks of the way in which a fable of comparison can make "the ideal requirement . . . sound like a fairy tale" (*J/P*, V, 366; n. 5976 [1847]). If it cannot be used in the service of faith, the study of fairy tales, Judge William reminds "A," merely goes off "in a brilliant display of fireworks" (*E/O*, II, 203). Teleologically bypassing the shallow social world of multiple distinctions and busyness, the fairy tale can serve as a conductor between demonic and divine. Perspectives in Kierkegaard's literature, as in all religious literature, are characters and are as pregnant with anxiety and pain as any hero of a novel.[32] When Sarah or the merman is shifted from

---

31. Kenneth Burke and Stanley Romaine Hopper, "Mysticism as a Solution to the Poet's Dilemma," in Stanley Romaine Hopper (ed.), *Spiritual Problems in Contemporary Literature* (New York, 1957), 109.

32. See E. J. Raymond Cook, "Kierkegaard's Literary Art," *Listener*, LXXII (November, 1964), 714.

one position to another in *Fear and Trembling*, our psychological interest follows the possibility, not the character. The subservience of character to position assures the impossibility of stopping with literature as an ultimate value.

Position is a dramatic register of ethical possibility, because the world is real only as it situates itself "before God." That is why Kierkegaard says in *Christian Discourses* and elsewhere, "The most important thing in life is to be in the correct position, to assume the correct position" (*CrD*, 76). He illustrates this with his manipulation of the birds and lilies that first set off the Christian from the heathen, then move to teach us silence, patience, and obedience, virtually representing the dearest Christian virtues. The bird does not have to fly through anxiety. It has, then, a higher station than that of the heathen stuck in "ungodly melancholy" (*CrD*, 25), but a lower station than that of the Christian who sees the bird's freedom as light-mindedness. From the perspective of the simple Christian, the bird's silence is inferior to his prayers of thanksgiving; it is a higher stage to become ignorant than to be ignorant (*CrD*, 29). And most of all "the lowly Christian is himself *before God*. In this wise the bird is not itself; for the bird simply *is* what it is. By the aid of this mode of being it has every instant evaded the difficulty of the beginning, but in this wise it did not attain the glorious end of the difficult beginning, to be doubly itself" (*CrD*, 43). The Christian must come to understand that "hating the world and oneself . . . in order to love God, that precisely this is blessedness, something entirely different from enjoying the world *au niveau* with the sparrow and the lily" (*J/P*, III, 48; n. 2437 [1852]).

Yet in the last section of *Christian Discourses* the natural silence, patience, and obedience of the bird and the lily teach man, by comic humiliation, the nature of worship. That Christianity is *unnatural* in relation to man's aesthetic expectations is a thesis that can make good use of nature's creatures. It reveals to us immediately, as well, like the whole design of *Works of Love*, what a strain it was for Kierkegaard to draw together his spiritual ethics and psychology as the only true reality. How to persuade his readers, where they are, that one should become un-natural? (*J/P*, II, 378; n. 1943 [1852]). The rhetorical means at hand is the humoring of the aesthetic world. As Christ humors us to a higher station through the birds and the lilies, so too, Kierkegaard puts them lovingly in his *Christian Discourses* and then places them in the parodic relation of the aesthetic to the spiritual.

> Let us then . . . think of the bird, which had its place in the Gospel and should have a place in the discourse. The bird is on high without the anxiety of highness; the Christian of high station, who in earthly highness is exalted above others, is on high without the anxiety of highness; the heathen of high station belongs with his anxiety to the abyss, he is not really on high but in the abyss. The bird is on high, the Christian of high station is on high, the heathen of high station is in the abyss. The bird's highness is a symbol of the Christian's highness, which in turn is a counterpart of the bird's highness, the one corresponding to the other with perfect understanding though with endless difference; thou canst understand the bird's highness by understanding that of the Christian, and by understanding the bird's thou canst understand the Christian's. (*CrD*, 61)

The brilliance of Kierkegaard's manipulation is that what we yearn for now is to be what we are *supposed* to be—real, not fantastic—and that means, from the aesthetic point of view, unnatural. Because the bird's first immediacy points us to the second, it takes its charmed place in Kierkegaard's typological cast as a lower version of Abraham's immediacy of faith, itself lower than the reflective faith of the believer in the Christian Paradox. Envy of these immediacies is perfectly in order, so that they may lead us to know ourselves more deeply, that is, more Christianly.

The graduated plan of exposing the landscape imitates God's education of man.

> If the eternal were to lay out the task for man all at once and on its own terms, without regard for his poor capacities and weaker powers, man would despair. But it is a wonderful thing that the eternal, the greatest power, can make itself so small, that it is divisible in this way and yet eternally one, that clothing itself in the forms of the future, the possible, with the aid of hope it educates the child of time (man), teaches him to hope (for to hope is itself instruction, is relationship to the eternal), if he does not arbitrarily choose austerely to be disheartened by fear or cheekily choose to despair—that is, withdraw himself

from the education of the eternal. In possibility the eternal, rightly understood, continually lays out only a small piece at a time. In possibility, the eternal is continually *near enough* to be at hand and yet *far enough away* to keep man advancing towards the eternal, on the way, in forward movement. (*WL*, 236–37)

This is, we recognize, the method and position of Kierkegaard as an author in relation to his reader, for he never tires of repeating that he has been educated in this way by God. The resistance to closure and climax, the persistence of possibilities, are the marks of the thankless aesthetic task for the maieutic poet. Abraham must approach Moriah in the imagination of Johannes de Silentio, again and again as "time passes," because "to relate oneself with existential pathos to an eternal happiness is never expressed by once in a while making a great effort, but by persistence in the relationship, by the perseverance with which it is put together with everything, for therein consists the whole art of existing and here perhaps it is that men are most lacking" (*CUP*, 476–77). The persistence of storytelling carries the impression of the persistence of suffering, which guarantees "that the individual remains in the correct position" (*CUP*, 397). That art, like the System, traditionally practices the "abbreviation of the pathological factors of life" (*SLW*, 404)—for even Lear dies at the end of his play, freed from his rack—makes it a treacherous friend; and it is the mark of Kierkegaard's unique literature that it changes the shape of expectation and takes the consequences of frustrated interest, anticipating, to some extent, the literature of twentieth-century existentialism. Through its cultivation of parodic reflection, its complementary turns of dialectical and pathetic transitions and of aesthetic self-irony, Kierkegaard teases art to its limit without authorizing its martyrdom.

When we watch Kierkegaard's efforts to reach men on their spots, in their positions, we have to think too of his relation to the literary masters who fed him from all ages, including the Romantic age in which he lived. In his excellent edition of *The Concept of Irony*, Lee M. Capel fully credits the efforts of contemporary Danish scholars to fill in Kierkegaard's literary ambience and notes that one might well claim that, on a primary level, the pseudonymous works are shaped by "polemical answers to philosophic and literary problems under discussion in the intellectual circle of his immediate environment" (*CI*, 15). Henning Fenger is right in his feeling that these relations are of most interest in the earliest work, when the voice is still unsure. This is true of most writers.[33] Louis Mackey, a reader sensitive to the literary designs of Kierkegaard, persuasively writes about his habit of adopting familiar texts as models, qualifying them for his critical needs, so that we end up with what amounts to a parody of the model.[34] This is most obvious with Hegel. When Mackey cites Billeskov Jansen's juxtaposition of Dante's *Commedia* and *Stages on Life's Way*, his own qualifications indicate the importance of concentrating on the uses to which the models are put. There is no question that the filling in of literary voices around the literature of Kierkegaard and the tracing of its echoes and parodies of earlier sources are important tasks that will continue to add resonance to Kierkegaard's literature.[35] But it is crucial to keep in mind the action of Kierkegaard, so that we do not feel his needs were created by the literature.[36]

Kierkegaard's original attraction to Goethe may be a natural one in light of the admiration of his contemporaries and his strong presence in the philosophy and literature of the period, but to say that Kierkegaard soon devised his scorn of the poet-existence in order to turn it against this dominance would be to deny the deep impulses of his drive for self-examination, expiation, and transcendence. He found others to diminish on this score, like his contemporary Hans Christian Andersen and Goethe (*J/P*, II, 159; n. 1458 [1844]), but he measured himself by it most of all.[37] Each influence helped him to sharpen and develop his imperial psychological and spiritual needs to public purpose. It is certainly helpful to see the meeting of these needs by the contrasting and open modes and tones of the German Romantic writers—of Friedrich

33. See Fenger, *Kierkegaard: Myths and Origins*, xi.

34. Louis Mackey, *Kierkegaard: A Kind of Poet* (Philadelphia, 1971), 273–76. Mackey primarily discusses Kierkegaard's use of Goethe.

35. See F. J. Billeskov Jansen, "The Literary Art of Kierkegaard," in Johnson and Thulstrup (eds.), *A Kierkegaard Critique*, 13–15.

36. Gerhard vom Hofe, *Die Romantikkritik Sören Kierkegaards* (Frankfurt, 1972), 79, notes that while Jean Paul saw in Christianity the mother of Romanticism, Kierkegaard saw Romanticism as a source of Christian hope.

37. The best and fullest discussion of Kierkegaard's self-consciousness as a religious poet is still that of Emanuel Hirsch, *Kierkegaard-Studien*.

Schlegel, for example, in his criticism and in *Lucinde* (whose moral implications Kierkegaard severely censured) and in his aphoristic manifestoes of progressive mixed forms and moods, supervised by a self-conscious irony looking impassively on spanned finites and infinites, romantic chaos and classical controls.[38] It would be difficult to believe that the author of *Either/Or* was not affected by the notion that the novel should be a poem that unites all genres, like *Wilhelm Meister*,[39] or by fragments that assert: "Novels are the Socratic dialogues of our time. Practical wisdom fled from school wisdom into this liberal form," or, "Many an excellent novel is a compendium, an encyclopedia of the entire spiritual life of an individual genius."[40] Schlegel's version of Socrates as one whose irony "incites a feeling of the insoluble conflict of the absolute and the relative, of the impossibility and necessity of total communication"[41] complemented those of Hamann and Hegel, patently strong presences for Kierkegaard. That Kierkegaard had a deep attraction to the Romantic position and its poetic ideals no reader could miss, nor that he had to struggle powerfully to transform this attraction, essentially aesthetic[42] (for very quickly he turned historical Romanticism into a psychological stage), into a Christian advantage. He repeated aesthetic paradox, parody, irony, into transcendental agents and categories.[43] It seems probable too that because, like Hegel, he began as a Romantic, he was particularly sharp when he turned against Romanticism.[44] Hegel helped him considerably to formulate his criticism of Romantic irony. Although Hegel's criticism of Romantic irony is directed against its

38. See Friedrich Schlegel, *Lucinde and the Fragments*, trans. Peter Firchow (Minneapolis, 1971), and *Dialogue on Poetry and Literary Aphorisms*, trans. and ed. Ernst Behler and Roman Struc (University Park, Penn., 1968).

39. See Mackey, *Kierkegaard: A Kind of Poet*, 273.

40. Literary aphorisms from the "Lyceum," in Schlegel, *Dialogue on Poetry*, p. 123, no. 26.

41. *Ibid.*, p. 131, no. 108.

42. vom Hofe, *Die Romantikkritik*, 96, 107.

43. See F. J. Billeskov Jansen, *Studier i Søren Kierkegaards Litteraere Kunst* (Copenhagen, 1951), 23 and *passim*.

44. Wahl, *Etudes kierkegaardiennes*, 135, makes an interesting transposition of this qualification when he says of Kierkegaard's attitude toward the Hegelian "unhappy unconsciousness" that the thought of Kierkegaard might be viewed as a protestation by such a consciousness against the idea of this temper as a moment in the evolution and education of the whole consciousness, against the idea of evolution itself.

scorn of the universal moral world and Kierkegaard's against its escape from the inner spiritual world, they had a great deal in common.[45]

Kierkegaard's notion that the poet-existence, which outside of guilt, dissipates its ethical self in aesthetic reveries about the ideal (an existence he felt vulnerable to: "poetically to present the ideal which he himself is far from being" (*J/P*, I, 373; n. 817 [1849]), and is therefore an unhealthy alienation, abstraction, fantasy, certainly echoes Hegel's complaint in the *Aesthetics*. It does not really matter how much of this absorption of the Hegelian censure came directly from Hegel and how much from Hegelians; still the denial of continuity of character by an irresponsible and empty irony escaping the wear and tear of history attracted a common charge. Hegel's view that the mannerisms of Jean Paul ("we see nothing develop; everything explodes") and that the struggle between idea and form which abandons character to contingency are symptoms of the alienated ego would certainly accord with that of Kierkegaard: "When the *ego* that sets up and dissolves everything out of its own caprice is the artist, to whom no content of consciousness appears as absolute and independently real but only as a self-made and destructible show . . . earnestness can find no place, since validity is ascribed only to the formalism of the ego."[46]

This is the perspective that colors Hegel's criticism of Ludwig Tieck, Karl Solger, and Schlegel and comes into Kierkegaard's thesis, with some characteristic touching up. "Because the ironist poetically produces himself as well as his environment with the greatest possible poetic license, because he lives completely hypothetically and subjunctively, his life finally loses all continuity" (*CI*, 300–301). The Romantic's feelings "are as accidental as the incarnations of the Brahma" (*CI*, 301). Again taking up Hegel's attack, Kierkegaard is especially hard on Schlegel's *Lucinde*, which "seeks to abrogate all ethics, not simply in the sense of custom and usage, but that ethical totality which is the validity of mind, the dominion of the spirit over the flesh" (*CI* 306). We note

45. See Edo Pivčević, *Ironie als Daseinsform bei Sören Kierkegaard* (Gütersloh, West Germany, 1960), 35. Also see Malantschuk, *Kierkegaard's Thought*, 204, who suggests that in reading Tieck, Schlegel, Solger, "Kierkegaard is also able to recognize his own romantic tendencies, and therefore his criticism of this movement in its various formations must be regarded as a showdown with himself." I agree with this judgment.

46. Hegel, *Hegel's Aesthetics*, I, 602, 65.

that he is, from the beginning of the authorship, intently looking for the religious individual who "does not have his infinity outside himself but within himself" (*CI*, 313). So, too, he speaks of Tieck's "impotent ideal" (*CI*, 322), slightly qualifies Hegel's loving criticism of Solger's negative and nihilistic irony, and playfully grants Solger martyrdom by calling him a "sacrifice for Hegel's positive System" (*CI*, 335).

For Hegel, the Romantic sensibility is a vessel for the subjectivity associated with Christianity; for Kierkegaard, it can merely start the idealism that must leap to a strenuous Socratic inwardness.[47] In tracing the rise and dissolution of Romantic art from its Christian content to humor, Hegel typically grants credit for the exploration of the human heart, for the attempt to reconcile man and the divine spirit, for the painting of the "history of mentality" with depth and subtlety, and gives demerits for the unbalanced relations between the external world and the soul, an imbalance that eventually leads to the contingency of both outer and inner worlds.[48] But the essential problem, as always in Hegel, is that Romantic art finally proves *inadequate* to represent the Spirit as fully as religion and philosophy can. Its "absolute inwardness" in various forms of subjectivity of character and author formally distorts the rhythms of the ideal dialectic. With the use of the dispassionate measure *inadequate*, we are reminded once again that as much as Kierkegaard used Hegel to criticize the Romantics, so too did he use the Romantics, as many have pointed out, to criticize Hegel. Steering between the two abstractions, aesthetic and speculative, in his thesis, "Kierkegaard speaks for neither while endeavouring to master both."[49] The Romantic sensibility in the literature of Germany, France,[50] and England would give Kierkegaard his forms of disguise and the structure of repetition and of compulsive

47. See Jean Wahl, "Kierkegaard et le romantisme," *Orbis Litterarium*, X (1955), 301: "La pensée religiouse telle que la conçoit Kierkegaard, apparaît à la fois comme la destruction et l'achèvement du romantisme" ("Religious thought, as Kierkegaard conceives it, appears to be at one and the same time the destruction and completion of Romanticism" [author's translation]).

48. Hegel, *Hegel's Aesthetics*, I, 525–29. See also vom Hofe, *Die Romantikkritik*, 78, who reminds us of the similar views of Kierkegaard and Hegel on the symptomatic isolation of the aesthetic sphere that features the dissolution of the classical relations of parts to the whole.

49. Lee M. Capel, Introduction to *CI*, 34.

50. See Ronald Grimsley, *Søren Kierkegaard and French Literature* (Cardiff, Wales, 1966).

story telling, with its strategies of quest for the redemption of fallen man and his guilty words. It would also help him sanction types of doubt and despair, play out seduction and secret sin, the moral exile of Faust and the Wandering Jew, and the aesthetic boredom of Don Juan, with which, as a young man, he could identify. He could give energetic assent to authorial self-consciousness and the hyperconsciousness of dreams and disruptions, to the tease and twist that turn the world upside down, that scorn bourgeois morality as sophistic, that stimulate a yearning for the ideal and an adequate language for the ineffable.[51] But all this the Romantic sensibility enjoys at the price of negating true spirit as it enjoys the flesh, so that, ironically, "poetry is precisely what it misses, for true inward infinity proceeds only from resignation, and only this inward infinity is in truth infinite and in truth poetic" (*CI*, 305).[52]

What is most important here is that, serving both as a demonic possibility for the spirit and as its preparation, the Romantic aesthetic derides the measure *adequacy* and favors the misunderstanding and mis-relationship that, for Kierkegaard, stir the consciousness of the need for God. Kierkegaard's fierce requirements wiped off *his* face the self-satisfied smile of Romantic irony that pretends to accept the inability of the aesthetic medium to express the poet's seriousness and depth of inspiration. But he can delight in discovering that even Hegel seems to suggest "the deficiency of pure thought" for grasping actuality, in a passage in the *Aesthetics*. "Not even philosophy is alone the adequate expression for human life, . . . consequently personal life does not find its fulfillment in thought alone but in a totality of kinds of existence and modes of expression" (*J/P*, II, 215; n. 1593 [1841–42]). The Romantic forms gave Kierkegaard a way of registering the anxiety of his literature in its service to religion, an anxiety that did not interest Hegel, who did not want to be Jean Paul's humorist, "both his own court jester and his director (prince)."[53] He would repeat aesthetic motions up to infinity

---

51. See *J/P*, III, 766; n. 3801 (1836): "The romantic actually arises from the two halves of one idea being kept apart by some intervening foreign element."

52. See Pivčević, *Ironie*, 11: "Das romantische Subjekt dichtet alles; das christliche Subjekt lässt sich dichten" ("The Romantic subject composes all; the Christian subject lets himself be composed" [author's translation]).

53. Jean Paul Richter, *Horn of Oberon: J. P. Richter's School for Aesthetics*, trans. and ed. Margaret R. Hale (Detroit, 1973), 94.

and exploit irony, no longer as an empty release or negative register of yearning for the immanent union of human and divine, but as a weapon of faith.

More than anyone else, Schlegel publicized the Romantic favoring of forms, like dialogue and aphorism, that break up artificial notions of the world's unity and show up "the producer along with the product," irony flashing the infinite into the world;[54] but it was Hamann's forms and tone that most attracted Kierkegaard, largely because of his Christian humor, his love for Socrates, and his own Socratic nature. "My soul clings to Socrates, its first love, and rejoices in the one who understood him, Hamann" (J/P, II, 204; n. 1555 [1844]). Hamann's love for the idea of misrelationship between God and man, despite its mystical overtones, no doubt appealed to Kierkegaard, as did his acknowledgment of anxiety as a holy hypochondria, his oblique pleas for passion in faith, and his intense attraction to the divine descent into words.[55] It was probably from Hamann that Kierkegaard learned to appreciate the skeptical Hume's contribution to the necessary ignorance that precedes faith. But most of all, perhaps, he was drawn to the subjective quirkiness of Hamann's style that amounts to indirect communication: "I have written about Socrates in a Socratic manner." Clearly Hamann is a lover of contradiction, dialectic, and paradox. In writing of the paradox that the redeemer suffers, that a man of "wounds and stripes" is the hero of his people's expectations, he says, "Through the cleverly devised myths of their poets, the heathens were accustomed to such contradictions until their Sophists, like ours, condemned such things as a parricide which one commits against the first principles of human knowledge."[56] His style of "crumbs, fragments, fancies, sudden inspirations," is deliberately set against systems, and this gives the personal and deep insight a penetration it could not have in paragraphs.[57] Kierkegaard felt obliged to "correct" his reluctance to carry through an idea. "Hamann rightly declares: Just as 'law' abrogates 'grace,' so 'to comprehend' abrogates 'to

54. "Athenaeum," no. 238, in Schlegel, *Dialogue on Poetry*, 145.

55. Hamann, *Schriften*, VII, 59.

56. J. G. Hamann, *Socratic Memorabilia*, trans. James C. O'Flaherty (Baltimore, 1967), 143, 157.

57. J. G. Hamann, Letter to J. G. Lindner, October 12, 1759, quoted in R. G. Smith, *J. G. Hamann: A Study*, 22.

have faith.' It is, in fact, my thesis. But in Hamann it is merely an aphorism; whereas I have fought it out of a whole given philosophy and culture and into the thesis: to comprehend that faith cannot be comprehended or (the more ethical and God-fearing side) to comprehend that faith must not be comprehended" (*J/P*, II, 205; n. 1559 [1849]). But he was delighted to use Hamann's aphoristic insights, with Jacobi's dialectic, against the paragraphs of the System. "The primitivity of genius is in his brief sentences, and the pregnant form is in entire correspondence with the desultory flinging out of a thought. With all his life and soul, to the last drop of blood, he is concentrated in a single word, the passionate protest of a highly gifted genius against an existential system. But the System is hospitable; poor Hamann, you have been reduced to a paragraph by Michelet" (*CUP*, 224).

The concentrated passion in a single word reflects the pressure of the unconditional requirement on the single subjective soul, and it is Kierkegaard's appreciation and use of this tempo and contraction, his willingness to cut diagonally through paragraphs, that puts him in the line of modern antisystematic philosophers of aphorisms, of which Nietzsche and Ludwig Wittgenstein are perhaps the most salient examples.[58] If Edith Kern's argument—that the short forms of letters, diaries, and aphorisms that Kierkegaard uses are, like soliloquies and dreams, symptoms of the absence of relationships in the literature, of the restricted relationships of reader to possibility alone, and of the imperious jealousy of the ethics of actuality—has any validity, and I think it does, we must remember that this "poverty" of the literature, the sacrifice to Kierkegaard's deepest spiritual intentions, carries his deepest pathos and pas-

---

58. I agree with this opinion of Susan Sontag, in Introduction to E. M. Cioran, *The Temptation to Exist*, trans. Richard Howard (New York, 1956), 11. See also Richard Rorty, *Philosophy and the Mirror of Nature* (Princeton, 1979), who perhaps borrows the term *edifying* from Kierkegaard, a term opposed to *systematic* as a designation for the philosophers he most admires. Rorty notes that thinkers like Kierkegaard, Nietzsche, and the later Wittgenstein are reactive and use the forms of satires, parodies, and aphorisms as reflections of "distrust of the notion that man's essence is to be a knower of essences" (367, 369). Kierkegaard is grouped with the philosophers who intentionally make themselves peripheral to traditional thought, who become pragmatic as a protest against the foundational pretensions of systematic philosophy. See also the anti-Hegelian attack of Michel Foucault, in *The Archaeology of Knowledge and the Discourse on Language*, trans. A. M. Sheridan Smith (New York, 1972), 215–37.

sion.[59] The sacrifice itself is felt, *because* it is an artistic liability or weakness.

Yet another advantage of the aphorism and paradox is that they promote territorial collisions. In his earliest writing, Kierkegaard characterizes the romantic as "essentially flowing over all boundaries" (*J/P*, III, 765; n. 3796 [1836]), and this attribute will serve as a basis for his severest criticism, equivalent to that launched by Hegel against the bad infinity of the endlessly creative romantic "I." He complains in his thesis of Solger: "He seeks to bring about the absolute identity of the finite and the infinite, seeks to destroy the boundary which in many ways would hold them apart" (*CI*, 325). We know how crucial such boundaries are for Kierkegaard's topography, for they prevent false reconciliations before faith. A beautiful illustration of the aesthetic perspective that leaves the spiritual need in empty longing and looking (again, like the bad infinite) is one Kierkegaard chooses from the Book of Judith, one that poignantly reflects his watching of Regine, of married life. "And Judith went out, she and her maidservant with her; but the men of the city watched her until she came down from the mountain, until she came through the valley and they could see her no more. And they proceeded onward in the valley" (*J/P*, III, 771; n. 3822 [1842]). To see how he spiritualizes this perspective, we need only respond to the intense relation between Abraham and his watcher in *Fear and Trembling*. Kierkegaard consistently protested against the blurring of boundaries in varieties of philosophical idealisms (*J/P*, I, 5; n. 7 [1850]), pantheisms, mysticisms. Even the boundary between art and religion, the most frightening of all boundaries to Kierkegaard, is passed without fear and trembling in Hegel.

It is the dialectical pattern in its Socratic rather than Hegelian model that, because it crucially includes the speakers in the process of questioning, keeps boundaries bristling.[60] Sartre vividly suggests the manner in

59. Edith Kern, *Existential Thought*, 24.

60. See Hermann Diem, *Kierkegaard's Dialectic of Existence*, trans. Harold Knight (Edinburgh, 1959), 41: "Kierkegaard's own dialectic grew out of the dialectical practice of Socrates as it is most clearly expressed in the first so-called dialogical dialogues. It is a dual dialectical movement, as contrasted with the single ones of Hegel or of the later Plato, for the firmly maintained dual relation of the enquirer to the object, on the one hand, and to the conversational partner, on the other, results in a two-fold dialectical

which this form frees the reader, a gesture that deeply interested him, for
he allows us to link the conscious heterogeneity of Kierkegaard to others,
to himself, and to what he writes by our act of seizing ourselves as we try
to seize Kierkegaard.[61] In *Concluding Unscientific Postscript*, Johannes Climacus spoke of communication as the "art of taking away" (*CUP*, 245),
and of the task of the reader to "overcome the opposition of the form" in
order to assimilate a new ethic. Of the dialectical union of the comic and
the serious in Socrates, Quidam observes:

> In the case of an immediate existence it is important not to see the
> contradictions, for with that immediacy is lost; in the existence of
> spirit the important thing is to hold out and to endure the contradic-
> tions, but at the same time to hold them off from oneself in freedom.
> Hence the narrow-minded seriousness is always afraid of the comic,
> and rightly so; but the true seriousness itself invents the comic. If this
> were not so, stupidity would be the privileged caste with relation to
> seriousness. But seriousness is not mediation—that is a poor jest and
> a new motive for the comic. Mediation has no place in the existence-
> sphere of freedom, and only in a ludicrous way, coming from meta-
> physics, can it intrude into the sphere where freedom is constantly in
> process of becoming. (*SLW*, 335–36)

Not that this form excludes passion and pathos. Far from it. And it is
certainly true that Kierkegaard added will and feeling to Socrates' dialectic.[62] For Quidam confesses that his "belligerent understanding has often
wanted to whirl the whole thing away in laughter, but precisely out of
this whirlwind has [his] tragic passion developed more strongly" (*SLW*,
336). In such a way is the reader to be inspired by the literary offense.

Because Kierkegaard thought of poetry as essentially undialectical in
its ideal matter and resolution of readers' expectations, he called himself
a dialectical poet. "I cannot repeat enough what I so frequently have said:

---

movement." See Stanley Cavell's definition in "Kierkegaard's *On Authority and Revelation*," in Thompson (ed.), *Kierkegaard*, 387, in which he astutely distinguishes the
dialectical structure of the religious questions from the undialectical attack on politics:
"The criticism of religion . . . is inescapably dialectical . . . because everything said on
both sides is conditioned by the position (e.g., inside or outside) from which it is said."

61. See Sartre, "The Singular Universal," in Thompson (ed.), *Kierkegaard*, 233–35.
62. See Diem, *Kierkegaard's Dialectic*, 23.

I am a poet, but a very special kind, for I am by nature dialectical, and as a rule dialectic is precisely what is alien to the poet" (*J/P*, VI, 38; n. 6227 [1848]). His job is not to feed illusions, like the poet, "beloved foundling of the human heart" (*AC*, 201) but, like Socrates, to starve "the life out of all illusions in which Christendom has run aground" (*J/P*, VI, 39; n. 6228 [n.d.]). The most remarkable of all the dialectical reduplications is that the religious author uses aesthetic means to get rid of illusions (*PVA*, 17). To break off the normal resolution of the story prematurely and to debate possibilities is a consistent technique of Kierkegaard, and at these junctures he likes to say, in the guise of whatever pseudonym, "But here I break off—I am not a poet, I go about things only dialectically" (*F/T*, 99) In fact, Kierkegaard himself tenses his view of a standard poetry against its dialectical breakup. This is beautifully illustrated by the difference between the lyricism of Sarah's poetic gaze after Abraham, still romantic like that of the watchers of Judith, and the multiple dialectical possibilities that come out of the watching of Johannes de Silentio. The dialectical relationship of Kierkegaard's voice to poetry and its possibilities keeps faith in the subjunctive. The persistence of the dialectical striving indicates a preoccupation with the eternal like that of Socrates, who puts everything, consequently, on the side of humanity into an *if*. "To have faith is this very dialectical suspension which is continually in fear and trembling and yet never despairs" (*J/P*, I, 108; n. 255 [1848]). Once again we see how constantly Kierkegaard made the movement of his literature work for the movement of faith. Literature must, like Christianity in this world, render the truth and its access more difficult "in order, finally . . . to make it easier" (*ED*, 149). Literature's truth can be defined only formally; if that resolution is denied, the truth is complicated by infinite possibilities.

Thus it is a conduit of striving, refusing its generic grace. And its grace is displaced outside its body to Providence, Governance, God, who gives the resolution of form to the life that the life denies to literature. No accident is unused; no loss unrecovered; no despair wasted. Most men, says Kierkegaard, live like the grass: "Only the trees catch the storm, and they experience a great deal, but the grass experiences practically nothing" (*J/P*, IV, 39; n. 3899 [1849]). The reason is that the life does not let Providence get hold of it, does not let the wind catch its sail. It does not understand that Providence is dialectical to fortune. "My unhappiness became my blessing. I am saved, humanly speaking, by one who is dead and gone, my father, but it is impossible for me to conceive of any living person's being able to save me. Then I became an author, precisely according to my potentialities; then I was persecuted—but without it my life would not have been my own. Melancholy shadows everything in my life, but that, too, is an indescribable blessing. That is precisely how I became myself by the indescribable grace and help of God" (*J/P*, V, 11; n. 6161 [1848]). The self's possibilities, tested in literature, rise to the indescribable pen of Providence that draws the self past literature to God. This is exactly what Kierkegaard means when he says: "Again and again I am educated by God and formed by possibility. Many a time it is almost mad, this disproportion—the corresponding actuality and the possibility by which I am educated" (*J/P*, VI, 49; n. 6239 [1848]). Stretched between striving and grace, literature and being (silence), the dialectical poet suffers providentially, for only "aesthetically, suffering stands in an accidental relation to existence" (*CUP*, 397–98). The possibilities started up in the literature, both demonic and divine, are the freedom that calls down grace. We experience the antideterminism of a universe where Providence can only be chosen to be felt. In return, *because* of this order, any true literary production can derive only from a continuous life-view, a notion akin to Hegel's, which Kierkegaard developed in his books on Andersen and Adler. "And after all a world-view, a life-view, is the only true condition of every literary production. Every poetic conclusion is an illusion. If a life-view is developed, if it stands out whole and clear in its necessary coherence, one has no need to put the hero to death, one may as well let him live: the premise is nevertheless resolved and satisfied in the conclusion, the development is complete."[63]

We may simply be speaking here of continuity and authenticity of voice; but what is interesting is that Kierkegaard took the lack of

63. Søren Kierkegaard, *On Authority and Revelation: The Book on Adler*, trans. Walter Lowrie, (New York, 1966), 4. Cf. this passage from Kierkegaard's book on Andersen, *Af en endnu Levendes Papirer*, in A. B. Drachmann, J. L. Heiberg, and H. O. Lange (eds.), *Søren Kierkegaard: Samlede Vaerker* (Copenhagen, 1963), I, 33: "Den samme glaedløse Kamp, som Andersen selv, kaemper i Livet, gjentager sig nu i hans Poesie" (The same joyless battle which Andersen himself fights in life, repeats itself now in his art [author's translation]).

aesthetic resolution literally as a way to affirm the superiority of a life-view to art, to keep art's content an agent of ignorance. If life could have the humility to remain in ignorance, it would not need art. A true life-view can be built only on the ignorance that resists sophistic knowledge. So the Romantic, open dispositions of Kierkegaard's literature do not compete with their content, for they are secretly controlled by a life-view that uses them to lead us to the spiritual world; they are perfectly classical in that their "form is the reduplication of the content" (*BA*, 43*n*). Kierkegaard lets us see how he himself might have become a literary Adler, a demonic author, if he had not had a personal and providential life-view that could procure "an infinite self-consistency" (*SD*, 238). "The abnormal man may be instructive when he is controlled and forced to take his place in a total life-view; but when he bluntly claims the authority of a teacher without being able to teach anything else but abnormality and its pain, one is painfully affected by the importunate reality of such an ex-author, who personally is in mortal danger and quite personally wants to claim our aid, or by the fact that he knows no way of escape, wants to make us uneasy, to make us suffer as he does" (*BA*, 11). The poet, says Johannes Climacus, uses fortune or misfortune, "investing immediacy with an ideality such as is never found in the finite world" (*CUP*, 389). But could he "make suffering the point of departure for a view of life" and remain a poet? "The joy of poetry, art, and scholarship stands in an accidental relationship to suffering, because one person becomes a poet without suffering, another by suffering" (*J/P*, I, 255; n. 625 [1844–45]). Kierkegaard always restricts poetry to aesthetic ideality because he wants the ethical contrast, but as an avid reader of Shakespeare, he certainly knew how powerfully suffering could be depicted by literature. Even Lear, however, remains obedient to the good fortune of his generic death. The passage between suffering in art and in life is the richest and most anxious of all Kierkegaard's dialectical and pathetic transitions, and it is here that we come to know him most fully.

How ridiculous for a poet to want to seize hold of
Socrates—Socrates' whole intention was to put an end
to the poetic and to apply the ethical, the whole point
of which is that it is actuality.
Journals and Papers

4 · *The Pathos of Unfulfilled Possibilities*

O NE of the most difficult of all the misunder-
standings in Kierkegaard's high reality was the
misrelationship between his art and Truth. The
apology of art to religion has a long history, but
Kierkegaard's anxiety gave to his art a unique and
passionate quality. Dialectically pressed between
his need for art to turn private torment into spir-
itual service and his guilt for exploiting imperfect analogies to the
divine, he struggled fearfully to identify the checking of his aesthetic
powers with the reflection of faith. He tortures his literature as he
tortures his heroes, giving it no rest, so that its utter frustration might
ransom both psychological and spiritual justification. The quality of
Kierkegaard's aesthetic distress is the predominant register of his passion. To "establish a relation to the religious through the imagination"
(*CUP*, 347) is impossible, yet the imagination must be used for faith.
The border-guards between aesthetic pathos and religious pathos are
merciless, thriving on the "frontier disputes inherent in [Kierkegaard's]
nature" (*J/P*, VI, 371; n. 6718 [1851]).[1] If "religious pathos does not
consist in singing and hymning and composing verses, but in existing"
(*CUP*, 348), the poetic production viewed as accidental, must not this
pathos be described by a literature that renounces itself and, like all
transvaluating agents, longs to die into a new life?[2] What it cannot do is

1. See Hirsch, *Kierkegaard-Studien*, for the long history of this relationship.
2. In *Self-Consuming Artifacts: The Experience of Seventeenth-Century Literature* (Berkeley,
Calif., 1972), 24, Stanley Fish gives this version of a classical contest: "To enjoy the

to compel, like Grundtvig's poetry of immediate feeling, a compensatory response of "craving for . . . superstitious security" (*CUP*, 43) in the lap of history; it despises magical communal solutions.

The literature features the Abraham-watcher Johannes de Silentio, who reminds us often that, for the knight of faith, silence is the holy medium of the unconditional God-relationship, while words are mediation with the world. Ever tormented, then, by the guilt of expression that might give personal relief, cheat renunciation, mediate the absurd, and foreshorten the ethical task, Kierkegaard, through his pseudonyms, wishbones himself into the dialectical tension between poetry and life. "Aesthetically it would be the highest pathos for the poet to annihilate himself, for him to demoralize himself if necessary, in order to produce masterpieces. Aesthetically it would be in order for a man to sell his soul to the devil, to use a strong expression which recalls what is perhaps still done more often than is ordinarily supposed—but also to produce miracles of art. Ethically it would perhaps be the highest pathos to renounce the glittering artistic career without saying a single word" (*CUP*, 349). It is no accident that this view so markedly resembles that of Otto Rank, who speaks of the retreat of the ego into artistic production to hide from life and hails the new "creative type who can renounce this protection by art and can devote his whole creative force to life and the formation of life." [3] The dilemma that Kierkegaard works through is as much psychological and ethical as religious. The enormous strain Kierkegaard manifests in his form and style derives, in part, from his attempt to rest his spiritual beliefs on a psychological basis that would credit the full complexity of reality.

Perhaps this is the reason for the singular quality of Kierkegaard's aesthetic struggle, historically related to the positions of Socrates, Augustine, Dante, Herbert, Hamann, Rousseau, but altogether more intense and agonizing; for who has found it so difficult to "plainly say, *My God, My King*"? [4] One of the ways in which Kierkegaard brings the psychological and religious needs together is by anatomizing the story of

---

things of the world is to have a *rhetorical* encounter with them; to use them is to have a *dialectical* encounter."

3. Otto Rank, "Deprivation and Renunciation," in *The Myth of the Birth of the Hero and Other Writings*, 244. The epigraph of this essay is a citation from Kierkegaard.

4. This is part of the last line of George Herbert's poem "Jordan I," in *The Temple*.

his guilt.[5] But art makes the suffering worse before it helps, in imitation of faith, for it becomes, strung through a hundred possibilities, a lure, not a solution, to anxiety. It hangs enviously between heroic action and holy silence. The dissembling of the aesthetic transformation of intimate pain into a distant critical position is "dearly bought" (CrD, 327). Kierkegaard must view his life as a "stumbling-block" to his art, a dialectically opposed mockery of its seriousness, so that the hidden life-view which gives the art depth and continuity can free his suffering to serve the spirit, not to justify the self (J/P, V, 323; n. 5892 [1846]). For most of the authorship, the art and the life must be held apart from each other in public. The literature that carries Christianity's ideals "poeti-cally" must call attention to its inferiority to ethical action by taunting the life that produced it. "I am only a poet, alas, only a poet. Do not look at my life—and yet, do look at my life only to see what a mediocre Christian I am" (J/P, VI, 377; n. 6727 [1851]). A more cynical entry is one that, admitting the "poetic strain," confesses:

> I am not spiritual enough to be able to slay it or ever really to understand . . . that it is contrary to God's will for me; neither am I spiritual enough to live as an ascetic.
>
> On the other hand I am exceptionally informed as to the nature of Christianity, know how to present it, and in that respect have rare aptitudes.
>
> So, with the help of God, I use these gifts to present it to men so that they at least get an impression, become aware.
>
> Thus I believe there is one thing I still will be empowered to do, to provide a constant reminder: just when I get people to accept it, then to remind them gently, kindly, but in loving truth, that the reason they are now accepting it is simply that I myself am not a true religious on any great scale but something of a poet who has used more lenient means, consequently less authentic means in the highest sense; whereas the authentic religious would be badly treated and persecuted because he used absolutely authentic means, was truly

5. See Fritz Billeter, *Das Dichterische bei Kafka und Kierkegaard* (Winterthur, Switzer-land, 1965), 31. He says of both Kafka and Kierkegaard: "Sie sind nicht nur schuldige Dichter, sondern auch Dichter ihrer Schuld" ("They are not only guilty poets, but also poets of their guilt" [author's translation]).

earnest, actualized everything ethically, instead of conceding to himself and to others a somewhat poetic relation to it. (*J/P*, VI, 334–35; n. 6647 [1850])

And in a late entry he speaks of the necessary powerlessness of the negative body, maimed by sadness and endowed with satire. "No, just as sadness and satire, this one-and-the-same twofold power, is the stopping power, so he in whom this stopping power resides must not be a power but an impotence, a weakness—a poet" (*J/P*, II, 291–92; n. 1800 [1853–54]).

The anxiety of the religious poet, caught between making and being, is a distress often described by religious writers, by Jacques Maritain, for example. Christian art, he says, is "doubly difficult . . . because it is difficult to be an artist and very difficult to be a Christian, and because the whole difficulty is not merely the sum but the product of these two difficulties multiplied by one another, for it is a question of reconciling two absolutes."[6] We have seen some of the ways in which Kierkegaard denies the satisfactions of the absolute to his art. We have spoken of the poignant withholding in Kierkegaard that goes beyond that of other religious writers, a withholding surely related to his sexual repressions and attendant anxieties, his fear of illegitimate justification. But it is also a withholding that aggressively holds out for the embodiment of the Incarnation, for the meeting with the Paradox, an expressive climax in which the poet participates by giving up the self, so long in the making. His need, not his song, is God's favored communication (*J/P*, II, 127; n. 1414 [1850]). But art, rather than prayer, must carry the need and is the only expressive body Kierkegaard will allow himself to have. He will then, as in his engagement, refuse to let it come to fulfillment. It must be humiliated, as if it were his own body, yet serve to transport the soul to its highest trust.[7] Is it any wonder we feel the tenuousness of his position so often in the *Journals*? "I am a poet. But long before I became a poet I was intended for the life of religious individuality. And the event

6. Jacques Maritain, *Art and Scholasticism*, trans. J. F. Scanlan (London, 1947), 53.

7. Nothing could be further from the mediation recommended by Denis de Rougemont, "Religion and the Mission of the Artist," in Stanley Romain Hopper (ed.), *Spiritual Problems in Contemporary Literature* (New York, 1957), 186: "Art is an exercise of the whole being of man not to compete with God, but to coincide better with the order of

whereby I became a poet was an ethical break or a teleological suspension of the ethical. And both of these things make me want to be something more than 'the poet,' while I also am learning ever more anxiously to guard against any presumptuous arrogance in this, something God also will surely watch over" (*J/P*, VI, 371; n. 6718 [1851]).

The medium of expression must, then, at the same time be the medium of renunciation. Offense is the best transition between the two, for if Kierkegaard's art denies the satisfaction of fulfillment through metaphor, it does use metaphor's traditional repulsion of the reader eager to grasp the "truth" quickly and intellectually. Art regularly retards this kind of understanding. But this difficulty is heightened in Kierkegaard's movement, for the art itself depends on a higher offense, the Paradox, "faith's protection and weapon of defence . . . so equivocal that all human understanding must be brought to a halt by it, must stumble— so as either to be offended or to believe" (*TC*, 107–108). It is the task of the Christian writer to lure men only with the understanding that he will not, like the orators, leave out the last difficulty (*WL*, 186). The art cannot embrace the reader, cannot give him premature embodiment, for such a closing, over the mere difficulties of fortune and misfortune, solves suffering. The literature must keep the spiritual wound open, and this aggravates the offense of traditional art, no matter how open the form or content. That the climactic bodily marriage of metaphor, image, character, gesture, pattern, to understanding must be avoided is under-lined in passages like this:

> But now, now, when Christianity has lived through centuries in extensive intercourse with human understanding, now when a fallen Christianity—like that fallen angel who married mortal women— has married human understanding, now when Christianity and hu-man understanding are on intimate terms: now Christianity above all must itself watch for the collision. If Christianity is going to be preached out of the enchantment of illusion (alas, it is like the fairy tale about the castle enchanted for one hundred years) and its dis-

---

Creation, to love it better, and to reestablish ourselves in it. Thus art would appear to be like an invocation (more often than not unconscious) to the lost harmony, like a prayer (more often than not confused), corresponding to the second petition of the Lord's prayer—'Thy Kingdom come.'"

figured alterations, the possibility of offense must again fundamentally be preached to life. (*WL*, 192)

The major metaphor of marriage reminds us that Kierkegaard has transformed into scorn his fear of marriage as intimate understanding without innocence. The possibility of offense is the "antidote to apologetics' sleeping potion" (*WL*, 192). Like the spoken word of Socrates, the offense of Kierkegaard's literature must not stimulate the reader to yearn more for the embodiment he expects in art, but for the embodiment beyond it.

Since poetry is to Kierkegaard essentially undialectical (even Hegel's description of *Antigone* does not manifest the paradoxical structure of the Abraham story, for the requirements do not come from the same source), Socrates cannot be its subject (*SLW*, 380). But he is the very model for Kierkegaard's literature, for he simultaneously refuses embodiment and multiplies possibilities. His spoken word, his conversation, are specifically directed against those who would turn life into poetry; therefore, he satisfies the emphatic antirhetorical strain in all transvaluators. The *Phaedrus* and the seventh letter of Plato are the *loci classici* of the mistrust of the written word in favor of the spoken. What is most eagerly appropriated by Kierkegaard is the intimate connection between the spoken word and the individual; the dialogue form precisely invents and caters to the category of the single individual and to his freedom. By contrast, the written word is for the race. Thus Socrates is to be admired because he left nothing "from which a later age can judge him" (*CI*, 49), no system by which professors can grab him (*J/P*, IV, 224; n. 4303 [1854]). His extempore speech is a rejection of the prepared speech "which both distracts him personally and leads the listener's thoughts to something other than what is important" (*J/P*, IV, 215; n. 4283 [1851]). From Socrates' point of view, this is how the age of Kierkegaard appears: "Instead of men, everywhere fantastic abstractions. Book—world—the public—as soon as one writes he is no longer an individual human being himself, nor does he think of a reader as an individual human being, either—here the means of communication is at fault; it is much too ambitious" (*J/P*, I, 278; n. 650 [1847]). So "unambitious" is the speech of Socrates that it is really a metaphor for silence, the language of the spirit. Even Shakespeare, offering fig leaves of words to his characters, "seems to have shrunk back from the genuinely religious collisions." The language of the gods, says Kierkegaard, "no man can speak; for, as a Greek already has said so beautifully, 'From men man learns to speak, from the gods to keep silent'" (*SD*, 258).

In an early *Journal* entry, Kierkegaard notes that "Christ did not go in for writing—he wrote only in sand" (*J/P*, I, 125; n. 281 [1837]), and the parabolic ambiguity of concealing and revealing, a spur to unknowing, is meant to free faith from learning to living. The writing down of Christ's words is a reluctant act, a formidable prototype for Kierkegaard's literary guilt, for as Luther notes:

> St. Luke says in his preface that he was moved to write his Gospel because of some who had dared to write the story of Christ, doubtless because he saw that they did not manage it too well (Luke 1 : 1 – 4). Similarly, the epistles of St. Paul make the point that the purpose of his writing is to preserve what he at first preached; without a doubt he preached far more fully than he wrote. If wishing could help, he could wish nothing better than that all books might simply be abolished and nothing but the pure, simple Scripture or Bible remain throughout the world.[8]

In the *Christian Discourses*, Kierkegaard chastises the poetic eloquence that thinks it accommodates the lilies and the birds; if only "the Gospel might succeed with the aid of the lilies and the birds in teaching thee, my hearer, seriousness, and me too, in making thee perfectly silent before God" (*CrD*, 330). If it cannot be silent before men, Kierkegaard's literature refuses to master the lilies and the birds, leaving them free to humiliate, distinguish, discriminate, by their example. The poet "cannot come to an understanding with the Gospel," for what he wishes is what the gospel says is literally true. It commands the poet to be as the birds are, while the poet wishes he could be like them (*CrD*, 320–22). But the gospel's literal command does not suppress our differences from the bird. Unlike nature, we must *choose* silence, being.[9] The desire for

8. Martin Luther, "The Gospel for the Festival of the Epiphany (Matthew 2 : 1 – 12)," trans. S. P. Hebart, in Pelikan and Lehmann (eds.), *Luther's Works*, LII, 206.

9. I like Stanley Cavell's claim in "Kierkegaard's *On Authority and Revelation*," in Thompson (ed.), *Kierkegaard*, 393, that "what . . . Kierkegaard's portrait of Abraham shows is not the inevitability of his silence, but the completeness of his wish for di-

perfect communion that must always wear the mask of misunderstanding in this world becomes an immediacy attained through renunciation, through the willingness to be annihilated before God. There is nothing in between except "a striking talent for conversation" (*J/P*, VI, 522; n. 6896 [1854]). It is important to stress that Kierkegaard's literature is not an exorcism, as is the literature of the many writers who hunger for the innocence of direct communion, because he is intent upon keeping it in a state and rhythm of anxiety. It explores possibilities of justification, but it never releases these into security. At times he might hope, like the Pharisee who desired self-justification, to have a long and wordy reply to his question, "Who is my neighbour?" (Luke 10:29), so that he might "find an escape . . . , waste time" (*WL*, 104). But Christ immediately "imprisoned the questioner in the answer which contained the task." Without authority, Kierkegaard cannot rivet with "the single eye." But he desires to do it, as it is done unto him. He would speak directly of love, and this desire is in his literature. But he must consciously exploit the aesthetic promise, a loitering, "a momentary stimulation, which in the next moment is a deception, a momentary blazing-up which is followed by langor, a leap forward which leads backward, an anticipation which, retarded, blocks its own way, an introduction which does not lead into the matter" (*WL*, 105). All this is the necessary maze of the literature, which reflects the ways we fall away from faith. It is a dangerous game, but it is in the service of the love that would offend the listener into disbelief. The literature must disappoint those who hunger to become themselves.

The gift of speech is decidedly demonic in relation to the silent immediacy of the beasts, and "only the most outstanding personalities of the human race are able to bear this advantage" (*J/P*, III, 14; n. 2337 [1854]). But the tension between life and speech is heightened in the relation between life and art, for it is more tempting to take art's ideality as an absolute than the babbling of self-righteousness. All the more must the service of art be marked by severe qualifications. As much as Plato, Kierkegaard knew the dangerous "pseudo-spirituality and . . . plausible

---

rectness, his refusal of anything less." He adds that this is especially relevant to our age, in which "every indirectness is dime-a-dozen, and any weirdness can be assembled and imitated on demand—the thing we must look for, in each case, is the man who, contrary to appearance, and in spite of all, speaks."

imitation of direct intuitive knowledge" that art could stimulate.[10] Listening to orators and poets of the crucifixion made Kierkegaard want to banish them from the state (*J/P*, VI, 161; n. 6412 [1849]). He calls attention to that fascinating paradox of Plato who, as a poet, curtailed his powers in his theory but not in his practice (*J/P*, III, 527; n. 3328 [1850]).[11] Plato even dares to treat the ethics of Socrates poetically, confirming the latter's wisdom in wanting to be rid of the poet. The application to Kierkegaard's own case is evident: "I have always recognized that there is a poetic strain in me. But in me there is a struggling forward. I do not spontaneously imitate a Socrates and let the matter regress. No, in the boundless turbulence of the religious I am one position ahead. I point out the turn, the swing, which has to be made; but almost collapsing myself under the enormous intellectual task of clearing the terrain, I point out the simple ethical existence as the higher life" (*J/P*, III, 527; n. 3328 [1850]). Plato is another who illustrates the closeness of the aesthete to the speculator, for "Socrates concentrates essentially upon accentuating existence, while Plato forgets this and loses himself in speculation," which Kierkegaard defines as "the lure of recollection and immanence" (*CUP*, 184–85). Kierkegaard, wedged between Socrates and Plato, is then forced to use a literary art, but in the service of existing. The strenuous life dialectically braced against the wit, the irony—this is the body shared by Socrates and Kierkegaard.

To enrich our view of Kierkegaard's uniqueness, it might be helpful, while examining the Christian traditions of art's ministrations to religion, to look at him once again in relation to Dante. As the pilgrim,

10. This is the claim of Iris Murdoch, *The Fire and the Sun: Why Plato Banished the Artists* (Oxford, England, 1977), 66. She calls Kierkegaard a "fore-runner of much modern unease about art" because he "sensed these problems and deliberately used art as a destructive anti-theoretical mystification, to promote a more direct relationship to the truth and to prevent the dogmatic relaxation of tension brought about by a hard aesthetically burnished theology. (But art is tricky stuff; did he succeed?)" (p. 70).

11. That Kierkegaard, like us, too loosely defines the term *poet* in relation to Plato's argument is the implication of Eric A. Havelock's discussion on the question of the banishment of poets. Since it is the mimetic *losing* of the self in the passion of characters for the sake of memorized moral education that Plato opposes, he is really quite Socratic. For he cares about choosing the self while facing the Ideal. But his conceptual emphasis on the *form* of justice and beauty moves him away from the pragmatic ethical being Kierkegaard cares so much about. See Eric A. Havelock, *Preface to Plato* (Cambridge, Mass., 1963).

Dante is moving through the terrace of Pride and Humility in the *Purgatorio* and gazing with great admiration at the craftsmanship of the carvings depicting humility. Granted, these were not sculpted by man, but the enjoyment and wonder at the rendering and the conviction of its representative power are testimonies to the authority of art to serve as a stirring incentive to spiritual ascent, as a handmaiden to the Lord,

> Mentr'io mi dilettava di guardare
> l'imagini di tante umilitadi.
> e, per lo fabbro loro a veder care.
> (X, 97–99)[12]

Dante himself is reminded by Oderisi in Canto XI that his own pride in his art will be blown away by time, humbled by spirit; yet here there is a comfortable sense that if art serves the spirit, it holds a glorious and guiltless place in the divine order. Nothing could be further from the anxious place of art in Kierkegaard's literature.[13] Again and again he will distinguish, chastise, warn, humiliate, and expose the image that attempts to reproduce life. He is heavily sarcastic when he refers to Heiberg in an 1843 *Journal* entry as Denmark's Dante, who, an aestheticizer of the spirit, peered through his apocalyptic poetry into the secrets of eternity.[14] In *The Concept of Anxiety*, Kierkegaard speaks of the perpetrators of bad infinities in art (which can only meekly anticipate eternity, prematurely reconciling us to its claims on life). "Some paint eternity elaborately with the tinsel of the imagination and yet yearn for

12. This is John Sinclair's translation, in "Purgatorio," *The Divine Comedy of Dante Alighieri* (3 vols.; Oxford, England, 1970), II, 135: "while I was taking delight in gazing at the images of so great humilities, dear to sight, for their Craftsman's sake."

13. T. S. Eliot's "modern" belief is as parallel to Dante's as it is antithetical to Kierkegaard's: "For it is ultimately the function of art, in imposing a credible order upon ordinary reality, and thereby eliciting some perception of an order *in* reality, to bring us to a condition of serenity, stillness, and reconciliation, and then leave us, as Virgil left Dante, to proceed toward a region where that guide can avail us no farther." "Poetry and Drama," in *On Poetry and Poets* (New York, 1957), 94. A return to the rich cooperation of literature and religion, abandoned by the modern world, is the bias that makes Eliot a hero of John Coulson's book *Religion and Imagination: In Aid of a Grammar of Assent* (Oxford, England, 1981).

14. This is my translation. In P. A. Heiberg, V. Kuhr, and E. Torstig (eds.), *Søren Kierkegaards Papirer* (Copenhagen, 1968), IV, B46 (1843), p. 203, we read that Heiberg is Denmark's Dante, *"der i sit apokalyptiske Digt skuede ind i det evige Livs Hemmeligheder."*

it. Some envision eternity apocalyptically, pretend to be Dante, while Dante, no matter how much he conceded to the view of the imagination, did not suspend the effect of ethical judgment" (*CA*, 153).[15] One can see that Kierkegaard offers a justification for Dante because he feels so uneasy with the high dignity of art in the *Commedia*.

In a *Journal* entry, Kierkegaard discusses at some length the common defenses for the use of art in depicting the religious spirit. "The spirit penetrates a man in such a way that one sees what sort of man he is" (*J/P*, I, 64; n. 170 [1850]). Kierkegaard calls this a concession and warns that it must not be taken too literally, for "if it transformed a man in this way, then also his enemies might immediately see the same thing." Kierkegaard is even more strict when it comes to the "object of faith," for then we have the claim for ocular proof satisfied. "The object of faith is not available for artistic presentation." Further, "even in the relations among men, to the extent to which a man in relationship to something may be the object for a kind of faith, to the same extent he cannot be painted or depicted in this relationship. For the fact that there must be accompanying faith signifies precisely that there is no direct immediacy; otherwise everyone would have to see the same thing" (*J/P*, I, 64; n. 170 [1850]). The ugliness of Socrates is a perfect disguise for inwardness, is a testimony that such a quality cannot be depicted or be directly recognizable. An extended passage in *Training in Christianity* sketches a youth imagining perfection before he has yet experienced the daily, unformed persistence of actual suffering. The portrait of Christ's perfection cannot reveal the endurance of suffering, the "daily indignity and maltreatment and vexation throughout a . . . life" (*TC*, 185). Suffering cannot be represented in art because it is already perfected there, foreshortened. It is Johannes de Silentio's task to disturb the picture of perfection and to put Abraham through possibility after possibility, to make him start again and again in our minds, to put him thoroughly in time. And when Abraham struggles with time and rises above it by belief, art's consoling foreshortening is denied by the deliberately tedious repetition of "time passed . . . Abraham believed." (*F/T*, 32). Nor can humility be represented because, here again, we are dealing with an act whose reality is its repetition. The pictures of pride Dante views on the pavement tombs

15. See *E/O*, II, 139.

might be represented because they have climaxes, but poetry and art cannot recreate the unclimactic persistence of humility, which "constantly remains." So that, "when it is shown in its ideal moment the beholder senses the lack of something, because he feels that its true ideality does not consist in the fact that it is ideal in the moment but that it is constant" (E/O, II, 138).

Judge William makes the same distinction between romantic and conjugal love. With poignant self-knowledge, Kierkegaard, through the judge, identifies married love with the humility and faith beyond his grasp, for it is a prolonged rejection of the pride that refuses understanding with forgiveness. It ought not to surprise us that, even as Kierkegaard mocks marriage as mediation, he can envy its courage, just as he notes that his aggressive disguise as a dialectic poet, which *can* be represented, is a demonic defense. But the tortured, celibate life best knows the long suffering that cannot "be represented artistically, for the point of it is incommensurable with art; neither can it be poeticized, for it requires the long, protracted tedium of time" (E/O, II, 138). Only when we are living our parts in the drama that the "Deity composes, where the poet and the prompter are not different persons" (E/O, II, 140), do we really represent the ethical; and this is internal history, incommensurable with poetry. Even more cause for concern arises from the sermon, for when the orator "illustrates this sublimity, that is, represents it with the Poet's aloofness from reality, people then are moved—but in reality, in the actuality of daily life, to perceive this sublimity in Copenhagen, in Amager market, in the midst of the week-day business life!" (TC, 63). The problem for the religious artist is that he sees time as always doubled by eternity. Kierkegaard stubbornly binds art in a dialectical constraint, for while eternity's ever-present tense is both uninteresting aesthetically and undemonstrable, time's passage is fixed. "The truly eternal cannot be painted or drawn or carved in stone, for it is spirit. But neither can the temporal essentially be painted or drawn or carved in stone, for when it is presented in these ways, it is presented eternally; every picture expresses a fixation of that particular moment. If I paint a man who is lifting a spoon to his mouth or blowing his nose, it is immediately eternalized—the man continues to blow his nose this one time as long as the painting endures" (J/P, I, 61; n. 161 [1847]). Eternity and its requirements on the ethical life sap the integrity of Lessing's anatomy of aesthetic media, for Kierkegaard simply will not allow time to be idealized in art, lest accident, climaxes of fortune and misfortune, be honored by ethics. From the point of view of eternity, the complaint about the foreshortening is reversed: eternity foreshortens not for interest but in the interest of salvation. It amounts to the same scolding if we remember the constant doubling of Kierkegaard's transvaluated cosmology. "One suffers only once—but is victorious eternally. Insofar as one is victorious, this is also only once. The difference, however, is that suffering's once is momentary (even though the momentary were seventy years)—but the victory's once is eternity. Suffering's once (even though it lasted seventy years) can therefore not be pictured or portrayed in art. On the altar in Vor Frelsers Kirke there is a work which presents an angel who holds out to Christ the cup of suffering. The error is that it lasts too long; a picture always endures for an eternity" (*J/P*, IV, 372; n. 4594 [1847]).

Behind the recalcitrant refusal of aesthetic convention is Kierkegaard's impatience with the contemporary refusal of the shock of misrelationship. The age introduces "triumph within the temporal" (*TC*, 206) by the conceit of the triumphant Church. "Men are not on such intimate terms with the sublime that they really can believe in it. The contradiction therefore is this: This sublimity on the one hand; and, on the other, the fact that this is daily life, quite literally daily life, in which it manifests itself" (*TC*, 63). One of the tasks of Kierkegaard's art, then, is to deny the aesthetic flight of the image to the boundless infinite in the name of spirit and, instead, to force the image to set into relief the wonder of the literal, which is habitually eased into the symbolic by the congregations of Christendom. Among the most characteristic and unique rhythms of Kierkegaard's art is the long, winding journey through images to the emphatic repetition, with graduated intensity, of the facts of Christ's being, of his situation. Typically, Kierkegaard is not as interested in the Passion itself (a climactic symbol) as in getting us there. He wants to work us back from the picture of Christ that traumatized the mind of the child, in order to make us *feel* our life stretched between imitation and grace. In doing this, he really inverts the process of Dante. This does not represent merely another Protestant protest against rhetorical flourish, a return to the directness and simplicity of the gospel, to the plain style, though Kierkegaard's anti-oratorical laments are obviously in this line. We must remember that Kierkegaard compels his literature to work itself through mazes of possibilities, of aesthetic and speculative distortions, as the way, in such a fallen world, to get to the literal. We are so far from the literal body that was, in Christ and in his presence, one with the spiritual, that we would not recognize it if we vividly projected contemporaneity with him. The density of Kierkegaard's world, its resistance to abstraction, is measured by the long and terrible journey to simplicity—a journey filled with anxiety and yearning, with envy of immediacy, with stops and starts, and backslidings. These complications are at once his psychological, his historical, and his spiritual realism. To recover the literal, he retards it in his literature. The reiterated imperative that Kierkegaard imposed upon himself is to make Christianity simpler by making it more difficult. The individual is, finally, the literal. Christ, like Socrates, confronts him, and the literature has this task: to "begin with the individual and through the race arrive at the individual again" (*CUP*, 383), repeatedly.

Although the Reformation intensified the tension between art and religion, Augustine's favoring of multiple interpretations of Scripture is really based upon his sense of the difficulties inherent in the rendering of divine truths by language.[16] His deepest desire is to move from words to silence back to the direct, the literal bonding of the word and the spirit.[17] That the Scriptures have both plain and difficult passages is a recognition of the need to stimulate the higher vision. For Saint Thomas, the disproportion between metaphor and divine reality, their misrelationship, indeed stimulates the higher vision, forcing us to look beyond the literal since we cannot grasp the twinship of spirit and word that is Christ. For both Augustine and Aquinas, then, the figurative was a means of forcing the mind beyond human understanding and formula. The inadequacy of language to express the spirit can be used as a guide to spirit.

---

16. See Barbara Kiefer Lewalski, *Protestant Poetics and the Seventeenth-Century Religious Lyric* (Princeton, 1979), 75. Although this is ever a problem for the religious writer, it is helpful to see Kierkegaard's Romantic situation historically, as it has been charted by language theorists, as a natural development from the anxious separation between *les mots* and *les choses* in the seventeenth century, when similitude and analogy are felt as possible sources of error instead of the very mark of things. See Michel Foucault, *The Order of Things*, trans. A. M. Sheridan Smith (New York, 1970).

17. See Joseph Mazzeo's chapter, "St. Augustine's Rhetoric of Silence," in *Renaissance and Seventeenth-Century Studies* (New York, 1964), 1–28.

As Dionysius says, it is more fitting that divine truths should be
expounded under the figure of less noble than of nobler bodies; and
this for three reasons. First, because thereby men's minds are the
better freed from error. For then it is clear that these things are not
literal descriptions of divine truths, which might have been open to
doubt had they been expressed under the figure of nobler bodies,
especially in the case of those who could think of nothing nobler than
bodies. Second, because this is more befitting the knowledge of God
that we have in this life. For what He is not is clearer to us than what
He is. Therefore, similitudes drawn from things farthest away from
God form within us a truer estimate that God is above whatsoever we
may say or think of Him. Third, because thereby divine truths are the
better hidden from the unworthy. [18]

If the Protestant motion of pulling eloquence down to the level of the
gospel is related to Kierkegaard's descents into the literal, this Catholic
emphasis on the misrelationship between art and truth as a useful apology for art also touches him decidedly. Or, to take the example of two
seventeenth-century attitudes to the contest, could we not say that
Kierkegaard, a hyperbolically self-conscious user of art and an anxious
apologizer, hangs between John Donne, who exclaims, "My God, my
God, Thou art a direct God, may I not say a literall God. . . . But thou
art also . . . a figurative, a metaphoricall God too," and George Herbert, who wants to say plainly, My God, My King." [19] Whatever their
forms of apology, these religious authors somehow allowed the acceptance of language as an essential, if insufficient, medium for the journey
into spirit, and they sometimes enjoyed it. [20] But Kierkegaard could
foreshorten neither the suffering of the word in the service of the spirit
nor the suffering of the poet. Never, not even at the end, could he feel the
divine justification for his indirect medium that Dante felt, or else he
would not have abandoned it.

   For this reason, in the most lyrical versions of Kierkegaard's three-

   18. "Summa Theologica," Q. I, Art. 9, Obj. 3, in Anton C. Pegis (ed.), *Introduction
to St. Thomas Aquinas* (New York, 1945), 17.
   19. The Donne citation is from his *Devotions*, Expostulation 19, and the Herbert is
from the last line of "Jordan I."
   20. See Marcia L. Colish, *The Mirror of Language: A Study in the Medieval Theory of
Knowledge* (New Haven, 1968), 63.

leveled repetitions—in the *Edifying Discourses* or *Works of Love* or *Christian Discourses*—the relentless redoings of the tension between the unconditional and conditional vocabulary betray an anxiety more patently present in an apology like *The Point of View for My Work as An Author.* Never do we feel in him the humility of which Maritain speaks: "The truth is that such conflicts can be abolished only on condition that a deep humility make the artist as it were unconscious of his art, or if the all-powerful unction of wisdom imbue everything in him with the repose and peace of love."[21] Like celibacy, art might protect pride. The circumlocutions of guilt have made him a genius of reflection, not of spontaneity, and it is obvious that reflection breeds demonic as well as religious dialectic. "But it does not follow that a man, if he has this reflection, is supposed to stop using it; he must simply learn humility before God and then do what he unselfishly acknowledges to be the wisest thing" (*J/P*, VI, 45; n. 6235 [1848]). Reflection can register the need for God's grace. On this side of the Paradox reflection must talk, but it allows the Paradox—that perfect binding of body and being, of word and spirit—to keep it yearning for silence, for Paradox reminds us of the inadequacy of speech to express spirit.

Kierkegaard is brutal on aesthetic analogy and comparison, and he is intent upon driving Christianity back to its literal beginnings, for its *telos* is clearly to have us believe that Christ came into the world in order to suffer, a purpose turned by our metaphors into the poetry of Passion. The aesthetic analogy must always be undone in Kierkegaard and rolled back to that purpose by the apology of literal reversal: "A childish orthodoxy accentuates Christ's suffering erroneously. By the most romantic definitions, which are anything but apt to enjoin silence upon the human understanding . . . it accentuates the frightfulness of the suffering, Christ's delicate body which suffers so prodigiously; or it accentuates, qualitatively and comparatively, the fact that He who was holy, the purest and most innocent of all, had to suffer. The paradox is that Christ came into the world *in order to suffer.* Take this away, and then an army of analogies takes by storm the impregnable fortress of the paradox" (*CUP*, 529). Perhaps only a literary imagination like Kierkegaard's can feel the full brutality of the descent from the comparative to the literal, for it

21. Maritain, *Art and Scholasticism*, 12.

knows well the deep comfort of metaphor ("Thou hast nor youth nor age, / But, as it were, an after-dinner's sleep, / Dreaming on both"[22]) and the pain of facing death itself, unprotected by words.

Because the martyrs suffered in the world but did not enter it in order to suffer, even they are not analogies to Christ, nor is the suffering believer. For "the absolute paradox is recognizable by the fact that every analogy is a fallacy" (*CUP*, 529). Yet the analogy must be used, doubled by its humiliation. The miracle behind the Incarnation—that God in all his majesty cares for each soul and that each soul is forgiven—this draws us up not by our poetry but by the paradox of Christ's entrance into history, of his own humiliation put into words. Christ knows the comfort of our poetry; he tenderly shows us the lilies and the birds before he says "Thou shalt." As the Christian upbringing progresses, the shielding metaphors of earth's fatherhood drop and the literalness of God's unchanging oneness confronts the believer. This is, oddly, one of the most difficult of all confrontations to the understanding, even when it is lyrically hammered home in the rhythm of the child's catechism of the responsive reading of the *Edifying Discourses*, a rhythm that has temporarily overcome metaphor and comparison. "What then is the good? It is that which is from above. What is the perfect? It is that which is from above. Whence comes it? From above. What is the good? It is God. Who is it who gives it? It is God. Why is the good a gift, and this expression not a figure of speech, but the only real truth? Because it is from God" (*ED*, II, 37).

That God's grief at the suffering of the learner cannot be "named in the language of the multitude of men," a selfish language (*PF*, 34), means that the poet has the task of finding "some point of union, where love's understanding may be realized in truth" (*PF*, 35). Kierkegaard uses the impossibility of this task for the poet, even the dialectical poet, as a major technique *and* theme, sanctioning his words by their impotence and envy. Even in the direct communication, the language agonizes to be worthy of the imperative. *Judge for Yourselves!* is filled with figures trying again and again to express the unconditional in its tormented attempt to use poetry to reflect eternity's prose.[23]

22. This is spoken by the Duke to Claudio in Shakespeare's *Measure for Measure*, III, 1, 32–34.
23. See *WL*, 35–36.

It is not the absolute which intoxicates, but it is the absolute which reveals that we are drunk, which we know well enough ourselves, and therefore shrewdly keep a hold on finite things, rub along the walls of the houses, remain in narrow alleys, never venture out into the infinite. And it is Christianity's opinion that it is precisely the absolute which makes sober, after it had first revealed that we are drunk. Oh, how cunning we men are, and how cunningly we know how to employ language! We chatter as nearly in imitation of the truth as possible; heard cursorily it is as though we were saying the same thing. We leave out the little subordinate clause, "it reveals," and so we say, "The absolute makes one drunk." This is thieves' Latin. Christianity says: "The absolute reveals that thou art drunk, and there is only one thing that can make a man entirely sober: the absolute. (*SE/JY*, 130)

Kierkegaard's art will at least express despair in its forms, as the Greeks expressed doubt in a doubting form (*SE/JY*, 130); and if it cannot reveal, it can stimulate the need for the absolute, the unconditional.

The most extensive emphasis on the distorted representation of ethics by aesthetics emerges from discussions of the notion of comparison in the discourses on the lilies and the birds in *The Gospel of Suffering* and *Works of Love*. It is a poignant reminder of the need in Kierkegaard to transpose his own envy of the normal up to envy of being in faith. Most often, he uses the silence of the birds to chastise the babble of human comparison, but Kierkegaard is quite aware that he must use a simile to make his charge. Therefore, he provisionally puts the bird into the role of the lily's seducer by the conversation of comparison (*GS*, 181–82). Pulled out of its expected position, the bird is able to call attention to the differences between poetry and being. And it tells us, too, that the finest poetry can only be an unreliable narrator. "The poetic is like the bird's story, true and untrue, poetry and truth: that is, it is true that distinctions exist, and that much may be said about them, but it is poetic to say that passionate distinctions, in despair or joy, are the highest; and this is eternally untrue" (*GS*, 182). God's simile is not comparative, for he allows only the invisible in man (which cannot be described) to be in his image. It is absolutely reliable. "Since God is invisible, no one can *visibly* resemble Him. That is exactly why the lily does not resemble God, because the glory of the lily is the visible; and that is why the pagan still spoke imperfectly about the human, even when he spoke most perfectly about the glory of the human body, but said nothing about the fact that the invisible God created every man in His own image. To be spirit, that is man's invisible glory" (*GS*, 211). The discourses on the birds and lilies are the finest examples of Kierkegaard's conscious and consistent use of comparison in order both to give us the texture of man's life splayed between time and eternity and to deny us its adequacy to describe our God-relationship. The bird, a fine teacher of obedience, being, and silence, is silly as a seducer, for he cannot know despair and anxiety. And these, the curses of man, are also blessings, for they can lead him past metaphor to faith. The bursting of flower and bird into visible glory calls attention to the kingdom of God but can serve only as a comparative agent for man's invisible glory.

The horizontal *as if*'s of comparison are countered by the *thou shalt*'s of divine imperative, hammering the head of every figure and fable. To deal in aesthetic categories, to love like the poet, is to love with the "passion of preference" (*WL*, 65), a form of self-love. Against this we have the lyric Pauline reminders that love and charity do not compare. To use degree to describe love is again a poetic misunderstanding; "to have faith in an *extraordinary* degree destroys the integrity of faith as an imperative" (*WL*, 48). And it is a constant temptation. "Comparison is the worst of all seductions. And no seducer is so readily at hand; no seducer is everywhere present the way comparison is as soon as your side-glance beckons" (*WL*, 181). The metaphor that exposes itself to time, suffers its qualifications and attritions, can well aid in the representation of anxiety in ethical choice. But the imperative of the unconditional requirement partakes of the eternal characteristic of being "in itself . . . its character-istics" (*WL*, 261). No more than Christ's divine nature can be separated from human nature can the act be separated from the speech, a separation coaxed by analogy (*WL*, 261). Metaphor drops out of the equation of love in faith. "What the lover does, he is or he becomes; what he gives, he is or, more accurately, this he acquires" (*WL*, 262); and the integrity of this identity is strengthened by its immediate sinking comparison to a proverb. The young girl who wastes away as a victim of erotic infatuation is a sacrifice that "does not have the solemnity of the eternal and therefore is not inspiriting and upbuilding." Her case has the "sadness of temporality and thus is inspiring to the poet" (*WL*, 289). Self-renunciation is pitted against talent in the representation of love. "Only in self-renunciation can a man effectually praise love. No poet can do it. The poet can sing of erotic love and friendship, and ability to do this is a rare gift, but the poet cannot praise love" (*WL*, 335).

To praise love by being it is not a talent; it is open to everyman by "self-renunciation's relationship to God or in self-renunciation to be related to God" (*WL*, 335). The lack of preference and comparison in that relationship is fatal in poetry; their presence is fatal to ethical seriousness. Therefore, if an ethicist sees that men tend to admire him ("which is quite all right for a poet, an artist . . . since the relation is to that which differentiates"), he must himself perceive "that this is a deception" (*J/P*, IV; 290; n. 444 [1847]). For it is the ethicist's task not to solicit admiration but to goad into freedom. The renunciation of the muse of comparison is the renunciation of the value, rather than the necessity, of time. "When the penitent has withdrawn himself from every relation in order to center himself upon his relation to himself as an individual . . . he becomes responsible for every relation in which he ordinarily stands, and he is outside of any comparison. The more use one makes of comparison, the more indolent and the more wretched his life becomes. But when all comparison is relinquished forever then a man confesses as an individual before God—and he is outside any comparison, just as the demand which purity of heart lays upon him is outside of comparison" (*PH*, 216). At this point the aesthetic and psychological comparisons are metaphor; envy, like admiration, is simile. "Admiration," says Johannes Climacus, "has its very proper place in connection with differential achievements, but it is a misunderstanding when brought into relation with what is universally human," the sphere of ethical requirement (*CUP*, 320).

If language serves God by calling attention to itself as an inadequate medium for spirit, so too can the fictional character, the historical character, by being qualified as possibility. To be taken as real, and then to be admired, prevents the ethical requirement from seizing the individual. "A communication in the form of the possible, operates in terms of the ideal man (not the differential level, but the universal ideal), whose relationship to every individual man is that of a requirement. In the same degree as it is urged that it was this particular man who did the deed, it becomes easier for others to make him out an exceptional case" (*CUP*, 321). Here we have an important justification for Kierkegaard's refusal to flesh out his characters and pseudonyms. Whether or not this is a cover-up for unsustained fictional talent, and whether or not it saps aesthetic autonomy, it seems consistent for Kierkegaard to insist that the particular, the individual in his ethical-spiritual journey, is not to be lured by his aesthetic double who has all the trappings of particularity, for this attraction competes against ethical freedom. "Ethically speaking there is nothing so conducive to sound sleep as admiration of another's ethical reality. And again ethically speaking, if there is anything that can stir and rouse a man, it is a possibility ideally requiring itself of a human being" (*CUP*, 322).[24]

The contemporaneity that Kierkegaard urged on the ethical and spiritual levels—that is, the transposition of Christ's historical coming into time to each generation, to each individual, as ever-present spirit and requirement, and the choosing of the self by the journey backward and forward from psyche to spirit of each individual—this is both complemented and betrayed by literature. When literature exposes mythologizing, keeps figures possible rather than full-bodied, and is content to say, "Look, but then this is not life!" it can be a stimulus to faith. But if it tries to foreshorten the ethical task and misrepresent the spirit, it is treacherous. If the past becomes truly present, how then "can it occur to the poet to want to poetize," for to be present means to "become engaged, suffer, and act" (*J/P*, III, 643; n. 3578 [1852]). From this perspective, it is clear that art as a medium for faith is under great stress. But we have seen that it can use its weaknesses as strengths. The more Abraham is called back to try once again the journey to Moriah, the more possibility he has, and the more contemporaneity. The splicing in of perspective on perspective, the shifts of level and view within books, between books—these too carry with them the rhythm of urgency that marks the contemporary presence of faith. The poet can bring distant things near, though he is also adept at distancing, by this means, ethical requirement. That is why Kierkegaard so insistently calls his stories "experiments instead of *actual* histories" (*J/P*, I, 323; n. 691 [1848]), so that literature does not console life, but tempts to it. The artist is, in this

24. See Kern, *Existential Thought*, 57.

case, an acceptable middleman. But if the contemporaneity of the scene is to be admired instead of stimulating to faith, its present tense is demonic.

The continuity of the self in relation to the spirit, its transformation, is ever present though constantly renewed, like the love "which had undergone the transformation of the eternal by becoming duty" (*WL*, 47). Only the eternal can truly draw life into the present tense, though it aesthetically disguises itself as the future to keep a relation with time (*CA*, 89). When the poet describes the sensuous life, he speaks of its enjoyment in "the instant," and this instant is a parody of the eternal instant, the moment when Christ came into time, forcing time to intersect with eternity. The true present tense, like true immediacy, must be attained through the repeated experience of the false one flanked by the anxiety of unresolved guilt in the past and fearful anticipation of the future. When, in the last years, Kierkegaard writes his attacks in his paper "The Instant," he himself parodies journalistic notions of time by working against Christendom in the false instant. "I call it the *Instant.* Yet it is nothing ephemeral I have in mind, any more than it was anything ephemeral I had in mind before; no, it was and is something eternal: on the side of the ideals against the illusions" (*AC*, 90). Clearly the "immediacy" of artistic presentation and the "look, here" of possibilities pay a price for usefulness to faith, for true contemporaneity scorns that poetry, and in the last phase Kierkegaard's art suffers from having to be, rather than reflect, his ethical action.

A fine example of the critical regulation of Kierkegaard's art as it reflects the experience of contemporaneity is the Deer Park outing for the religious individual, an outing that takes as long as Abraham's journey. Johannes Climacus makes this apology:

> Up to this point I have kept my exposition still somewhat abstract, and shall now refer to my problem as if it were an occurrence of today, for today is Wednesday in the Deer Park season, and our religious individual is to take a pleasure outing, while I experimentally observe his psychological condition. It is easy enough to talk about it, to do it is something else. And yet, in a certain sense talking about it may not be quite so easy; I understand very well the risk I take, that I risk the loss of my little bit of reputation as an author, since everyone will find

it extremely tiresome. It is still the same Wednesday in the Deer Park season, the whole thing is about taking an outing there, and yet so many pages have already been filled that a novelist would have had space to recount the highly interesting events of ten years, with great scenes and tense situations and assignations and clandestine childbirths. (*CUP*, 442)

Later, he admits that he senses, if he cannot reenact, the hard hidden inwardness of the hero of the outing, and remarks, "I who merely sit and experiment with it, and thus essentially keep myself outside, feel the strenuousness of this labor" (*CUP*, 445). This kind of watcher's strain is a constant in many of the pseudonyms and gives Kierkegaard the protection of being no authority while suggesting the possibility that the strenuousness of living out Christianity is something he knows about, even if only by its contemporary absence. Johannes Climacus is critical of the "false medium" of *Fear and Trembling*, which allowed Johannes de Silentio too much power of illusion. More patently experimental, Johannes Climacus' excursion is less complete (*CUP*, 447). Yet even Johannes de Silentio had censored those who would have the whole of Abraham's journey over as quickly as possible, would have Abraham "mount a winged horse, the same instant one is at Mount Moriah, the same instant one sees the ram; one forgets that Abraham rode only upon an ass, which walks slowly along the road" (*F/T*, 62). The length and difficulty of the narrative must explode aesthetic satisfaction to reflect the contemporaneity of the true instant. Literature must "retard the thought" (*GS*, 162) that would get too soon to joy. In a sense even this is a parody of how God educates through experience, for what is striving in art—the long drawn-out trials and expeditions—can be mercy in life. The youth is tried by life gradually, for "if existence had done this at once, it would have crushed him" (*TC*, 189).

The metaphor has its pathos too as a symptom of the split between intention and effect. In the discourse "Every Good Gift and Every Perfect Gift Is from Above," Kierkegaard, probably thinking of his own father, speaks of the sadness in the possibility that the best of men may injure unintentionally, and he contrasts the health of divine literalness with the recourse to figure. "'So your heavenly Father gives good gifts.' It does not state that so your heavenly Father knows how to give good gifts, but it states that so He does give the good gifts; for His knowledge is not different from His gift" (*ED*, II, 37). When this is grasped in its unchangeable integrity, the "figure of speech which made it intelligible to the young," the comparison to the earthly father, is dropped. It is extremely difficult to accept the requirement of the pattern, to say nothing of grace, without retreating to figure, without relating it through the imagination in order not to have to relate to it in actuality. It is terrifying to be alone with the Scriptures. "When I turn up a passage in it, whatever comes to hand—it catches me instantly, it questions me (indeed it is as if it were God Himself that questioned me), 'Hast thou done what thou readest there?'" (*SE/JY*, 56). And to be alone in this way means to be without recourse to poetry's protections. His poetry has to fall in "party clothes" (*J/P*, II, 377; n. 1942 [1848]) or its serious uses and abuses will not be recognized, but it must fall away from the gospel. It must be good enough to move us to desire the pattern, and frustrating enough to keep us from making it the pattern. The Paradox scorns Aristotelian probability and might speak in the words of Hamann, "Comedies and romances and lies must needs be probably, but why should I be probable?" (*PF*, 65). To insure the separation between poetry and Paradox, Johannes Climacus allows an interlocutor to accuse him of plagiarism, for he appears to quote words of the offended consciousness written by those who honored the absurd—Tertullian, Hamann, Shakespeare, Luther—that Paradox is allowed to "take the bread from the mouth of the offended consciousness" (*PF*, 67). This is a technique Kierkegaard had successfully used as a device to criticize Hegel. Kierkegaard's words must regularly tease us out of habitual thought, but God's word grips and requires us directly if we do not let interpretation defend us against the divine imperative (*SE/JY*, 61). Kierkegaard often refers to himself as being a little more than a poet, a penitent, adding, "but of this I cannot speak" (*PVA*, 160). It is, ironically, the poet who must lead his listeners beyond poetry.

When he sets against his own art the requirement to become what one already is, Kierkegaard draws not only from Socrates and the Christian traditions but from Romantic literature itself, which, from Rousseau on, struggled with the problem of bringing together sincerity and expression, of finding the language of the heart. Besides being drawn to the theological structure of Rousseau's *Confessions*, Kierkegaard was no doubt drawn to the search for social as well as psychological innocence, for the way to be what he appeared to be.[25] Rousseau felt that he had solved the dialectical struggle, but Kierkegaard never could, not even in his last period, for his vision of life could not be immanently cured. Kierkegaard's anxiety could not let him thrill either to the wonder of the poet's signs in relation to spiritual signs, drawn though he was to Hamann, or to that writer's mystic curiosity and enthusiasm about the ambiguities of speech.

Of utmost significance is the association Kierkegaard made between the Romantic poet and the poet-existence, an identification that allowed him to separate himself from his aesthetic designs, which had given him so much body. After an initial embrace of Goethe, Kierkegaard had used him as an example of one who "poetizes guilt away" (*J/P*, II, 159; n. 1485 [1844]), and by doing this, Kierkegaard draws our attention to the tendency of Christendom to poetize Christ away (*TC*, 128). If suffering is brought into the aesthetic medium, it hangs upon accident and fortune, while all who want to be Christians must necessarily suffer. For most of the authorship, Kierkegaard felt the anxious possibility that he might have made an accidental condition a providential one, without authorization, and perhaps he was so fierce about the democracy of suffering ("equality of the equal suffering . . . constitutes the victory of the religious over this jest about fortune and misfortune" [*CUP*, 392]) in order to counteract all suspicion that he was not just aesthetically extraordinary. He must separate himself from Mynster: "Dazzled by the aesthetic in him, people believe that he is a religious personality, alas, even an *outstanding* personality, although perhaps he is not religious at all" (*CUP*, 348). He could hold the private and public purpose together only by turning accidental suffering into a chosen one. In this way he, like Rousseau, could serve humanity while isolating himself from it. But the constant dialogue between the world of accident and providence in his art was the willing display of his impotence. He could not claim, like Rousseau, to be an awkward conversationalist, to transvaluate without the help of eternity, to be a humbler of self-idealizations. In effect,

25. See Rousseau, *The Confessions*, 29, 87, 388. Kierkegaard could also identify with the way in which Rousseau presents the compelled writing of *The Confessions* as a bad situation, equivalent to all those that thwart desire, while he uses it to make himself transparent in the passage from private justification to public revolution.

Rousseau becomes what he is by aestheticizing guilt, by assuming that it is a question of being guilty on Tuesday or Wednesday instead of existentially guilty every day (*CUP*, 478). Kierkegaard's art is dialectical, not just because it assumes this guilt, but because it works at its task of leading others to this consciousness. The literature pits varieties of aesthetic guilt (like the dream of innocence) against religious guilt.

While Schlegel and Novalis deem poetry an immediate conveyer of historical and spiritual transformation in culture, Kierkegaard viewed it as a fruitful obstacle to ethical transformation, which could be harnessed for faith, like offense.[26] The aesthetic intention could not be denied by a spiritual realist; instead, it had to be outlived. "What once was the content of paganism is experienced again in the repetition of every generation, and only when it has been outlived is that which was idolatry reduced to a careless existence in the innocence of poetry" (*SLW*, 458). For this reason Kierkegaard could not really ban the poet. What good is it if his exile creates longing for him? His presence serves as a test for Christian ethics, for every would-be Christian ought to ask himself, "How does he relate himself to the poet, what does he think of him, how does he read him, how does he admire him?" (*WL*, 61). Since the preference in love that the poet idolizes is countered by the Christian *thou shalt love*, he gives us a useful dialectical term (*WL*, 63). Unlike poetry, Christianity, the true ethic, "knows how to shorten deliberations and cut short prolix introductions, to remove all provisional waiting and preclude all waste of time" (*WL*, 64). And Kierkegaard's art must use the circumlocutions of the poet to make us *feel* this distinction. The poet will not find a word in the New Testament to inspire his notion of love, but he might well steal one and misuse it (*WL*, 59).

The Apostle does not have the problem of the poet-existence, which, in one place, Kierkegaard defines like this: "to have one's own personal life, one's actuality, in categories completely different from those of one's poetical production, to be related to the ideal only in imagination, so that one's personal life is more or less a satire on the poetry and on oneself" (*J/P*, VI, 85; n. 6300 [1849]). So he does not have Kierkegaard's poet-anxiety. "As an Apostle St. Paul has no connexion whatsoever with Plato or Shakespeare, with stylists or upholsterers, and none

26. See vom Hofe, *Die Romantikkritik*, 182.

of them . . . can possibly be compared with him" (*PA*, 90). In contrast to the Genius, who has only an immanent teleology, the Apostle is "placed as absolute paradoxical teleology" (*PA*, 91) He is what he is through divine authority. The envy of this authority, as of Abraham's immediacy of faith that can, like that of the Book of Tobit's Sarah, even embrace marriage, helps us to measure Kierkegaard's specific density. *Without authority* had to become, like the wound, hyperbolically attached to his body as a hysterical compensation for authority's absence. As a category, then, it has presence. The beauty of a simile is utterly indifferent to Saint Paul, for he is not one who uses aesthetic equipment self-consciously: "Whether the comparison is beautiful or whether it is worn and threadbare is all one, you must realize that what I say was entrusted to me by a revelation, so that it is God Himself or the Lord Jesus Christ who speaks" (*PA*, 94). Clearly, authority has sprung him free of Kierkegaard's dialectical dealings with art. Unlike the Apostle, Kierkegaard can never be sure that he is to write "in order that." He is doomed to suffer the ambivalences of his service and its medium, an "unauthoritative poet who moves people by means of the ideals." If he is advanced over the average, it is only poetically, which means "I know better what Christianity is, and know better how to present it," but this is an "unessential difference" (*SE/JY*, 46). Kierkegaard is trapped in his telling because he can *be* neither in the average world nor in that of the Apostle.

   The most central apology for art in all of Kierkegaard is that which insists that, though it is a "deceit," it is a "necessary elimination" (*PVA*, 73). From the beginning of the authorship, claims Kierkegaard, the religious "waits patiently to give the poet leave to talk himself out" (*PVA*, 74). This *udtømmelse*, emptying, is decidedly an imitation of Christ's *kenosis*. The soul humiliates itself by entering the body of art (without the demon's delight of infiltration), the work in which Kierkegaard explores all his private possibilities in infinite subjunctives and stretches them to public possibilities. He is not as good at loving his ironic designs as Christ was at loving men, and because he is some distance away from purity of being, he can never be sure that he is revealing and concealing in the right way. Perhaps one could say, even, that in the late period, his real body becomes jealous of the body in the art and pulls away in an imitation of that direct apostolic action he always envied. In the role of John the Baptist, who must decrease as Christ increases (a phrase Kierkegaard uses for himself and for man in his approach to God (*J/P*, II, 138; n. 1432 [1852]), Kierkegaard forces the body of his literature, even at its fullest, to shrink from authority. "If what I describe is higher than my life, then for the sake of truth I must admit that I am only a poet. And above all I must not suppress the highest and make my little no. 2 or no. 3 or no. 10 into the highest" (*J/P*, VI, 231; n. 6503 [1849]).

The humiliation of the life in literature is its cast of reflection, its long purgatory of possibilities, when it longs for direct communication and the simplicity of Christian action. Yes, poetry is Kierkegaard's purgatory. The literary works are viewed from the perspective of *The Point of View for My Work as an Author* as an interim activity, "a necessary process of elimination" (*PVA*, 87), (*en nødvendig udtømmelse*), but as an activity prolonged by the difficult relations between psychological insecurity and religious imperatives. The religious waits for literature's death—"Are you not now through with that?" (*PVA*, 84)—but knows the ledges of purgatory are long and narrow.

The incognito of the public life that is taken for the reality of the private life is mirrored by the incognito of the teasing art that hides its ethical and religious purpose (*TC*, 128–29). In *Fear and Trembling*, the poet and the hero are imaged as two halves needing and loving each other. The poet, brooding over his pain, "lets everything . . . echo" it; and "the echo of this pain is the poem; for a mere scream is not a poem, but the endless echo of the scream within itself, that is the poem" (*CrD*, 330). Unlike the epic hero, who can act undialectically, the poet is eloquent out of regret (*CrD*, 329), for he is the "unfortunate lover" of historical achievement. "Out there in the silence he devises great plans to transform the world and render it blissful, great plans which never are realized—no, they become in fact the poem" (*CrD*, 330). Now, telling the story of his suffering is the only act available to the religious poet whose arsenal of words is solely in the service of turning it into example. The poet, by compensation, is a hero torturer, putting him through possibility after possibility to free him from his admirers. The hero, though, has been a poet torturer, for his immediacy and action stir envy in the reflective artist, the "repeated" envy of the normal lovers in the world. The religious Kierkegaard hides as a hero in the belly of the poet in the hope that, in a fit of consumption, he can devour his way out. He knows that he cannot do this without being nourished by the poet.[27] Is this not the texture and tension of Kierkegaard's art that is suggested by this body made up of mutual yearning and envy? It is a powerful courtship. Could anything be more different from this than the relationship between Dante the poet and Dante the pilgrim? Even direct communication, the word its own hero, does not cancel the dialectic, and because ethics and its expression cannot be one in this world, the word must struggle to its heroism, like the *thou shalt* in *Works of Love*. In the indirect communication, however, Kierkegaard's body is more richly trapped. Furthermore, the religious hero does not want to become a legend. His silence is set against the aesthetic silence of the sacrificial hero of romance (*F/T*, 121–22).

The religious Kierkegaard never reaches this indifference, which would permit him to live peacefully in art, in hidden inwardness. As a poet, his "sole joy" is in "pointing out what is a quality higher" (*J/P*, II, 299; n. 1812 [1854]). He must suffer this dialectic, for if art makes him suffer, it prevents him from being a carrier of the ideal who, by reaping the rewards of mob love and earthly pleasure, "destroys the ideal by concealing it" (*J/P*, II, 297; n. 1809 [1854]). No, Kierkegaard's concealing would not be a distortion of the ideal itself. To us it seems a rueful pathos that, in his last years, Kierkegaard would talk about the carrier who does not hide the ideal "in any way with his carnality or finitude" (*J/P*, II, 297; n. 1809 [1854]). Art *is* his finitude and carnality, hounded into flesh by the spirit's hunger.

In the epic poet's tradition of self-belittling, Kierkegaard always reduces his power and that of his pseudonyms, a version of Dante's claim that he is not Paul, not Aeneas. In typical epic envy, the contemporary reflective poet sees the old heroes as giants of immediate faith. "I doubt very much that there could be found among us one single person who in the old Christian or Jewish sense is able to have anything to do personally

---

27. See Walter L. Reed, *Meditations on the Hero: A Study of the Romantic Hero in Nineteenth-Century Fiction* (New Haven, 1974), 80–84. The emphasis on telling anticipates the epistemological emphasis in modern literature in which the relation between the teller and hero is the central concern of the novel. Our interest in Conrad's *Lord Jim*, Proust's *Remembrance of Things Past*, and Gide's *The Counterfeiters* suggests a reason for this aesthetic interest in the form of *Fear and Trembling*.

with a personal God. In relation to those heroes, we are a bunch of old rags, duplicates, a heap of bricks, mass-men, a school of herring, etc." (*J/P*, II, 142; n. 1437 [1854]). In 1848 he feels as a particular affliction his long suffering from reflective melancholy and senses a turning point—not a restoration of the child's immediacy, which he never had, but the attainment of the second immediacy of faith, *after* reflection. "As poet and philosopher I have presented everything in the medium of imagination, myself living in resignation. Now life draws nearer to me, or I draw nearer to myself" (*J/P*, V, 447; n. 6135 [1848]). While it was the job of the literature to draw us near to the knight of faith, now Kierkegaard hopes to annihilate the watcher in him. Dreading to be left to assistant professors of his life, even as commentators become professors of the Crucifixion, he himself shares some of the "shadow-existence" of the novelist creating possibilities. He will not, like those novelists, act as a vampire toward his fiction, "weep buckets over one or another remarkable character (just as shadows in the underworld sucked the blood of the living to continue living" (*J/P*, I, 265; n. 646 [1848]). By giving elasticity to the position of his figures while denying them autonomous body, he prevents literature's usurpation of life.

As a psychological experimenter in literary models, Kierkegaard describes a technique in *The Concept of Anxiety* that is remarkably similar to psychoanalytic transference.

> He imitates in himself every mood, every psychic state that he discovers in another. Thereupon he sees whether he can delude the other by the imitation and carry him along into the subsequent development, which is his own creation by virtue of the idea. Thus if someone wants to observe a passion, he must choose his individual. At that point, what counts is stillness, quietness, and obscurity so that he may discover the individual's secret. Then he must practice what he has learned until he is able to delude the individual. Thereupon he fictitiously invents the passion and appears before the individual in a preternatural magnitude of the passion. If it is done correctly, the individual will feel an indescribable relief and satisfaction, such as an insane person will feel when someone has uncovered and poetically grasped his fixation and then proceeds to develop it further. (*CA*, 55–56)

How does the experimenter achieve immediacy ethically denied him? He draws out individuals that are seduced into chatting by his silence. Soon, with experience, he is able to abandon "literary repertoires and . . . half-dead reminiscences," construct a type, and "bring his observations entirely fresh from the water, wriggling and sparkling in the play of their colors" (*CA*, 55). This is more than a mere aesthetic immediacy, for he leads, like the poet, his subject and his reader beyond him. He frees them from his office, his literature. Behind the poet and experimenter in the texts is Kierkegaard, who binds them with the hero and subject through *his* passion, *his* envy, and *his* ironic humility. So, we might think that his generalization about the necessity to raise the individual to type in order to be free from the book and the street, from history itself, is like that of many writers, for example, Henry James, who reminds himself in the face of the hard facts of the social world he wanted to picture in *The Princess Casamassima*: "What it all came back to was, no doubt, something like *this* wisdom—that if you haven't, for fiction, the root of the matter in you, haven't the sense of life and the penetrating imagination, you are a fool in the very presence of the revealed and assured; but that if you *are* so armed you are not really helpless, not without your resource, even before mysteries abysmal."[28] But it is more. For Kierkegaard is not merely speaking of the persuasion of scene or character. He is asking the writer to put at the center of his art the maieutic intention to free subject and reader from the art. He must rise from the role of seducer in *Either / Or*, who strands the seduced with her phantom passions, in order to be "repeated" into the ethical seducer, who strands his victims for faith. This act, by consuming his literature, also might free him from the thrall of its irony into an immediacy outside of the literature. He seduces out his own passion by seducing that of another.[29] He effects his own transference by using himself as a vessel through which pass his projections. In the process of magnification, he poetically comprehends himself. But true self-knowledge waits on God, beyond words.

28. Preface to *The Princess Casamassima*, in R. P. Blackmur (ed.), *The Art of the Novel: Prefaces of Henry James* (New York, 1934), 78.

29. See Aage Henriksen, "Kierkegaard's Review of Literature," in *Orbis Litterarium*, 82–83.

Kierkegaard's literary immediacy, pushed beyond the aesthetic, derives from his concentration on the relationship between poet and hero, experimenter and subject, bound together in an interminable transference and counter-transference pattern, and the relationship is itself, as subject of the work, a block to idealized projection. He will not paint Christ, but the relationship of the individual to him. In a diatribe against the painters and professors of Christ, Kierkegaard speaks of the artist's "unnatural intercourse with the holy." Yet, he remarks: "The artist admires himself, and all admire the artist. The religious point of view was entirely superseded; the beholder contemplated the picture in the role of a connoisseur—to determine whether it is a success, whether it is a masterpiece, whether the play of colours is just, and the shadows right, whether blood looks like that, whether the expression of suffering is artistically true—but he found no incentive to become a follower" (TC, 248). When he tries to describe Christ, he humiliates his "poem" by having it called "plagiarism" and by prostrating it before the Miracle itself (PF, 45). Only at the end will he abandon this relation between the hero and the poet as his major subject, and even then it stands in the wings, because "the most difficult of tasks is this: from 'poet' to Christian; for the poet clings fast to this world even though he suffers in it. A poet can endure much in this respect. The one thing he cannot do is to let go of the world as Christianity requires. The poet can become more and more unhappy but nevertheless through imagination continue to relate himself to the world—real renunciation he never achieves" (J/P, I, 63; n. 168 [1849]).

Because he cannot utterly renounce the world in his mind, he must interiorize the hero in his literature, but his own life must be told between the hero and the poet. Of his rendering of the story of Abraham's sacrifice he writes: "In calling attention to the difference between the poet and the hero a truth has already been said. There is a predominating poetic strain in me, and yet the real hoax was that *Fear and Trembling* actually reproduced my own life" (J/P, VI, 221; n. 6491 [1849]). The pathos is that the real life of Kierkegaard cannot stand without the literature that makes it into a story, while Abraham's could very well stand alone. Kierkegaard hides his passionate anxiety in the unavailable immediacy of Abraham's faith. The most moving and penetrating of all his discussions on this relationship is a *Journal* entry of 1849. Here he forthrightly calls his *kenosis* a humiliation, for as an author he "may not venture . . . to express in actuality that which I present and according to the criteria I set forth, as if I myself were the ideal" (*J/P*, VI, 148; n. 6391 [1849]). He terms the reconciliation of the authorship and the lived ideal a "superhuman task which perhaps never will be worked out." He admits that normally "the hero comes first, or the ethical character, and then the poet—I wanted to be both; at the same time as I need the 'poet's' tranquility and remoteness from life—and the thinker's composure, at the same time I wanted to be, right in the middle of actuality, that which I wrote and thought. Self-tormenting as I have always been, in my depression and very likely, too, with an admixture of pride, I devised this task to plague me" (*J/P*, VI, 148; n. 6391 [1849]). God's help gave him a compensatory task—to use this tension to depict in the body of art the difficulty of becoming Christian out of that body. "I became the unhappy lover with respect to becoming personally the ideal Christian, and therefore I became its poet. I will never forget this humiliation and to that extent will be unlike the usual orator who wantonly confuses talking about something with being it" (*J/P*, VI, 148; n. 6391 [1849]).

A telling comment in relation to the final years is this proof that he did not confuse his life with his authorship. Speaking of *Either / Or II* and *Stages on Life's Way*, he reminds us, "I did not get married, but I became the most enthusiastic champion of marriage." His passionately desired role as witness to the truth, a role he vehemently denied to Mynster, is denied to him as well, and he must take the consolation of confessing "that in the strictest sense I am not a witness to the truth." It is the pain of this confession that is "precisely the condition for the poet's and the philosopher's creativity" (*J/P*, VI, 149; n. 6391). The sigh of the Christian poet for this loss, like that of the poet remembering his "own unhappy love," is heard in his work. Even the persecution—called out, we suspect, partly by Kierkegaard himself to effect the transition from poet to martyr and witness—cannot absolutely transform this sigh to pure anger, justified and triumphant, nor to its counterpart, silence.

The relationship of Kierkegaard's voice to that of his pseudonyms is another facet of this obsessive subject. It has been the most controversial aesthetic device in Kierkegaard's repertoire, though he has amply justi-

fied its use for maieutic purposes.[30] Putting aside the problem of Kierkegaard's talents for fiction, the reader might well suspect the meager
embodiment of his figures as a symptom of his fear of loving the world's
body. It might also reflect a fear of that world's judgment, for Kierkegaard might lose control of his game, the protection of his guilts and
passions, to full-bodied characters. In a jesting letter to Regine, Kierkegaard encloses a hasty stick-drawing of himself looking through a
spyglass on the Knippelsbro, and he comments: "Several art experts have
disagreed as to why the painter has not provided any background what-
soever. Some have thought this an allusion to a folk tale about a man who
so completely lost himself in the enjoyment of the view from Knippelsbro that at last he saw nothing but the picture produced by his own
soul, which he could just as well have been looking at in a dark room.
Others have thought that it was because he lacked the perspective necessary for drawing—houses."[31] And he lacked the faith that sees as possible the marriage of author with character, with Regine, the reader.
This self-irony might not tame the skepticism of the reader, but there is
no question that its anticipation on Kierkegaard's part led him to work
out carefully the ethical justification of his pseudonyms. Most often the
pseudonyms have much of the humorous experimenter about them, a
role that keeps the systems at bay and the written word itself vulnerable.
If humor is the incognito of the religious man (*CUP*, 447), then the
pseudonyms themselves are in large part its agent. They are expert
observers of the incommensurable relations between the relative and the
absolute, between poets and heroes, between Christianity and Christendom. They are adept at distinguishing extraordinary individuals and
measuring their own limitations against them. The pseudonyms are not
moral enthusiasts whose direct assaults on misguided ethical standards
are, to their hearers, boring and indifferent. Instead, they jest while
serving as exchange centers for transactions between the relative and the
absolute. Except for Anti-Climacus—and even he is not immune from
irony—they are themselves short of a God-relationship.

In a sense, the pseudonym is the presence assuring humility in the

30. The best defense of the pseudonyms is by Josiah Thompson, "The Master of
Irony," in Thompson (ed.), *Kierkegaard*, 103–63; see esp. 109–11 and 160–61.
31. Kierkegaard, *Letters*, 63.

passage from private to public service. He must check his author's voice, but cannot compete with it. Kierkegaard himself cannot go directly to Abraham, but must pass through the medium of the observer. He worried about the reader's identification of the voice of the pseudonym with his own, chiefly because that act might lead one to identify the eager singling out of the extraordinary as self-promotion. In *The Point of View for My Work as an Author*, he carefully distinguishes between the association of the pseudonym with the extraordinary, and the association of his voice in the *Edifying Discourses* with the individual as everyman, noting the complementary relationship between them (*ED*, 124). The experience of incommensurability between poetry and being is the major check on Kierkegaard's voice in the pseudonymous works, and Kierkegaard himself inhabits this space of humor. He is not justified in relation to true faith, but "is justified against everything that courts recognition" as faith (*CUP*, 465). Thus the pseudonyms help to "illuminate faith negatively" (*J/P*, I, 7; n. 10 [1850]). They must, then, have a negative body, accentuate his posture, "a point, a stance, a position" (*J/P*, VI, 167; n. 6421 [1849]). From this perspective, wonder is a major weapon against sophistic knowledge. Johannes de Silentio explains that he cannot make the leap of faith, but he can make the leap from the springboard, "the great leap whereby I pass into infinity, my back is like that of a tight-rope dancer, having been twisted in childhood, hence I find this easy" (*F/T*, 47). As distinguished from Abraham, he cannot "perform the miraculous, but can only be astonished by it." Kierkegaard comes to see the pseudonyms mainly in their maieutic function, and the maieutic, by nature, can have neither too much body nor any disciples, for it must stimulate "a phase of poetic-emptying" (*J/P*, VI, 338; n. 6654 [1850]) in the education of both the author and the reader.

   If the voice of Kierkegaard is studiously regulated by positions of humor, it is like the voice of John the Baptist announcing the embodiment to come, but not itself filling it. The suspension of the voice from bodily hosts is an aesthetic weakness turned into a powerful and poignant preparation for the movements of faith. Throughout the work, restriction and withholding are strenuously exercised to make straight the way of the Lord, to open a path through the literature to Christ's body. Because the metaphors, figures, pseudonyms, fulfill only half the desired function of the artistic agent, that of luring and obstructing, but not fulfilling, aesthetic humiliation is ethical humility. "Everything you communicate which is existentially higher than your own existence you dare communicate only in such a way that you use it to your humiliation, in such a way that no meritorious light falls on your saying it" (*J/P*, III, 712; n. 3694 [1851]). This humility comes as much out of the position of Anti-Climacus, who is higher than Kierkegaard (though he is not free of demonic self-idealization), as out of that of Johannes Climacus, who is lower (*J/P*, VI, 147; n. 6433 [1849]).[32] The pseudonyms testify, too, to Kierkegaard's lack of complete ethical integrity. In a passage remarkable for its psychological diagnosis of depression as the sense of a split and haunted self, Kierkegaard notes:

> For many years my depression has prevented me from saying *"Du"* to myself in the profoundest sense. Between my *"Du"* and my depression lay a whole world of imagination. This is what I partially discharged in the pseudonyms. Just as a person who does not have a happy home goes out as much as possible and would rather not be encumbered with it, so my depression has kept me outside myself while I have been discovering and poetically experiencing a whole world of imagination. Just as a person who has inherited a great estate is never able to become fully acquainted with it, so I in my depression have been related to possibility. (*J/P*, V, 369; n. 5980 [1847])

We feel somewhat uncomfortable about his last period, not only because it is shrill and extreme, but because it appears to be Kierkegaard's attempt to move into his great estate, to express himself through a positive rather than a negative body, and the humility is in danger of being lost. We feel that in his wish of 1849: "It will help me if God will enable me to work more humanly so that I do not always need to make myself a third person, so that I personally can enter into things" (*J/P*, VI, 176; n. 6435). In fact, this is the work that seems least human.

To keep the authorship from internal incarnation, Kierkegaard places himself, in *Repetition* and in "Guilty?/Not Guilty?" of *Stages on Life's Way*, between an older man and a youth. He also assigns his capacity to arouse expectations, create pathos, to the experimenter, and his capacity for suffering to the younger man, imagined into life by the experimenter.

---

32. See Mackey, "The Poetry of Inwardness," in Thompson (ed.), *Kierkegaard*, 92.

This dialectical relationship keeps Kierkegaard's person from usurping the scene and instead allows his fractured voice "to point beyond [me] at the decisive moment: I am not that" (*J/P*, VI, 242; n. 6525 [1849]). I am not Christian, the voice says. The works are filled with figures who call attention, like the art at large, to the difficulty of the Christian position and who then indicate by their mere possibilities, "I am not that." Johannes de Silentio never tires of reminding us that he cannot get higher than his resignation. "I am unable to make the movements of faith, I cannot shut my eyes and plunge confidently into the absurd, for me that is an impossibility" (*F/T*, 44). The book is essentially about his efforts, from such a position, to project the difficulties of the life of faith, and is not about Abraham himself. The failures, the fallings, beg for grace outside the books, and force us beyond understanding, beyond literature, to the need for God.[33] The pseudonyms press us to the desire to get beyond their irony, and in this way they are Socratic teachers. But they are also *poetic* voices that indicate the difficulty and necessity of being an "*I*," so that, for all their distancing, they compel us to consciousness of the requirements of contemporaneity (*J/P*, I, 302; n. 656 [1847]). For all their lack of body, they are acknowledgments of the need for personality in an anonymous world.

To refuse disciples is not to sell out to objectivity. "The New Testament insists that the person who is to be a teacher in Christianity should be prevented in every way from being permitted to slip into objectivity, from withholding, hiding his personality" (*J/P*, III, 490; n. 3228 [1855]). The personality of the pseudonym, precisely like that of Kierkegaard, comes through the concentration on the relation to the absolute, through the struggle and slipping recorded in denials of capacity. However thin the pseudonyms may be, they certainly are not impersonal like the age. They are full of tone. Their names are the names of watchers, and they are poets and experimenters, but they project the personal

33. See Thompson, "The Master of Irony," in Thompson (ed.), *Kierkegaard*, 160–61. It is interesting to compare a secular version of the relation between posture and need with that of the pseudonyms. Hegel greatly admired the character of Lui in Diderot's *Rameau's Nephew*, who from hunger and necessity becomes a master of pantomimed positions whereby he can win his way into the society he hates but off which he must live. These positions are a reproach and a body block to the philosopher's "universals," as those of Kierkegaard's pseudonyms are to philosophy's speculation.

by calling attention to their restrictions.[34] Even when Constantius' young man in *Repetition* rebukes him with the words, "Is it not mental derangement to be so normal, to be a mere idea, not a human being, not like the rest of us, pliant and yielding, capable of being lost and of losing ourselves?" we are immediately reminded that this coldness has, precisely, called out the work of passion in the youth, and that the relation between the idea and its pathos is charged with the difficulty of coming into oneself. When Constantine Constantius speaks of his connection with the young man, he notes of him:

> He represents the transition to the more properly aristocratic exceptions, namely, the religious exceptions. The poet is generally an exception. People commonly rejoice over such a man and over his productions. I think therefore it might be worth while for once to bring such a figure into being. The young man whom I have brought into being is a poet. More than this I am unable to do; for at the utmost I can get as far as to imagine a poet and through my imagination produce him. I cannot become a poet myself, and moreover my interests lie elsewhere. (*Rep*, 134)

Now he confesses: "I have had a purely aesthetic and psychological interest in this task. I have brought my own person into the theme; but if thou, my dear reader, wilt look more closely, thou wilt easily see that I am only a serviceable spirit and am far from being indifferent to the young man, as he fears. This was a misunderstanding to which I gave occasion in order by this means to bring him out." By calling attention to its aesthetic sphere, the literature can then offer not just demonic temptation but lyrical transition through a maieutic transference. "Even where all ends in melancholy, there is a hint about him, about his condition. For this reason all movements take place lyrically, and what I say about myself one is to understand obscurely of him, or by what I say one is to understand him better" (*Rep*, 134–35). He offers to the reader a similar service as a different person, for each need is accommodated. The maieutic watchers in Kierkegaard are not impersonal, for their presence

---

34. Mackey, *Kierkegaard: A Kind of Poet*, 249: "The direct writings provide the ultimate *what* and the ultimate *why* of the pseudonymous books, while these latter supply the *how*."

is felt through the transition from their objectivity to the subjectivity they serve. In the meantime, of course, they are also subjects as they measure themselves against the ideal. They keep the movements of subjectivity in the realm of possibility to raise the need for faith. The pseudonym, drawing out the personal in the reader by direct address, is master of the transitions of mood that, demonically, could be exploited as aesthetically interesting or as seduction for a purpose other than the subject's freedom. But he is also a *lyrical* catalyst of subjectivity, which is why "all of the pseudonyms have an unqualified linguistic value in having cultivated prose lyrically" (*J/P*, V, 345; n. 5939 [1846]). So Father Taciturnus is able to give to Quidam a passionate style he himself cannot use, a style that he is able to

> construct rhetorically upon a conditional clause and then have the main clause amount to nothing, an abyss from which the reader as it were once again shrinks back to the antecedents; to plunge into a tentative effort as if this wealth were inexhaustible and then the very same second discontinue it, which is like the trick of pulling up short at full gallop (most riders fall off—usually one first breaks into a gallop and then into a trot); to be at the head of a cavalry of predicates, the one more gallant and dashing than the other, to charge in, and then swerve, the leap in modulation; the turning to the concept in one single word; the unexpected stop, etc. (*J/P*, V, 345; n. 5939 [1846])

In an early *Journal* entry Kierkegaard, speaking of Schleiermacher's "Vertraute Briefe über die *Lucinde*," a commentary on Schlegel's novel, calls it a model and productive review "in that the author constructs a host of personalities out of the book itself and through them illuminates the work and also illuminates their individuality" (*J/P*, IV, 13; n. 3846 [1835]). The reader's judgment is free to develop because it is not mastered by any one point of view. Although Kierkegaard is not, like Schleiermacher, an admirer of *Lucinde*, it is not surprising that he is stirred by this indirect method of criticism that moves the reader to liberate himself from the book by participating in it. Schleiermacher's discussion deals, in several instances, with the way in which poetry moves infinity in us, prompts the readers to an original poem, as it were, fashioned out of their own love. Kierkegaard would always be wary of an easy aesthetic usurpation of spiritual tasks, of the possibility that the book itself might be taken for actuality and be lyrically admired. But the way in which the form of the letters seems to discourage this usurpation was something he would always remember and from which he would profit. The pseudonyms serve this purpose, too: they become themselves the letters of various viewpoints, which see further than they can be. Like Don Quixote, like their own author, they are vessels of possibility. "To be victorious does not mean that *I* am victorious, but that the idea is victorious through me, even though I am sacrificed" (*J/P*, V, 314; n. 5885 [1846]).

Johannes Climacus reminds the reader that, though he is by no means a Christian he has, by not going further than the idea, served it. "It is always something to have called attention to the difficulty, even if this is done, as here, only in the edifying *divertissement*, brought forward essentially with the aid of a spy whom I send out among men on week days, and with the additional assistance of a few dilettantes who are made to play a role against their wills" (*CUP*, 417). The pseudonyms people his world with orators and speculators who either advance beyond Christianity or abolish it. Their "positive" example gives negative body to him whose irony serves faith. And they keep Kierkegaard, for the major part of his authorship, in the right position. "The whole matter of publishing with or without my name perhaps would have been a bagatelle. But to me in my ideality it is a very taxing problem so that above all I do not falsely hold myself back or falsely go too far but in truth understand myself and continue to be myself" (*J/P*, IV, 164; n. 6416 [1849]).

In 1849 Kierkegaard records in his *Journal* the story of his fierce debate with himself about the indirect authorship, his role, his finances, his worry about publishing *Training in Christianity* and *Sickness Unto Death*, and he decides, at least, to use Anti-Climacus as a wedge between himself and ideality. "The difference from the earlier pseudonyms is simply but essentially this, that I do not retract the whole thing humorously but identify myself as one who is striving" (*J/P*, VI, 181; n. 6446 [1849]). He is straining to come out of literature, so long holding him back by its humor. The emphasis now is that the great debates over mode of communication are to be seen as an education—an education that teaches him that he cannot ever, by himself, finally judge whether his forms guarantee his humility. He is ready to hand them over to grace, which has no need of retraction to prove good faith. A dialectical relation to the idea, a tormenting tease for himself and the reader, has had the great service of frustration, which if accepted, is some check on self-righteousness and a testimony to a better author, Providence.

> If I had been only a poet, I may well have ended up in the nonsense of merely poetizing Christianity without perceiving that it cannot be done, that one has to take himself along and either existentially express the ideal himself (which cannot be done) or define himself as one who is striving. Had I not been a poet I may well have gone ahead and confused myself with the ideal and have become a zealot. What, then, has helped me in addition to what is of greatest importance, that a Governance has helped me? The fact that I am a dialectician. (*J/P*, VI, 282; n. 6577 [1850])

His body, twisted by dialectics, will continue to affirm the ideals, though always poetically, to some extent, even as it struggles to be free from the literature (*J/P*, VI, 403; n. 6753 [1851]). The tension between judgment and grace is starkly present in the religious poet's late rendering of Christianity's prose, even more because some of the particularities of life that Johannes Climacus brought together with the absolute (*CUP*, 431) are hardened to allegory, pathos to anger. But what more than ever attracts the pain of the trapped poet is the envied affirmation—"What He said, He was"—heard again and again: "No, Christianity takes the absolute requirement seriously, and though it may be that not a single person has been able to fulfil the requirement—yet One has fulfilled it, fulfilled it absolutely, He who uttered the saying, 'No man can serve two masters,' He who here, as in every situation, not only uttered the truth but was the truth. He who was the Word also in this sense, that what He said, He was" (*SE/JY*, 170).

One of Kierkegaard's favorite stories from the Old Testament is a chastisement of poetic distance by ethical contemporaneity. Nathan tells David the fable of the rich man and his herds, and the poor man and his one lamb. David, the poet, is charmed. "There was perhaps a particular trait which he thought might have been different, he perhaps proposed an expression more happily chosen, perhaps also pointed out a little fault in the plan, praised the prophet's masterly delivery of the story, his voice, the play of his features, expressed himself, in short, as we cultured people are accustomed to do when we criticize a sermon delivered before a cultured congregation, that is, a sermon which itself also is objective" (*SE/JY*, 63). Nathan then pulls David up and shocks him with the prose of the unconditional: "Thou art the man." Kierkegaard calls this sudden change from the proverbial to the indicative "a transition to the subjective," and it is this transition that the literature had worked for, had prepared. It was a patient formation, but it never hid the urgent envy of Christ's identity with his Word. Above anything in the world, Kierkegaard wanted this identity for himself, and for others: that what he said, he was. Since the *Corsair* persecution, he imagined it possible to consider that authorship, in fact, a deed (*J/P*, V, 314; n. 5887 [1846]). Now he wondered if the persecution could free his negative body from literature to transparency. Could the literature in which he found himself lose itself and release him to God?

A certain outliving [*Udlevethed*] is necessary in order really to feel the need for Christianity.
Journals and Papers

The more one thinks about it the stranger does the earthly life and the human language become.
Edifying Discourses

If an individual defrauds possibility by which he is to be educated, he never arrives at faith.
The Concept of Anxiety

5 · *Educated by Possibility*

 rich dialectical literature of possibilities was a sign that Kierkegaard still played with possibilities of life. There might be a real reconciliation with Regine; there might be a country parish; there might be a trusted intellectual friend. But when the first dream was exploded by the return of his letter to Regine's husband and the third by the misinterpretations of Rasmus Nielsen, and when the pastorship was not forthcoming, with money running out, the latencies that literature protected were used up, and the energy that kept them alive turned to direct attack. Indirect communication had been a continuing and sly courtship of Regine, his ideal reader—the world. Now, however, the literary deceits began to seem to him more uncomfortable and ambiguous in their relation to life, but always his aesthetic depiction of possibilities had been intimately related to the dreaded but urgent ethical and spiritual education by possibility that took place outside literature. Typically, Kierkegaard had taken the traditional philosophical categories of possibility and invested them with the passion and imagination of "terror, perdition, annihilation" (*CD*, 140), so that the aesthetic imagination would touch the ethical imagination, both pressed into the ser-

vice of actuality, the reality of full psychological and spiritual education.[1] The poet's seductive possibilities could be helpful servants of the
spirit because they quicken the infinite in us, but even the religious poet
is never free from the distortion of aesthetic priorities. "A religious poet
is a questionable figure in relation to the paradoxically religious, because
from the aesthetic point of view, possibility is higher than actuality and
the poetical consists precisely in the ideality of imaginative intuition"
(*CUP*, 514).

To signal the necessary education in dread, in the anxiety of freedom,
of choice, the ethical possibility is unprotected by aesthetic conventions.
For the sake of this emphasis, Kierkegaard turned from the Hegelian
identification of necessity as the unity of possibility and actuality to the
identification of actuality as the unity of possibility and necessity. When
the soul goes astray in sheer possibility, without submitting to the
psychological and ethical "necessary in oneself" (*SD*, 169), it goes astray
in fantasy and despair, volatilizing the potential self into a bad infinite
(*SD*, 164). For God only are all things possible, and that is why the
human education by possibility needs faith (*SD*, 171). If the learner
"cheats the possibility by which he is to be educated" by ignoring
necessity, he "never reaches faith" (*SD*, 141). The aesthetic hierarchies
are quite reversed by the presence of the Paradox, which consistently
"nullifies a possibility . . . as an illusion and turns it into actuality" by
making itself unavailable to understanding (*CUP*, 515). Where there is
no absurdity, there is no faith, no actuality, for the limits of understanding keep false knowledge and order in their aesthetic and speculative
confines.

By its constant attention to barriers and limits, the authorship stimulated the hunger of need. Like Luther, Kierkegaard understood from his
own life the pathos of need as a great mover to faith. While Luther insists
that the anguished conscience is the necessary hunger for God, Kierkegaard writes, "The need brings with it the nutriment, not *by itself*, as
though it produced the nutriment, but by virtue of God's ordinance

1. For interesting comments on this theme and on the relationship between the
thought of Kierkegaard, Freud, and Rank, see Ernest Becker, *The Denial of Death* (New
York, 1973). On p. 196 Becker links Kierkegaard's notions of sin with Rank's of
neurosis.

which joins together the need and the nutriment" (*CrD*, 249). Commenting on a common theological patronization, voiced by Jacobi, of Enlightenment morality—that ideas of the "good, the beautiful, the true" are merely responses to need—Kierkegaard claims that the need born of despair is the basis of faith (*J/P*, II, 8; n. 1113 [1844]). By anticipation, he criticizes Freud's notion that an education into reality allows the individual to live without the need for God.[2] But he moves toward the modern world, in some ways helps to create it, by disturbing the psychologically cold Socratic equation: self-knowledge is the knowledge of God, with qualifications inherent in the notion of need as the beginning of self-knowledge itself. No one more than Kierkegaard admired Socrates' moral passion—the classical fervor to distinguish between opinions, beliefs, and truth, a concern for discrimination lost to the modern world.[3] And he fully honored Socrates' courage to teach with his life, but he did complain that "Socrates does not make room for the will, or room within which the will can stir and move" (*J/P*, III, 466;

2. See Paul Ricoeur's answer to Freud's patronization of faith, in *Freud and Philosophy*, trans. Denis Savage (New Haven, 1970), 536: "Freud seems to me to exclude without reason, I mean without any psychoanalytic reason, the possibility that faith is a participation in the source of Eros and thus concerns, not the consolation of the child in us, but the power of loving; he excludes the possibility that faith aims at making this power adult in the face of the hatred within us and outside of us—in the face of death." And this statement of Ricoeur certainly has interesting resonances when placed beside Kierkegaard's pattern of accelerating repetition:

> For Freud, religion is the monotonous repetition of its own origin. It is a sempiternal treading of the grounds of its own archaism. The theme of the "return of the repressed" means nothing else: the Christian Eucharist repeats the totem meal, as the death of Christ repeats that of the prophet Moses which repeats the original killing of the father. Freud's exclusive attention to repetition becomes a refusal to consider a possible epigenesis of religious feeling, that is to say, a transformation or conversion of desire and fear. This refusal does not seem to me to be based upon analysis, but merely expresses Freud's personal unbelief. (534)

See also F. J. Hacker's comment on Kierkegaard's courage, "Freud, Marx, and Kierkegaard," in Benjamin Nelson (ed.), *Freud and the Twentieth Century* (New York, 1957), 138: "So for Kierkegaard anxiety was not just an inevitable state to be suffered. To be and to remain afraid became a command . . . an imperative: You *should* have anxiety . . . The atheist Freud was still protected from the last dizziness by his attenuated faith in Science. The Christian Kierkegaard was without such comfort."

3. See Gould, *The Development of Plato's Ethics*, 60. He compares Kierkegaard and Socrates on the importance of ignorance, for "to be mistaken in matters of moral import is the worst evil."

n. 3194 [1849]).[4] For Socrates, only ignorance can cure ignorance, but since we recollect eternity instead of repeating ourselves into it, distortions of man's spirit are not regulated by the Christian categories of sin and grace. For Kierkegaard, faith is born not of doubt but of the despair that is "the last psychological state out of which sin breaks forth with the qualitative leap" (*CD*, 83). He speaks often of that "most terrible kind of spiritual trial [*Anfaegtelse*]—before the point is reached where the same man is disciplined in faith, that is, to regard everything inversely, to remain full of hope and confidence when something happens which previously almost made him faint and expire with anxiety, to plunge fearlessly into something against which he previously knew only one means of safety, to flee, and so on" (*J/P*, II, 121; n. 1401 [1850]).

Self-knowledge is not really the knowledge of God, then, for that assumes an immanent recollection of the divine; rather, it is the consciousness of the *need* for God. The Paradox is met only when one can do nothing by himself, before God, after a life and literature of necessary striving. The giving of the self to God is a common Christian pattern, but in Kierkegaard it is a particularly moving one. Courageously he renders the movement as one that must be undergone again and again: "It is not done once and for all, for this is aesthetic" (*CUP*, 412). And we are stirred by the surrender because Kierkegaard ordered his life, his authorship, by such a fierce will. "For only a man of will has a will that can be broken. But a man of will whose will is broken by the unconditioned or by God is a Christian. The stronger the natural will, the deeper the break can be and the better the Christian" (*J/P*, VI, 569; n. 6966 [1855]). Self-knowledge is full only with the act of self-annihilation before God. That withdrawals are so easily practiced by the artist made Kierkegaard harsh from the beginning on the parodies of self-renunciation in Romantic irony. "The ironist constantly preserves his poetic freedom, and when he notices that he is becoming nothing, he includes even this in his poetizing" (*CI*, 298). Closer to his ideal movement is that of Socrates, who knew how, in his learned ignorance, to sink down into his own nothingness for the sake of exposing illusions (*ED*, 150), of maieutically freeing his listeners from his body. But John the

---

4. Ironically, Feuerbach would agree with this, only to use it as a justification for eliminating the notion of an autonomous God.

Baptist knew himself perfectly, for he knew he must decrease as Christ
increased: "He was the greatest at the moment of his decline" (*ED*, III,
134).

The linking of need, self-knowledge, and self-annihilation is one of
the most passionate and dramatic clusters in all of Kierkegaard's work,
for it is played out on the perilous border between literature and its
annihilation before God. To "come to oneself in self-knowledge, and
before God as *nothing*" (*SE/JY*, 122) is one of those hard-earned and
constantly qualified beliefs, cumulatively and successively gained
through jab after jab. The paradox before the Paradox is this: that the self
is more when it is closer to God and at that moment, it is dwarfed by
God's majesty. "The child who hitherto has had only the parents to
measure himself by, becomes a self when he is a man by getting the state
as a measure. But what an infinite accent falls upon the self by getting
God as a measure!" (*SD*, 210). One of the most affecting discussions of
this relationship is the edifying discourse, "Man's Need of God Constitutes his Highest Perfection." Kierkegaard gives to the language of
spiritual need an independent existence, as if it were a character, and
indeed it is. "It is because of man's impatience that the language speaks
of trying to rest content with the grace of God" (*ED*, 144). This is not
the common tongue, for "when a human being has fully awakened to its
import it calls him aside to a place where he no longer hears the earthly
mother-tongue of the worldly mind, nor the customary speech of men"
(*ED*, 145).

It is the language of transvaluation again, of inversion—the transferred language that allows the self this side of the consciousness of sin to
seem large, and on that side, small, as nothing. The self, annihilated
before God in its need, is the self at its highest perfection.

> So then it happens, little by little, for the grace of God can never be
> seized by force, that the human heart becomes in a very beautiful
> sense more and more discontented, more and more burning with
> desire, more and more filled with longing, for the assurance of the
> grace of God. And behold, now all things have become new, every-
> thing is changed. In the case of the earthly goods of life the principle
> obtains that man needs but little, and in proportion as he needs less
> and less he becomes more and more perfect. A pagan who knew only

how to speak of earthly things has said that God was happy because he needed nothing at all, and next to Him in happiness was the wise man, because he needed little. But in the relation between a human being and God this principle is reversed: the more a man needs God the more perfect he is. (*ED*, 145)

It is God now who is seen to educate through possibility, over the poet's raising of possibilities, for the poet, anxious and guilty about being a teacher, becomes a learner. "It is God Himself who best knows how to utilize a man's own anxieties for the purpose of extirpating all his self-confidence; and when he is about to sink down into his own nothingness, it is again God Himself who can best keep him from continuing to maintain a diver's underwater connection with his earthly self" (*ED*, 148).

The pseudonyms call attention to their limitations in order to create a higher need; they decrease so the divine can increase, and know very well how to demonstrate anxiety and despair. Kierkegaard knows how to frustrate the reader's expectations, like Socrates, to create a higher hunger. But God is the hardest of all authors before he is the kindest. "What is offered to us as a consolation, begins by making life more difficult, in order, finally, aye finally in truth, to make it easier" (*ED*, 149). Kierkegaard's literature can never give grace, can never, finally, make life easier, for it is meaningless to say that man needs it or that he must annihilate himself before it. But that it imitates difficulty by deliberately setting between itself and its readers "the awakening of misunderstanding" (*J/P*, I, 310; n. 662 [1848]) reveals and raises a need that is *its* highest perfection. Kierkegaard does not want to say that man's highest perfection is his knowledge of God. The word *need* is the dramatic and poignant longing that collides with the word *perfection*, as literature's analogies and possibilities collide with the actuality of faith. The literature itself is in need, and so it is bound to perfection in oxymoronic richness.

Without the density of anxiety and despair, the torment of guilt, and the envy of immediate faith, without the thick possibilities of double-mindedness and demonic descents, without this body of the will's distortions, a transparent self-knowledge cannot be reached, even sporadically. In any case, it cannot stay fast in this life. I think it worthwhile to see the whole literature of Kierkegaard as a demonstration of the body retarded, held back from fulfillment, while it goads its hunger for grace, for surrender. The busy churning of figure after figure, analogy after analogy, is a way of achieving an understanding that by itself, like the self, can do absolutely nothing. *Slet intet*, absolutely nothing, echoes as an emphatic refrain throughout the discourse. Yet a man writes this refrain in the lyrical hope that it might persuade the reader to need. It is only through this sensation of need, of helplessness, that the striving man "learns to know himself" (*ED*, 158). This is the most important justification for the literature. It works not for fulfillment and consolation but for need, and since need is absolutely identified in Kierkegaard with self-knowledge, the distant pairing can be spanned only by unlearning our expectation of closer pairings, by ignorance undoing worldly knowledge and preparing for the meeting of Paradox and incomprehension. Of this lesson he says: "It may seem that this is what a man must learn from a study of himself; why then praise self-knowledge? And yet it is so; and if the entire outer world conspired to teach him, he cannot learn from the world that he can do absolutely nothing" (*ED*, 167).

This recognition calls out God's forgiveness for the authorship that put the sickness to use, but to believe in that forgiveness, to hand over control, is the hardest of all Kierkegaard's tasks; for the mind must let go of its fictions, even those tormented ones, "to become spirit . . . the most agonizing of all the sufferings" (*J/P*, II, 506; n. 2222 [1852]).[5] The literature had always rolled backward in order to go forward, in an imitation of the journey from anxiety to repentance. The *Concluding Unscientific Postscript* and *The Point of View for My Work as an Author* call attention to their reviews of the perverse progress and purpose of the work. These are never free from the consciousness of the ways in which God constrains expression, for the acceptance of this constraint is the confession of need and the petition for grace. "An eternal symbol of the relation of the God-fearing to God (that this is education) is embodied in a characteristic of the language of God's chosen people: It must be read backward. To exist [*existere*] backward is actually the most rigorous

5. See Wahl, *Etudes kierkegaardiennes*, 399, *n*. 1, on Hirsch's interpretation: "L'extraordinaire est un élu sans révélation qui ait un contenu particulier. Tel fut Kierkegaard, un éducateur qui fait profiter les autres de sa providentielle éducation, sans qu'il ait une révélation propre à lui qu'il doive partager avec eux." (The extraordinary man is one elected, but without revelation, who has a particular content. Such was Kierkegaard, an educator who helps others to profit from his own providential education, though he has no personal revelation that he can share with them [author's translation].)

religiousness, the strongest expression for the way God constrains. He who is turned forward, boasting in exalted tones about what he will do in the future, etc.—he is by no means rigorously religious" (*J/P*, IV, 298; n. 4460 [1850]). The literature helps its author turn expression to obedience, teaching to learning. "Moses saw the back of God, not his face—that is, there is no agreement in advance, the religious man is only the unconditionally obedient instrument—and then afterward he sees how God has used him. To know that God is using one—this would be a dangerous thought for a man to have; this is why he does not get to know it until afterward" (*J/P*, IV, 299; n. 4460 [1850]). Like Moses, Kierkegaard cannot enter the Promised Land by the book, for it is not a fulfilled body, but a body in need. The acceptance of this necessity, which was instrumental in his education by possibility, is reflected in this qualification of ideal surrender: "No religious person, even the purest, has sheer, purified subjectivity or pure transparency in willing solely what God wills, so that there is no residue of his original subjectivity, a residue still not wholly penetrated, a remote portion of residue still uncaptured, perhaps as yet not even really discovered in the depths of his soul—out of this come the reactions" (*J/P*, IV, 272; n. 4384 [1854]). That is why man's perfection is only his need.

Read backward, from the view of God's eye, Kierkegaard becomes, in a movement dear to the mystics, known, as he knows himself; and it is this direction that is dominant at the end. "In paganism God was regarded as the unknown. More recently it has been assumed presumptuously that to know God is a trifle. Nevertheless, although God has revealed himself, he has taken some precautions, for one can know God only in proportion to one's being known, i.e., in proportion to one's acknowledging that he is known" (*J/P*, II, 100; n. 1351 [1847]). The spiritless who prosper are simply ignored by God; it is a punishment of which they are not even conscious. A God-forsaken world is a fantastic one, reveling in its spurious freedom (*J/P*, IV, 600; n. 5038 [1854]). But need, man's deepest self-knowledge, wants to be known and is the source of the real.

To be known by God is to recognize that one has been educated by his love—a love that is, in this life, suffering. Since divine love is "a love of the learner" (*PF*, 30), it is called "upbringing," a drawing up and a bringing up (*opdragelse*) by God. God has "only one pathos: to love, to be love, and out of love wanting to be loved" (*J/P*, III, 54; n. 2447 [1854]). Now the teacher through literature, the religious poet, passes the authorship to God. "I surrender it and myself to you in unconditional obedience; do with it what you will; in this way I am positive that even the most foolish action will eventually become good" (*J/P*, II, 107; n. 1372 [1848]). The authorship becomes the education as it suffers, a body caught between the world and the spirit. Kierkegaard would envy the Christ who teaches in the temple with such spirit and spontaneity that the Jews ask, "How knoweth this man letters?" (John 7:14–15). No one could ask that of Kierkegaard, filled as his literature is with the university wit he so hated, so these talents had to be undone by dialectical self-mockery. The higher educator annihilates his shrewdness and reminds him that the wordless martyr brings up not by his metaphors, but by his life, his pain, his patience, his obedience. When the teacher becomes a learner who "attends to himself . . . all instruction is transformed into a divine jest"—a jest reflected in Kierkegaard's maieutic irony—"because every human being is taught essentially only by God" (*CUP*, 92). Kierkegaard repeatedly divests himself of his extraordinary talent and in democratic Christianity professes: "I do not call myself a teacher, I am the person who is being brought up—but by God" (*J/P*, I, 310–11; n. 662 [1848]). As Socrates the teacher was the ignorant one, so too Kierkegaard would be a teacher only in the sense of one who is being educated. The edifying discourses are not called sermons, for Kierkegaard has no authority to preach; nor are they called discourses for edification, for he makes no claim to be a teacher (*TC*, 260).

The surrender to God, the self-annihilation before the Paradox— this is from the world's view a passive state and one particularly offensive to Hegel and Freud. But from the view of spirit, the realistic view to Kierkegaard, the offense of despair is passive ("it lacks the power to obey" [*SD*, 169]), and the shift from teaching to learning is active (*TC*, 80). The teacher is impotent; the believer is not. This is bound up with the view that freedom can be kept only if "in the very same second unconditionally and in full attachment [you] give it back to God and yourself along with it" (*J/P*, II, 69; n. 1261 [1850]). The granting of freedom in maieutic upbringing (Kierkegaard claims that Hegel is entirely unmaieutic, (*J/P*, II, 222; n. 1611 (1846)}) is acted out by Socrates, man to man, but only God by his omnipotent withdrawal can make a person completely independent (*J/P*, II, 62; n. 1251 [1846]). And what does upbringing into independence mean? It means to come to oneself, to become what one already is, to then be willing, like Socrates, to "perish . . . completely and wholly transformed into being simply an active power in the hands of God" (*WL*, 260). To have this power a person must expose himself fully to the suffering of existence, must plunge into seventy thousand fathoms of water, Kierkegaard's favorite measure of incommensurability. "As soon as a person acts decisively and enters into actuality, then existence can get hold of him and providence can bring him up" (*J/P*, II, 20; n. 1142 [1851], and I, 76; n. 188 [1850]).

No man can get hold of Socrates because he lets only God get hold of him. And Kierkegaard imitates his action. He makes himself a target in order not to be held by men, and "by the step of exposing myself to ridicule I proved at least that I had a conception of what it means to be a teacher" (*J/P*, III, 162; n. 2655 [1849]). The willingness to give and get pain in the name of spiritual freedom is the highest teaching one can do on earth. Socrates was the highest because "he loved [men] in the idea, after first being disciplined by the idea himself to be able to stand unconditionally alone, unconditionally to do without any other man" (*J/P*, I, 46; n. 109 [1851]). He must stand unconditionally alone in order to force each man to do the same, for only the individual can be brought up, not the race. In respect to existence, then, the teacher is a learner, "for anyone who fancies that he is in this respect finished, that he can teach others and on top of that himself forget to exist and to learn, is a fool" (*J/P*, I, 453; n. 1038 [1845]). Qualified by Christianity, Socratic ignorance is the sign of the learner. "Socratic ignorance, but, please note, modified in the spirit of Christianity—this is maturity, is intellectually what rebirth is ethically and religiously, is what it is to become a child again" (*J/P*, III, 637; n. 3567 [1849]). The bird and the lilies, Kierkegaard's most appealing teachers, can illustrate by their difference from man that to be ignorant is not the task of man. It is something more difficult—to *become* ignorant (*CrD*, 29). And the task of becoming ignorant is another way of saying that the writer is under orders to annihilate himself, is to have no authority. It is because this imperative always underlies Kierkegaard's expression that we are moved when

Johannes de Silentio proclaims: "I am as though annihilated trying to catch sight of the paradox of Abraham's life" (*F/T*, 44). How much more is he annihilated by the idea of the Paradox? Allowing God to rule is a most difficult task, one that is "learned in the school of suffering" (*GS*, 56–57). Again the birds and the lilies show us that to teach is to obey, but we must *learn* obedience. Obedience is the direct antithesis of seduction. It paradoxically frees the learner to become himself. Of course Kierkegaard will always envy the Jobs who teach solely with their bodies instead of their books, but his talent for giving offense allows his suffering body to teach that to teach is to learn. He imitates the motions of rebellion, like Socrates, by making his heterogeneity into a case in order to isolate the individual for God, but he must see this action as obedience.[6]

Always searching for justification for his melancholy reserve in its use for freeing others from discipled dependence, he is drawn to the case of Socrates, who transforms demonic reserve into a spiritual weapon; for his irony was "precisely the close reserve which [he] began by shutting himself off from men, by shutting himself in with himself in order to be expanded in the Deity, began by shutting his door against men and making jest of those who stood outside, in order to talk in secret" (*CD*, 120). No one was more aware of the demonic possibilities of teaching, of its temptation to seduction, false authority, and the lure of discipleship. Kierkegaard particularly admires in Socrates the transformation of these demonic stances. So he turns self-love into love of the neighbor by making his "self-love" a sign of renunciation (*WL*, 342–43). Again, this is an act that reassures Kierkegaard's own concern. And he is attracted to the Socrates who speaks of loving the ugly as a jest, not of loving the beautiful (to which one might be naturally inclined); for the ugly then stands for the neighbor whom one does not naturally love and reminds us of the imperative nature of the command, thou *shalt* love. These transformations leave the learner free of the teacher's person and make straight the way for God's upbringing love.

---

6. Cioran, *The Temptation to Exist*, 168, comments, "The fact remains that if his teaching leaves us indifferent, the argument he provoked about himself still affects us: he was the first thinker to make himself into a *case*, and it is with him that the inextricable problem of sincerity begins."

If the literature could chart these transformations, it would reveal the passion of the body behind the irony and lead him away, at least, from the professor who, a satire on the apostle, cannot "protect himself against illusions in communication" (*J/P*, III, 698; n. 3665 [1847]). In this sense Kierkegaard clearly wants to have the suffering of his authorship be his ethical act. To assure this, to bring his body closer to ethical act, he imagines that in his last journalistic polemics, "I did want to achieve an approximation of preaching in the streets" (*J/P*, VI, 563; n. 6957 [1855]), as Luther recommended.

Like the pseudonym, the human teacher is "a vanishing transition" (*CUP*, 508) giving way to the divine. He must never be regarded as an object of faith (*TC*, 142). Christ, of course, is the creative teacher, for his body gives a new being to the learner so that the "learner owes the Teacher everything. . . . the learner becomes as nothing and yet is not destroyed" (*PF*, 38). Christianity moves beyond the Socratic and brings with it a "new organ: Faith; a new presupposition: the consciousness of Sin; a new decision: the Moment; and a new Teacher: the God in time" (*PF*, 139). It is the recognition of this advance alone that gives Kierkegaard even the slightest right to present himself "for inspection before Socrates, that master of Irony" (*PF*, 139). The human teacher can begin the ethical task of self-knowledge, of striving to become what one already is (*CUP*, 116) and then letting Christ "help every man to become himself" by requiring of him "first and foremost that by entering into himself he should become himself, so as then to draw him into Himself" (*TC*, 160). In his greatest moments, Socrates, "with a heroism of soul which it requires courage even to appreciate" (*PF*, 127), prepared the individual to become contemporaneous with himself. In Kierkegaard's desire, he could thus become contemporaneous with Christ.[7]

Eternity is altogether in the present tense: Plato reminds us that "being is nothing other than participating in an essence in time present" (*J/P*, III, 526; n. 3324 [1842–43]). So that which is farthest from it

7. See Gould, *The Development of Plato's Ethics*, 66–67, who in several places draws parallels between Socrates and Kierkegaard: "I have tried hitherto to show that the fundamental factor in Socratic thinking was not, as some commentators have felt, intellectual, but a quality of faith." And see Popkin, "Kierkegaard and Scepticism," in Thompson (ed.), *Kierkegaard*, 345–46, 361.

must be dominated by the past and the future; and indeed the determination of anxiety and despair in Kierkegaard's view, as in psychoanalytic theory, is an inability to exist in the present, equivalent to the
aesthetic parody of living *for* the present. "All men desire to be or to
become *contemporary* with great men, great events, etc.—but only God
knows how many men really live contemporaneously with themselves.
To be contemporary with oneself (therefore neither in the future of fear or
expectation nor in the past) is transparency in repose, and this is possible
only in the God-relationship, or it is the God-relationship" (*J/P*, I,
456–57; n. 1050 [1847]). Most men, remarks Kierkegaard, are ahead
of themselves, and we see in all his literature demonic speculators striving to go further than faith, but the believer, who is present, "is in the
highest sense contemporary with himself"; he is "matured for eternity"
(*J/P*, VI, 575; n. 6969 [1855]). The lilies and the birds are joyful
because they exist in the present tense, and "teachers that exist, *are
today*, and are joy" (*CrD*, 351). Could Kierkegaard, as a poet, as a
teacher—exist "today," rendering the roles superfluous? He knew literature could not be produced out of the present tense alone. That is why his
body, imprisoned in his literature, so much longed for the body out of
literature. Christ himself is "an eternally present one" (*J/P*, I, 134;
n. 318 [1848]), a contemporaneity renewed in each heart of each generation that in no way denies the actual historical coming into the world.
One needs the poetry of the possible to be able to begin to experience a
reality that is raised over actual history. "The past is not reality—for me:
only the contemporary is reality for me. What thou dost live contemporaneous with is reality—for thee. And thus every man can be contemporary only with the age in which he lives—and then with one thing more:
with Christ's life on earth; for Christ's life on earth, sacred history, stands
for itself alone outside History" (*TC*, 68).[8]

Since Christ "does not answer *directly*" but "requires faith" to be heard
(*TC*, 96), then the religious poet, to preserve contemporaneity as an
individual act, must set up his barrier for belief, the offense of his irony.
He asks:

8. See Vernard Eller, *Kierkegaard and Radical Discipleship*, 333. Eller notes that
Kierkegaard reverses the Church's emphasis on Christ's descent to us in order to stress,
in our struggle for contemporaneity, our ascent to him.

What then can a contemporary do for a successor? (a) He can inform him that he has himself believed this fact, which is not in the strict sense a communication (as expressed in the absence of any immediate contemporaneity, and in the circumstance that the fact is based upon a contradiction), but merely affords an occasion. For when I say that this or that has happened, I make an historical communication; but when I say: "I believe and have believed that so-and-so has taken place, *although it is a folly to the understanding and an offense to the human heart*," then I have simultaneously done everything in my power to prevent anyone else from determining his own attitude in immediate continuity with mine, asking to be excused from all companionship, since every individual is compelled to make up his own mind in precisely the same manner. (*PF*, 128)

Christ's instruction depends upon his presence; the religious teacher, the poet, is only an occasion. And Christ is equally present in every generation, since truth is not cumulative knowledge, but the way (*TC*, 204). His life and words humble the poet and the teacher, but the philosopher scorns his being. "Never before has there been such an example of pure subjectivity and sheer negation carried to the utmost excess. He has no doctrine, no system, no fundamental knowledge; it is merely by detached aphoristic utterances, some bits of sententious wisdom, constantly repeated with variations, that He succeeds in dazzling the masses, for whom also He performs signs and wonders, so that they, instead of learning something and receiving instruction, come to believe in Him" (*TC*, 51).

The great and anxious purpose of Kierkegaard's literature is to bring words up to the body of Christ. The literature opens to the divine embrace and dies into belief. In contrasting the personal nature of his authorship with the impersonal one of the press, Kierkegaard comments that "the impersonal, which for the most part is irresponsible and incapable of repentance, is essentially demoralizing" and that anonymity is "the most absolute expression for the impersonal, the irresponsible, the unrepentant" (*PVA*, 44). How can we not feel the beauty, for Kierkegaard, of giving himself away in the act of repentance, of redoubling, as the life complements the literature despite all the tensions between them? And can we not imagine him at the end—the Christian learner, conscious of all his guilts of reserve and expression, doubled back, even at the new birth, looking backward in grief, as he understood backward, as he was read backward, a movement reflected in the word *repentance*.

> "For what is repentance but a kind of leave-taking, looking backward indeed, but yet in such a way as precisely to quicken the steps toward that which lies before?" (*PF*, 23).

BIBLIOGRAPHY

Abrams, M. H. *Natural Supernaturalism: Tradition and Revolution in Romantic Literature.* New York, 1971.

Adorno, Theodor. *Kierkegaard: Konstruktion des Aesthetischen.* Frankfurt, 1966.

Agacinski, Sylviane. *Aparté: conceptions et morts de Søren Kierkegaard.* Paris, 1977.

Bainton, Roland H. *Here I Stand: A Life of Martin Luther.* New York, 1950.

Barth, Karl. *Protestant Thought: Rousseau to Ritschl.* New York, 1959.

Battenhouse, Roy W. "*Measure for Measure* and the Christan Doctrine of Atonement." *PMLA*, LXI (December, 1946), 1032–50.

Becker, Ernest. *The Denial of Death.* New York, 1973.

Benjamin, Walter. "Goethes Wahlverwandtschaften." in *Schriften*, edited by Theodor W. Adorno and Gretel Adorno. Vol. I of 2 vols. Frankfurt, 1955.

————. *Illuminations.* Translated by Harry Zohn. Edited by Hannah Arendt. New York, 1969.

Bespaloff, Rachel. "En marge de 'Crainte et tremblement' de Kierkegaard." *Revue philosophique de la France et de l'Etranger*, CXVII (1934), 335–63; CXIX (1935), 43–72.

Billeter, Fritz. *Das Dichterische bei Kafka und Kierkegaard.* Winterthur, Switzerland, 1965.

Blanchot, Maurice. "Le journal de Kierkegaard." In Blanchot, *Faux pas.* Paris, 1943.

Bloom, Harold. *The Anxiety of Influence: A Theory of Poetry.* New York, 1973.

Bohlin, Torsten. *Kierkegaards dogmatische Anschauung.* Translated by Ilse Meyer-Lune. Gütersloh, West Germany, 1927.

Bonhoeffer, Dietrich. *Prisoner for God: Letters and Papers from Prison.* Translated by Reginald H. Fuller. Edited by Eberhard Bethge. New York, 1960.

Buber, Martin. *Between Man and Man.* Translated by Ronald Gregor Smith. Boston, 1955.

Burke, Kenneth. *The Rhetoric of Religion.* Boston, 1961.

Burke, Kenneth and Stanley Romaine Hopper. "Mysticism as a Solution to the Poet's Dilemma." In *Spiritual Problems in Contemporary Literature*, edited by Stanley Romaine Hopper. New York, 1957.

Butler, E. M. *The Tyranny of Greece over Germany.* Cambridge, England, 1935.

Christensen, Arild. "Romantismens og Søren Kierkegaard Opfattelse af Lidelse." *Kierkegaardiana*, I (1955), 16–41.

————. "Efterskriften Opgør med Martensen." *Kierkegaardiana*, IV (1962), 45–62.

Cioran, E. M. *The Temptation to Exist*. Translated by Richard Howard. New York, 1956.

Clive, Geoffrey. "The Teleological Suspension of the Ethical in Nineteenth-Century Literature." *Journal of Religion*, XXXIV (1954).

Cochrane, Charles N. *Christianity and Classical Culture*. Oxford, England, 1940.

Cole, Dennis. *The Problematic Self in Kierkegaard and Freud*. New Haven, 1971.

Colish, Marcia L. *The Mirror of Language: A Study in the Medieval Theory of Knowledge*. New Haven, 1968.

Collins, James. *The Mind of Kierkegaard*. Chicago, 1953.

Cook, E. J. Raymond. "Kierkegaard's Literary Art." *Listener*, LXXII (November, 1964, 713–14.

Coulson, John. *Religion and Imagination: In Aid of a Grammar of Assent*. Oxford, England, 1981.

Crites, Stephen. *In the Twilight of Christendom: Hegel vs. Kierkegaard on Faith and History*. Chambersburg, Pa., 1972.

Croxall, T. H. *Kierkegaard Studies*. London, 1948.

De Man, Paul. *Allegories of Reading: Figural Language in Rousseau, Nietzsche, Rilke, and Proust*. New Haven, 1979.

————. "The Rhetoric of Temporality." In *Interpretation: Theory and Practice*, edited by Charles S. Singleton. Baltimore, 1969.

de Rougemont, Denis. *Love in the Western World*. Garden City, N.Y., 1957.

————. "Religion and the Mission of the Artist." In *Spiritual Problems in Contemporary Literature*, edited by Stanley Romaine Hopper. New York, 1957.

Derrida, Jacques. *Of Grammatology*. Translated by Gayatri Chakravorty Spivak. Baltimore, 1977.

————. "Plato's Pharmacy." In *Dissémination*, translated and edited by Barbara Johnson. Chicago, 1981.

Diamond, Michael L. "Kierkegaard and Apologetics." *Journal of Religion*, LXIV (1964), 122–32.

Diem, Hermann. *Kierkegaard's Dialectic of Existence*. Translated by Harold Knight. Edinburgh, 1959.

Dillenberger, John, ed. *Martin Luther: Selections from His Writings*. Garden City, N.Y., 1961.

Dupré, Louis. *Kierkegaard as Theologian*. London, 1963.

Eliot, T. S. *On Poetry and Poets*. New York, 1957.

Eller, Vernard. *Kierkegaard and Radical Discipleship*. Princeton, 1968.

Elrod, John W. *Being and Existence in Kierkegaard's Pseudonymous Works*. Princeton, 1975.

————. *Kierkegaard and Christendom*. Princeton, 1981.

Erikson, Erik. *Young Man Luther*. New York, 1962.

Fabro, Cornelio. "The Problem of Desperation and Christian Spirituality in Kierkegaard." *Kierkegaardiana*, IV (1962), 63–69.

Fenger, Henning. *Kierkegaard: The Myths and Their Origins.* Translated by George C. Schoolfield. New Haven, 1980.

Feuerbach, Ludwig. *The Essence of Christianity.* Translated by George Eliot. New York, 1957.

Fish, Stanley. *Self-Consuming Artifacts: The Experience of Seventeenth-Century Literature.* Berkeley, Calif. 1972.

Foucault, Michel. *The Archaeology of Knowledge and the Discourse on Language.* Translated by A. M. Sheridan Smith. New York, 1972.

―――. *The Order of Things.* Translated by A. M. Sheridan Smith. New York, 1970.

Freud, Sigmund. *Civilization and Its Discontents.* Translated by James Strachey. New York, 1961.

Frye, Northrop. *The Great Code: The Bible and Literature.* New York, 1982.

Geismar, Eduard. "Wie urteilte Kierkegaard über Luther?" *Luther-Jahrbuch*, X (1929), 1–27.

Gill, Jerry H., ed. *Essays on Kierkegaard.* Minneapolis, 1969.

Gould, John. *The Development of Plato's Ethics.* Cambridge, England, 1955.

Gregory of Nyssa. "The Great Catechism." Translated by William Moore and Henry Austin Wilson. In *A Select Library of Nicene and Post-Nicene Fathers of the Christian Church*, edited by Philip Schaff and Henry Wace. 2nd series. Vol. V of 14 vols. Grand Rapids, Mich., 1892.

Grimsley, Ronald. *Søren Kierkegaard and French Literature.* Cardiff, Wales, 1966.

Hamann, J. G. *Schriften.* Edited by Friedrich Roth. Vol. VII of 8 vols. Berlin, 1821–43.

Harris, H. S. *Hegel's Development: Toward the Sunlight, 1770–1801.* Oxford, England, 1972.

Havelock, Eric A. *Preface to Plato.* Cambridge, Mass. 1963.

Hegel, G. W. F. *Hegel's Aesthetics.* Translated by T. M. Knox. 2 vols., Oxford, England, 1975.

―――. *G. W. F. Hegel's Early Theological Writings.* Translated and edited by T. M. Knox and Richard Kroner. Chicago, 1948.

―――. *Lectures on the Philosophy of Religion.* Translated by E. B. Speirs and J. B. Sanderson. 2 vols. London, 1895.

―――. *Lectures on the Philosophy of World History: Introduction—Reason in History.* Translated by H. B. Nisbet. Cambridge, England, 1975.

―――. *The Phenomenology of Mind.* Translated by J. B. Baillie. New York, 1967.

Henriksen, Aage. *Methods and Results of Kierkegaard Studies in Scandinavia.* Copenhagen, 1951.

―――. *Kierkegaards Romaner.* Copenhagen, 1969.

Herde, Heinz. *Johann Georg Hamann: Zur Theologie der Sprache.* Bonn, 1971.

Hirsch, Emanuel. *Kierkegaard-Studien.* 2 vols. Gütersloh, West Germany, 1933.

Hohlenberg, Johannes. *Søren Kierkegaard*. Translated by T. H. Croxall. New York, 1978.

Hyppolite, Jean. *Genesis and Structure of Hegel's Phenomenology of Spirit*. Translated by Samuel Cherniak and John Heckman. Evanston, Ill., 1974.

Inquiry. Vol. VIII, No. 1 (1965).

James, William. "Hegel and His Method." In *Essays in Radical Empiricism and a Pluralistic Universe*. Edited by Ralph Barton Perry. New York, 1971.

————. *The Varieties of Religious Experience*. London, 1961.

Jansen, F. J. Billeskov. *Studier i Søren Kierkegaards Litteraere Kunst*. Copenhagen, 1951.

Johnson, Howard A., and Niels Thulstrup, eds. *A Kierkegaard Critique*. Chicago, 1972.

Kant, Immanuel. *The Conflict of the Faculties / Der Streit der Fakultäten*. Translated by Mary J. Gregor. New York, 1979.

Kermode, Frank. *The Genesis of Secrecy: On the Interpretation of Narrative*. Cambridge, Mass., 1979.

Kern, Edith. *Existential Thought and Fictional Technique: Kierkegaard, Sartre, Beckett*. New Haven, 1970.

Kierkegaard, Søren. *Letters and Documents*. Translated and edited by Henrik Rosenmeier. Princeton, 1978.

Kierkegaard vivant: Colloque organisé par l'Unesco, 1964. Paris, 1966.

Lessing, Gotthold-Ephraim. *Gesammelte Werke*. Vols. IV, VII, VIII of 10 vols. Berlin, 1954–58.

————. *Lessing's Theological Writings*. Translated by Henry Chadwick. Stanford, Calif., 1957.

Levi, Albert W. "The Idea of Socrates: The Philosophical Hero in the Nineteenth Century." *Journal of History of Ideas*, XVII (January, 1956), 89–108.

Lewalski, Barbara Kiefer. *Protestant Poetics and the Seventeenth Century Religious Lyric*. Princeton, 1979.

Löwith, Karl. *From Hegel to Nietzsche: The Revolution in Nineteenth-Century Thought*. Translated by David E. Green. New York, 1964.

Lowrie, Walter. *Kierkegaard*. 2 vols. New York, 1962.

Mackey, Louis. *Kierkegaard: A Kind of Poet*. Philadelphia, 1971.

Malantschuk, Gregor. "Begreberne Immanens og Transcendens hos Søren Kierkegaard." *Kierkegaardiana*, IX (1974), 104–32.

————. *Kierkegaard's Thought*. Translated by H. V. Hong and E. H. Hong. Princeton, 1971.

————. "Søren Kierkegaards Teori om Springet og hans Virkelighedsbegreb." *Kierkegaardiana*, I, (1955), 7–15.

Manheimer, Ronald J. *Kierkegaard as Educator*. Berkeley, Calif., 1977.

Maritain, Jacques. *Art and Scholasticism*. Translated by J. F. Scanlan. London, 1947.

Mazzeo, Joseph. *Renaissance and Seventeenth Century Studies*. New York, 1964.

Miller, J. Hillis. *Fiction and Repetition: Seven English Novels*, Cambridge, Mass., 1982.

Mortensen, Viggo. "Luther og Kierkegaard." *Kierkegaardiana*, IX, (1974), 163–95.

Murdoch, Iris. *The Fire and the Sun: Why Plato Banished the Artists*. Oxford, England, 1977.

Nadler, Käte. "Hamann und Hegel: Zum Verhältnis von Dialektik und Existentialität." *Logos*, XX (1931), 259–85.

Nelson, Benjamin, ed. *Freud and the Twentieth Century*. New York, 1957.

Nietzsche, Friedrich. "Beyond Good and Evil." In *Basic Writings of Nietzsche*. Translated and edited by Walter Kaufmann. New York, 1968.

———. *The Birth of Tragedy and The Genealogy of Morals*. Translated by Francis Golffing. Garden City, N.Y., 1956.

———. *Twilight of the Idols and the Anti-Christ*. Translated and edited by R. J. Hollingdale. Baltimore, 1968.

Nordentoft, Kresten. *Hvad siger Brand-Majoren? Kierkegaards Opgør med sin Samtid*. Copenhagen, 1973.

———. *Kierkegaard's Psychology*. Translated by Bruce H. Kirmmse. Pittsburgh, 1972.

Olney, James, ed. *Autobiography: Essays Theoretical and Critical*. Princeton, 1980.

Ong, Walter J. *Fighting for Life: Contest, Sexuality and Consciousness*. Ithaca, 1981.

———. "Wit and Mystery: A Revaluation." *Speculum*, XXII (1947), 310–41.

Orbis litterarium. X, i, ii (1955).

Ostenfeld, Ib. *Søren Kierkegaard's Psychology*. Translated by Alastair McKinnon. Waterloo, Ontario, 1978.

Otto, Rudolph. *The Idea of the Holy*. Translated by John Harvey. Oxford, England, 1931.

Paulsen, Anna. "Kierkegaard in seinem Verhältnis zur deutschen Romantik Einfluss und Uberwindung." *Kierkegaardiana*, III (1959), 38–47.

Peliken, Jaroslav, and Helmut T. Lehmann, eds. *Luther's Works*. Vols. I–VIII, translated by George V. Schick; vols. XXII–XXIII, translated by Martin H. Bertram; vol. XXIV, translated by Jaroslav Pelikan; vol. XXV, translated by Walter G. Tillmanns and Jacob A. Preus, edited by Hilton C. Oswald; vols. LI–LII, translated and edited by John W. Doberstein. 55 vols. St. Louis, 1955–76.

Perkins, Robert L., ed. *Kierkegaard's "Fear and Trembling": Critical Appraisals*. University, Ala., 1981.

Pivčević, Edo. *Ironie als Daseinsform bei Sören Kierkegaard*. Gütersloh, West Germany, 1960.

Price, George. *The Narrow Pass: A Study of Kierkegaard's Concept of Man*. New York, 1963.

Rank, Otto. *The Myth of the Birth of the Hero and Other Writings*. New York, 1959.

Reed, Walter L. *Meditations on the Hero: A Study of the Romantic Hero in Nineteenth-Century Fiction*. New Haven, 1974.

Rehm, Walter. *Kierkegaard und der Verführer*. Munich, 1949.

Richter, Jean Paul. *Horn of Oberon: J. P. Richter's School for Aesthetics*. Translated and edited by Margaret R. Hale. Detroit, 1973.

Ricoeur, Paul. *Freud and Philosophy*. Translated by Denis Savage. New Haven, 1970.

Rorty, Richard. *Philosophy and the Mirror of Nature*. Princeton, 1979.

Rousseau, Jean-Jacques. *The Confessions*. Translated by J. M. Cohen. Baltimore, 1954.

Ruttenbeck, Walter. *Søren Kierkegaard: Der Christliche Denker und Sein Werk*. Berlin, 1929.

Said, Edward W. *Beginnings: Intentions and Methods*. New York, 1975.

Schlegel, Friedrich. *Dialogue on Poetry and Literary Aphorisms*. Translated and edited by Ernst Behler and Roman Struc. University Park, Penn., 1968.

———. *Lucinde and the Fragments*. Translated by Peter Firchow. Minneapolis, 1971.

———. *Friedrich Schlegel, 1794–1802; Seine Prosaischen Jugendschriften*. Edited by J. Minor. Wien, Austria, 1882.

Schleiermacher, Friedrich. *The Christian Faith*. Edited by H. R. Mackintosh and J. S. Stewart. Edinburgh, 1948.

Schrag, Calvin. *Existence and Freedom: Towards an Ontology of Human Finitude*. Evanston, Ill., 1961.

Schrey, Heinz-Horst, ed. *Søren Kierkegaard*. Darmstadt, West Germany, 1971.

Schröer, Henning. *Die Denkform der Paradoxalität als theologisches Problem*. Gottingen, West Germany, 1960.

Shestov, Lev. *Kierkegaard and the Existential Philosophy*. Translated by Elinor Hewitt. Athens, Ohio, 1969.

Shmuëli, Adi. *Kierkegaard and Consciousness*. Translated by Naomi Handelman. Princeton, 1971.

Sløk, Johannes. *Die Anthropologie Kierkegaards*. Copenhagen, 1954.

———. *Kierkegaard-Humanismens Taenker*. Copenhagen, 1978.

Smith, Joseph, ed. "Kierkegaard's Truth: The Disclosures of the Self." Essays by Paul B. Armstrong *et al. Psychiatry and the Humanities*, V (1981).

Smith, R. G. *J. G. Hamann: A Study in Christian Existence*. New York, 1960.

Sponheim, Paul. *Kierkegaard on Christ and Christian Coherence*. New York, 1968.

Starobinski, Jean. "Kierkegaard et les masques." *Nouvelle revue française*, XXV (1965), 607–22, 808–25.

Susini, Eugène. *Franz von Baader et le romantisme mystique*. 2 vols. Paris, 1942.

Taylor, Charles. *Hegel*. Cambridge, England, 1975.

Taylor, Mark C. *Journeys to Selfhood: Hegel and Kierkegaard*. Berkeley, Calif., 1980.

————. *Kierkegaard's Pseudonymous Authorship: A Study of Time and the Self.* Princeton, 1975.

Thomas, J. Heywood. *Subjectivity and Paradox.* Oxford, England, 1957.

Thompson, Josiah, ed. *Kierkegaard.* New York, 1973.

————, ed. *Kierkegaard: A Collection of Critical Essays.* New York, 1972.

————. *The Lonely Labyrinth: Kierkegaard's Pseudonymous Works.* Carbondale, Ill., 1967.

Thomte, Reidar. *Kierkegaard's Philosophy of Religion.* Princeton, 1949.

Thought: A Review of Culture and Ideas. LV (September, 1980).

Vlastos, Gregory, ed. *The Philosophy of Socrates: A Collection of Critical Essays.* New York, 1971.

vom Hofe, Gerhard. *Die Romantikkritik Sören Kierkegaards.* Frankfurt, 1972.

von Baader, Franz. *Sämtliche Werke.* Edited by Franz Hoffman and Julius Hamberger. Vols. VII–X of 16 vols. Aalen, West Germany, 1963.

Wahl, Jean. *Etudes kierkegaardiennes.* Paris, 1949.

Wild, John. "Søren Kierkegaard and Classical Philosophy." *Philosophical Review,* XLIX (1940), 536–51.

Wilde, Norman. *Friedrich Heinrich Jacobi: A Study in the Origin of German Realism.* New York, 1966.

INDEX

239